REFORMS AT RISK

PRINCETON STUDIES IN AMERICAN POLITICS:

HISTORICAL, INTERNATIONAL, AND
COMPARATIVE PERSPECTIVES

Ira Katznelson, Martin Shefter, and Theda Skocpol, eds.

A list of titles in this series appears at the back of the book

REFORMS AT RISK

WHAT HAPPENS *AFTER* MAJOR POLICY
CHANGES ARE ENACTED

Eric M. Patashnik

PRINCETON UNIVERSITY PRESS

PRINCETON AND OXFORD

Copyright © 2008 by Princeton University Press

Published by Princeton University Press, 41 William Street, Princeton, New Jersey 08540

In the United Kingdom: Princeton University Press, 6 Oxford Street, Woodstock, Oxfordshire OX20 1TW

Library of Congress Cataloging-in-Publication Data
Patashnik, Eric M.
  Reforms at risk : what happens after major policy changes are enacted / Eric M. Patashnik.
     p.   cm. — (Princeton studies in American politics)
  Includes bibliographical references and index.
  ISBN 978-0-691-11998-4 (hardcover : alk. paper) — ISBN 978-0-691-13897-8 (pbk. : alk.
  paper)   1. Political planning—United States.   I. Title.
  JK468.P64P38   2008
  320.60973—dc22   2008005148

British Library Cataloging-in-Publication Data is available

This book has been composed in Goudy

Printed on acid-free paper. ∞

press.princeton.edu

Printed in the United States of America

10 9 8 7 6 5 4 3 2 1

For Debbie

Contents

List of Figures and Tables

Acknowledgments

THIS PROJECT EXAMINES the political sustainability of domestic policy reforms. It explores why some reforms succeed and others unravel after they become law. This question has received surprisingly little attention. Most scholars and journalists have focused far more on the adoption of reforms than on their unfolding policy development. Yet the political aftermath of reform is no less interesting or important than the dramatic moment of enactment. If my book has a simple message, it is that even the most solid reform ideas require ongoing collective support to endure, but such support is not always provided. When it does come, it should never be taken for granted. I hope the ideas contained in this book will prove useful to scholars, policymakers, advocates, and journalists. If they do, it will be because of the considerable support I have received from a large number of individuals and institutions. Truly, they sustained me over the life of this project.

My research was supported by fellowships from the UCLA Center for American Politics and Public Policy, the Smith Richardson Foundation, the Earhart Foundation, and the D&D Foundation. Special thanks to Kim Dennis, Mark Steinmeyer, Joel Aberbach, and Barbara Nelson for their support on this project. I received outstanding research assistance from several University of Virginia graduate students, including Anne Peters, Justin Peck, and Hilde Eliassen Restad. Seminar audiences at Yale University, William and Mary, and Georgetown University provided great comments and suggestions. I have also benefited enormously from my participation over the years in various "new politics of public policy" conferences organized by Martin A. Levin, Marc K. Landy, and Martin Shapiro at Brandeis University and Boston College. I am very grateful for their support, as well as for the feedback I received from other scholars who have participated in these conferences and book projects, especially Eugene Bardach, Jacob Hacker, Alan Jacobs, Jonathan Macey, Christopher Howard, and Peter Schuck. I also appreciate the encouragement I have received for this project from Paul Pierson and Paul J. Quirk.

Julian Zelizer and Steven Teles read early drafts of the entire manuscript and provided many helpful suggestions. Many qualitative studies in political science explore a single policy episode or sector in depth, but I believed it was necessary to examine reform trajectories across a fairly large number of arenas to identify more general patterns of policy development. The challenge was to keep my larger themes in focus without making a hash of the individual cases. I am fortunate that a number of policy experts were willing to take the time to give me detailed comments on specific case-study chapters. I wish to thank

Dallas Burtraw, William Gale, Bruce Gardner, Darius W. Gaskins, Jr., Donald F. Kettl, Michael E. Levine, David Orden, Eugene Steuerle, John Witte, James Wooten, and George Yin for sharing their insights. I hasten to add that I alone am responsible for any errors of fact or interpretation. I also wish to thank the many congressional staff members, policy practitioners, and journalists who were willing to be interviewed about these reform episodes.

I appreciate the intellectual and professional support I have received from my University of Virginia colleagues, including Herman Schwartz, Gerard Alexander, Sid Milkis, James Ceaser, James Savage, David Breneman, Jeff Legro, Jeffrey Jenkins, and especially Martha Derthick, whose superb book (with Paul J. Quirk) *The Politics of Deregulation* helped motivate this study. Marylynn Sergent, Steve Morrison, Bruce Gardner, and other individuals I fear I have forgotten to name, generously provided data or factual information.

I received extremely helpful feedback from two anonymous reviewers for Princeton University Press. I also wish to express my deep appreciation to my editor, Chuck Myers, for patiently supporting this project from concept to completion. Portions of this book appeared in very different forms in two previous essays: "After the Public Interest Prevails: The Political Sustainability of Policy Reform," *Governance*, (April 2003): 203–34 and "The Day *After* Market-Oriented Reform; or What Happens When Economists' Reform Ideas Meet Politics," in *Creating Competitive Markets: The Politics and Economics of Regulatory Reform*, Marc K. Landy, Martin A. Levin, and Martin Shapiro, eds., (Brookings Institution Press, 2007), 167–289.

Finally, I wish to thank my family. My wonderful sons Michael and Josh have provided a steady stream of good-natured distractions and fun. My parents, Anne and Bernard Patashnik, my grandmother, Bertha Rosenblatt, and my brother David Patashnik have all been very supportive. This book is dedicated to my amazing wife Deborah Gordon. A book project is all-consuming. I am fortunate to have a wife who is not only my best friend, but a professional policy analyst who does not mind discussing an unromantic topic like emissions trading over a candlelight dinner. Debbie suggested the book's title, helped me create some of the graphs, and proofread the manuscript. She always seemed to know when to give me a well-deserved kick to motivate me to write another few pages before calling it a day—and when to nudge me away from the computer to take a much-needed coffee break or family walk. I am one lucky guy.

REFORMS AT RISK

Introduction: General-Interest Policymaking and the Politics of Reform Sustainability

> To innovate is not to reform.
>
> —Edmund Burke

> There is nothing more difficult to carry out, nor more doubtful of success, nor more dangerous to handle, than to institute a new order of things.
>
> —Niccolo Machiavelli

> The most dangerous moment for a bad government is when it begins to reform.
>
> —Alexis de Tocqueville

ON OCTOBER 22, 1986, lawmakers from both parties gathered on the South Lawn of the White House and applauded as President Ronald Reagan signed into law the most comprehensive revision of the federal tax code in a half century. The landmark Tax Reform Act of 1986 eliminated or curtailed dozens of shelters, loopholes, and other tax breaks enjoyed by powerful corporations and well-heeled investors. By withdrawing tax preferences from a favored few, the federal government was able to sharply lower tax rates for millions of low- and middle-income Americans without increasing the federal budget deficit. While the tax reform law was not flawless, it made the federal tax system fairer and more efficient. At the signing ceremony, Reagan called the Tax Reform Act "the best antipoverty bill, the best pro-family measure, and the best job-creation program ever to come out of the Congress of the United States." "At last. It's a day to stop and take unashamed satisfaction in a triumph of the whole over the parts," editorialized *The New York Times*.[1] Only a few months earlier, it looked like this historic day would never arrive. Hundreds of high-priced Washington lobbyists worked feverishly to bury the measure in committee. But Senate Finance Committee chairman Robert Packwood (R-OR), Ways and Means Committee chairman Dan Rostenkowski (D-IL), and President Reagan came together to defeat the special interests.

For scholars and journalists alike, the importance of general-interest reforms like the 1986 Tax Reform Act goes beyond their substantive policy accomplishments. These stunning reform victories signal that American national government has the capacity to overcome parochial concerns and serve a larger public interest. The American state can fulfill its core purpose of promoting the general welfare.

Unfortunately, many of the accomplishments of the Tax Reform Act of 1986 have been gradually eroded. The remarkable 1986 coalition between supply-side Republicans and tax-reforming Democrats has "disintegrated" over the past twenty years, leaving the reform vulnerable and defenseless.[2] Although important "vestiges" of the celebrated measure remain, tax policymaking dynamics have largely regressed to their pre-1986 ways.[3] Politicians of both parties have been keen to create special tax preferences for capital gains income, educational savings accounts, and the energy industry. Some of these new tax preferences have failed to achieve their own purposes because they offer subsidies to activities that would take place without them. Since the late 1980s, the core principles of tax simplification and horizontal equity have been honored mainly in the breach. The federal tax code has become less neutral, less economically efficient, and far more opaque and convoluted. While individual tax shelters have been curbed, tax shelters for corporations have proliferated. These developments have been demoralizing to politicians, public interest lobbyists, and policy experts alike. "The Tax Reform Act of 1986 was a great leap forward," said former Congressional Budget Office director Robert D. Reischauer. "Now we're slowly undoing the good that we did then."[4] "I feel like crying," said Senator Bob Packwood (R-OR), one of the prime movers of the 1986 reform.[5]

The failure of the Tax Reform Act of 1986 to consolidate its gains and reconfigure political dynamics is just one example of a larger and more worrisome phenomenon—the reversal or unraveling of general-interest reforms after their adoption. By general-interest reform, I mean *a non-incremental change of an existing line of policymaking intended to rationalize governmental undertakings or to distribute benefits to some broad constituency.* Examples of general-interest reforms include agricultural reform, transport deregulation, procurement reform, and private pension reform. The targets of general-interest reforms are the policy sins and social pathologies of the day before yesterday. The long-term sustainability of reform projects, however, depends on what happens to them tomorrow. By sustainability, I mean the capacity of a reform not only to maintain its structural integrity over time, but to use its core principles to guide its course amid inevitable pressures for change.[6]

The threats to reform sustainability are multiple and mutually reinforcing. They include interest group power, rent seeking behavior, and parochialism. Narrow interests can be expected to press their particular demands up to a point where the organizational costs in effort exceed the expected benefits of winning. But clientelism is not the whole of the sustainability problem. Threats to reform sustainability also include the rational ignorance and myopia of mass publics, the political allure of empty symbolism, and the temptation of politicians to serve the organized and meddle with markets rather than promote more general-interests.[7] In sum, the passage of a reform law is only the beginning of a political struggle. Reform enactment *could* indicate a sharp, permanent break with prior patterns of governmental activity. It *may* signal that the political climate has fundamentally changed in ways that will redound to the benefit of ordinary citizens. By itself, however, the passage of a reform act does not settle *anything*.

A PREVIEW OF THE ARGUMENT OF THIS BOOK

General-interest reforms are frequently adopted with great fanfare, but their success simply cannot be taken for granted. The losers from reform cannot be counted on to vanish without another fight, and new actors may arrive on the scene who will seek to undo a reform to further their own agendas. Rather than a one-shot static affair, policy reform must be seen as a *dynamic process*, in which political forces seeking to protect a general-interest reform may be opposed by forces seeking to undermine it. Indeed, sustaining reforms against the threats of reversal and erosion may be even tougher than winning the reforms' adoption in the first place. To draw an analogy from everyday life, losing weight is hard, but the real challenge is *keeping* it off.

Yet if making reforms stick is a formidable task, it is not an impossible one. The sustainability of reforms turns on the *reconfiguration* of political dynamics. Concentrated interests must be prevented from reasserting themselves. This may entail the disabling of power structures that shield narrow groups from democratic accountability. Equally important, the reforms must produce a self-reinforcing dynamic. Often that may involve a Schumpeterian process of "creative destruction" in which group identities and coalitional patterns shift, would-be rent seekers are divided, political expectations change, and social actors become invested in the new policy regime.

After reform, governance should become less particularistic or more technically or administratively rational. In some cases, the scope of the government's interventions may narrow. But reform does not extract public policy from ultimate dependence on the political process. All reforms require, at a bare minimum, rules and legal frameworks to support them. Some policy reforms even require the government to *expand* its capacities. Government's role *changes* after reform, but government does not disappear. As Alfred Kahn, the father of airline deregulation, has argued, reform "should not be understood as synonymous with total government laissez-faire."[8] Because government is inevitable after reform, politics is inescapable. Without the incentives for inefficient and inequitable policymaking that American politics often creates, general-interest reforms would be unnecessary. Without the creative coalition-building that the American political system makes possible, reforms could not be enacted. And without the economic and social transformations that American politics ideally permits, the reforms could not be sustained. *While policy reform may be intended to promote economic goals, it is a political project all the way through.*

While the political sustainability of general-interest reforms has been little-studied, this analysis joins a broader dialogue about the politics of policy stability and change, one to which scholars as diverse as Forrest Maltzman and Charles Shipan, Andrea Campbell, Suzanne Mettler, Jacob Hacker, Terry Moe, Karen Orren and Steven Skowronek, Christopher Berry, Barry Burden and William Howell, and Frank Baumgartner and Bryan Jones have made contributions. My analysis differs in subtle but important ways from these prior studies. In providing a detailed examination of how the rules, incentives, and norms embedded in reforms channel and constrain political dynamics over extended periods of time, my analysis departs from Maltzman and Shipan's important quantitative study of legal durability and why some major laws are more likely to be subsequently amended than others.[9] An emphasis on how sustainable reforms not only heighten the political activity of citizens that make affirmative demands on government but also disempower and divide rent-seeking clientele groups distinguishes this account from the compelling positive feedback studies of Campbell and Mettler.[10] With its emphasis that the sustainability of reforms turns as much on coalitional patterns and the play of uncoordinated market forces as on institutional changes, my analysis diverges from accounts that emphasize the politics of administrative structure (Moe) and shifts in formal authority (Orren and Skowronek).[11] In contrast to studies (Berry, Burden, and Howell) arguing that policy durability hinges on the continuity of initial enacting coalitions, I argue that the most resilient reforms upset inherited coalitional patterns and stimulate the emergence of new vested interests and political alliances.[12] Theoretically, my study of reform trajectories is related to Jacob S. Hacker's important work on how social policies evolve without the formal revision of laws, but my study investigates policy development across a broader set of arenas, providing an opportunity to sharpen our understanding of how policies reshape politics in different settings.[13] While I discuss the distributional consequences of reforms, my analysis also places unusual emphasis on the *efficiency* implications of policy feedback, thereby linking market and political models of policy analysis. Finally, in its focus on what happens years or even decades *after* the passage of major policy shifts, the account differs from Baumgartner and Jones's influential punctuated equilibrium model.[14]

JUST AN IMPLEMENTATION PROBLEM?

My analysis also differs from the traditional literature on policy implementation, which examines what can go wrong after laws are enacted. A major lesson of this literature is that implementation is politics by other means. As Jeffrey Pressman and Aaron Wildavsky argued, "continued skepticism [is warranted] when anyone suggests that inherent features of political life can be summarily abolished."[15] This lesson is certainly relevant to the present inquiry, but there are at least two subtle but important differences between my approach and how most scholars have studied the implementation process.

First, implementation has been conceived as a process of "assembling numerous and diverse program elements," such as administrative and financial accountability mechanisms and regulatory clearances.[16] While reform sustainability may also entail the building of a new "policy machine," as mentioned earlier, it usually involves a process of *disassembly*. Some extant policy system must be cleared away or at least contained before a reform can be safely established. Second, the implementation literature focuses mainly on the internal life of bureaus and the conditions under which statutory mandates are (or are not) translated into administrative actions. Classic implementation problems include bureaucratic resistance, tokenism, and delay.[17] These problems can affect the durability of reforms. Yet reforms may crumble not because of anything bureaucrats do, but rather because of the actions (or inactions) of *elected officials themselves*.

In the language of rational choice modeling, the implementation literature focuses primarily on "slippages" between the preferences of political principals and the actions of their less-than-faithful bureaucratic agents. My analysis, in contrast, gives more attention to agency slippages between the citizenry (the ultimate principal in a democracy) and the government, and especially to what theorists refer to as the "commitment problem," meaning the inability of a sovereign government to bind itself or its successors. Today's leaders may change their minds about the direction of public policy and, even if they don't, they will eventually be replaced by other leaders who hold different views. The commitment problem may not be a concern for rank-and-file lawmakers, who arguably benefit from voting to enact general-interest reforms and then benefit themselves, again, at a later stage, by retracting the policies to serve other goals.[18] But it is a serious problem for those policy entrepreneurs advocating reforms, who might stand to attract more political support if they could credibly demonstrate that reforms, once adopted, will endure.[19] And it is an even bigger problem for the intended beneficiaries of reforms, especially diffuse constituencies who may be poorly placed to defend their policy gains over time.[20] If the commitment problem could be better managed, society would be better off.

When the commitment to a general-interest reform unravels, three bad things happen. First, the substantive achievements of the reform are lost. Thus, all or most of the reformers' hard political work was for naught. This suggests it would have been better if the political system had focused its limited attention and information-processing capacities on some other problem.[21]

Second, the undoing of a reform undermines the stability that people need to plan for the future. There is a sense in which even a durable "bad" policy is better than a fragile "good" one. "The problem for America is that no one knows what will come next in terms of changes to the tax code. With Congress constantly twiddling with the tax controls, companies and individuals are unable to develop long-term strategies to build financial security. Even a bad tax law that is left in place is better than almost constant substantive changes that undermine investment strategies and business plans," states one professional association newsletter.[22]

Finally, the unraveling of reforms causes ordinary Americans to lose faith in the ability of public leaders to solve public problems. When tax reformers today talk about cleaning up the tax code again, for example, voters think they've seen that movie before, and they know how it turns out. "Achieving [a new comprehensive tax reform] would have to overcome the cynicism that's developed, because the grand compromise of '86 lasted . . . only a few years," lamented a tax expert who was one of the leading architects of the reform.[23] Similar statements could be made about farm subsidy reform, campaign finance reform, health care reform, administrative reform, and so on. *In sum, the unraveling of general-interest reforms harms the economy, squanders scarce political resources, and breeds public disillusionment with government.*

A NEW POLITICS OF PUBLIC POLICY?

How sustainable have the major U.S. general-interest reforms of the past thirty or so years been? Why have some domestic reforms produced a remarkable shift in political dynamics while others have barely left a trace on the policy landscape? What lessons do the post-adoption experiences of major policy reforms offer about the capacities and incapacities of American national government?

Despite their substantive and theoretical importance, these questions have received only limited attention in the American politics literature.[24] Most political scientists who study the politics of policy reform in the United States have focused on the logically prior question of how major general-interest reforms come to be enacted in the first place. The neglect of the second phase of reform is easy to understand. The first phase of reform typically involves the passage of major legislation. These public policy moves are ordinarily highly visible. When Congress adopts major reforms, it is front page news. But if the reforms are subsequently reversed or eroded in committee chambers, the story may get relegated to the back pages. In sum, important post-reform developments are relatively easy to miss.

A second important reason why scholars have focused on the first phase of reform is that they are drawn to the counterintuitive, and many reforms were widely believed to have little chance of adoption either because they imposed tangible losses on entrenched clienteles, or because they attempted to impart a greater degree of instrumental rationality to governmental undertakings. The passage of these reforms would seem to contradict much conventional political science wisdom.

The orthodox view found expression in the work of political scientists like Theodore Lowi, Grant McConnell, and David R. Mayhew.[25] In his classic 1969 book, *The End of Liberalism*, Lowi attacked the pluralists' contention that interest group politics is an acceptable method of making public policy in a democracy. According to Lowi, policymaking by group struggle renders the government unable to achieve collective goals, leads citizens to expect too little from elected officials, and weakens democratic institutions. In a similar vein, McConnell's 1966 book, *Private Power and American Democracy*, argued that interest group access undermines policy coherence and allows a privileged few to profit at the expense of the general public.

The argument of David R. Mayhew's 1974 classic, *Congress: The Electoral Connection*, had a different cast to it. Part 2 of the book (arguably even more insightful than the better-known Part 1) offers a penetrating analysis of the policymaking distortions endemic to an individualistic legislature in the American constitutional setting. According to Mayhew, members of Congress (due chiefly to information costs and the fragmentation of political accountability) tend to be rewarded more for delivering particularized benefits, taking pleasing stands, serving the organized, and engaging in symbolism than for effective problem solving: "Electoral incentives will detour members into small-bore distributive politics and feckless position taking."[26] One of Mayhew's more subtle points was that Congress is prone to incorporate popular understandings of means-ends relationships into laws (even when the public is misguided). Hence the congressional penchant for "blunt, simple" solutions (e.g., command-and-control pollution curbs) over less intuitive, expert schemes (e.g., emissions trading programs) that might be more effective.[27] While Mayhew suggested that dissatisfaction with congressional performance often provokes reform efforts to make government more universalistic, efficient, and rational—countervailing mechanisms are a key part of his story—he implied that the "ambitious 'public interest' aims" of many statutes seldom will be accomplished.[28]

The work of leading economists reinforced these pessimistic conclusions. In *The Logic of Collective Action*, Mancur Olson claimed that interest group politics undermines the public good.[29] The key problem has to do with the incentives for participation. According to Olson, rational individuals have no incentive to join large groups seeking to promote broad public concerns since they recognize that their contribution will not affect a particular group's chances of attaining its goals; moreover, if the group does succeed, those who did not join will benefit as much as those who did. The implication of Olson's analysis is that not all groups will be effectively represented in Washington. In particular, groups with relatively narrow interests will be much better represented than larger and more diffuse collectives, all else being equal. The process of partisan mutual adjustment, however valuable it may be in a heterogeneous society, will not ensure that the interests of average citizens will be represented. *The general-interest can suffer even when public policies win adoption, generate supportive constituencies and pass constitutional muster.*

Olson's analysis provided a powerful explanation for a number of disturbing features of American governance, including the underprovision of public goods and the vulnerability of some agencies to interest group capture. To be sure, "public interest" lobbies like Common Cause were founded in the 1960s and early 1970s to counteract these unfortunate tendencies. But the creation of these associations was heavily subsidized by donations from foundations and wealthy patrons, who had absorbed Olson's key lesson that organizations seeking to promote issues of broad public concern will have tremendous difficulty maintaining themselves if they must rely on the contributions of ordinary citizens. By the early 1970s, the received wisdom among social scientists and journalists alike was that clientele groups often get their way at the expense of the larger public and that Congress often produces laws that sound good but accomplish little.

But dramatic policy developments in the 1960s, 1970s, and 1980s challenged conventional wisdom about the power of narrow interests and the pathologies of governance. Congress enacted sweeping general-interest reforms in arenas ranging from taxation to transportation that intelligently addressed major national problems. These reforms upset many preexisting policy whirlpools and "cozy" subsystems. Many of the reforms reflected the sophisticated ideas of policy experts. This new view of American national government as responsive to dispersed interests and rational analysis provided a badly needed corrective to an older conception of policymaking as a giant pork barrel. To be sure, the political talents of policy entrepreneurs were often required to get the reforms onto the agenda. Under favorable political conditions, however, general-interest reforms *could* be adopted.

While some Chicago-school economists claim that the enactment of procompetitive deregulation and similar laws does not invalidate group theory, properly understood, most mainstream political scientists and economists accepted that the reforms constituted a genuine puzzle to be explained. A provocative new political science literature emerged to account for the reforms' surprising adoption. Martha Derthick and Paul Quirk's important 1985 book, *The Politics of Deregulation*, placed ideas at the center of the story.[30] Derthick and Quirk claimed that bold reform measures can be passed if leaders are able to link experts' prescriptions for policy change to salient public issues. R. Douglas Arnold's 1990 book, *The Logic of Congressional Action*, stressed the importance of anticipated public reactions.[31] In an important refinement of Mayhew's approach, Arnold argued that under certain special conditions even lawmakers focused on their own reelections will find it in their political interests to vote for general-interest legislation. Gary Muccaroni's excellent 1995 book, *Reversals of Fortune*, demonstrated that government could impose losses on powerful producer groups.[32] In a similar vein, Adam Sheingate's insightful book, *The Agricultural Welfare State*, shows that farm subsidies are more vulnerable to fiscal retrenchment than previously thought.[33]

Finally, Marc K. Landy and Martin A. Levin's provocative edited volume, *The New Politics of Public Policy*, claimed that American national policymaking experienced a regime shift in the 1960s.[34] As a result of changes in prevailing norms, institutions, and practices, old-style client politics had been thrown on the defensive. In his contribution to this volume, distinguished political scientist, James Q. Wilson, argued that the United States in the 1960s acquired a new political system, one in which major policy innovations could be enacted with greater ease than in the past. This new political system reflected the greater influence of expert analysis, the increased role of the courts in domestic policymaking, and the lowered cost of political mobilization due to technological advances. As Wilson put it, the American polity had been "rationalized in the sense that partial interests are now suspect and general-interests are thought paramount."[35]

In sum, general-interest reforms have served as the basis for broad generalizations about the fundamental character of policymaking in the American polity.[36] What the recent literature on American national government has largely neglected to investigate, however, is what happens *after* the reforms are signed into law. That is the central purpose of this book.

REFORM SUSTAINABILITY AND AMERICAN POLITICAL DEVELOPMENT

To some extent, my analysis represents a return to the themes of classic works by scholars such as Grant McConnell, Theodore Lowi, Mancur Olson, and David Mayhew. Like these analysts, I claim that it is not easy for American government to promote the general-interest or for dispersed constituencies to shape policy outcomes, especially when such groups find themselves in a struggle with better-organized clienteles. Yet the remarkable public policy changes that caught the attention of prominent scholars like Derthick and Quirk, Arnold, and Wilson *did* occur, and are a vital part of my story. These sweeping policy reforms should not be dismissed as mere aberrations. The key question is not *whether* general-interest reforms can ever be passed (we now know they can be), or even how often policy reforms are adopted, but the conditions under which the reforms can be successfully consolidated. This book addresses this critical question through a theoretically informed examination of canonic reform experiences in key areas of American national policymaking.

This study aims not to attack this recent line of scholarship, but just the reverse—to juxtapose U.S. policy reform experiences over time and across issue areas in order to promote knowledge accumulation. My major quarrel with the recent hopeful literature on general-interest reform adoption in the United States is that it takes a "snapshot view" of the reform process when what we really need, as Paul Pierson has persuasively argued, are "moving pictures."[37] The "new politics of public policy" literature appropriately emphasizes the fluidity and creativity of U.S. lawmaking processes and the potential for skilled policy entrepreneurs to make support for reform politically compelling. Yet it ignores or seriously downplays the historical and institutional obstacles to carrying out fundamental shifts in the larger political economy in which policymaking takes place. Reform is less a destination than a political journey. Scholars concerned about how, and how well, government works must pay far more attention to ongoing processes and dynamics.[38] Only by examining policymaking *developmentally* will we be in a position to obtain an accurate sense of the possibilities and limits of broad-based reform efforts in American government. Only then can we grasp why sweeping reforms sometimes fall short of their impressive aspirations.

Comparative politics scholars seem to have absorbed this lesson far better than Americanists.[39] When scholars examine the politics of governance in developing nations, in which millions of people live in dire poverty, it is impossible for them to be unaware of the gap between the government's promises and performance.[40] In the U.S. context, however, the unraveling of domestic policy reforms generally does not lead to such tragic consequences; it just causes our economic and political institutions to underperform relative to their potential. Because the consequences of democratic failure in the United States are less stark, they are easier for scholars to ignore. The lack of attention to the long-term consequences of U.S. domestic policy reforms may also reflect the American field's high level of specialization. For example, students of Congress typically focus on committee assignments and the determinants of roll call votes, not on the requisites of policy sustainability.[41] The result is an unfortunate tendency among many legislative specialists to conflate lawmaking with definitive and decisive public action.[42] Implementation experts in the public administration subfield, for their part, do recognize that the game doesn't end when laws are adopted. But these scholars mainly focus on the internal life of bureaus. They rarely study broader political dynamics or policy feedback mechanisms.

One place where U.S. policymaking *is* regularly examined from a developmental perspective is in the vast literature on the U.S. welfare state. Scholars have demonstrated that a deep understanding of the government's role in providing and regulating social benefits requires close attention to the influence of both political institutions and policy feedback effects.[43] However, this political science literature focuses mainly on *distributional* issues: the level of social provision, and the degree to which benefits are targeted at the truly needy. These are obviously important questions in a democratic polity, and I touch on them in chapter 8 in my discussion of ERISA and the Medicare Catastrophic Coverage Act. Yet government exists to do more than impose distributive standards. It also supplies public goods, corrects negative externalities, and provides the institutional foundations that allow markets to function and create the economic growth that makes redistribution feasible. Economists study these questions, and they bring a welcome attention to the complex role of market forces (which many American Political Development [APD] scholars downplay or ignore). Yet many economists pay little attention to how policy choices reshape the capacities of government and the incentives and engagement of key political actors. This book seeks to bridge the divide between APD and policy analysis by using historical-institutional concepts to shed light on the politics of economic growth, deregulation, and market efficiency.

WHY STUDY THE EVOLUTION OF POLICY REFORMS?

Two compelling reasons for studying the evolution of general-interest reforms are to better understand the consequences of past reform efforts, and to improve the direction of public policymaking in the future. By examining the experience of prior reform moves, we can learn why some reforms have persisted while others have come undone. The analysis should also help advocates of general-interest reforms anticipate political sustainability problems at the early stages and so design against the problems for more durable reform legislation.

General-interest reforms do not fit easily into a conservative or liberal camp. The reforms often attract bipartisan support among policy elites—a rare occurrence in this age of ideological polarization. Conservative elites may support general-interest reforms because they wish to unleash market forces or discipline spending demands. Yet the same reforms may also draw support from liberal elites who seek to terminate unwarranted public transfers (sometimes called "corporate welfare") to privileged clientele groups who should not require governmental assistance. Just as both liberals and conservatives can find reasons to support general-interest reforms, so efforts to erode the reforms also can be a bipartisan affair. Liberal and conservative politicians may disagree about the appropriate scope of government, but both camps are equally adept at scrambling to protect powerful lobbies from losses come election time.

General-interest reforms are not about dismantling government programs *per se*. Nor, as I mentioned earlier, are they fundamentally about redistributing wealth from the rich to the poor (or vice versa). Rather, the reforms are about promoting the general welfare. The policies often draw support from experts at both the Brookings Institution (a center-left think tank) and the American Enterprise Institute (a center-right think tank).[44] While some intellectuals and critics of American democracy might argue that any policy idea that can attract support from across the ideological spectrum *must* be suspect, most citizens would disagree. The American ethos features support for both capitalist *and* democratic values.[45] Americans expect government to permit competitive markets to function smoothly *and* to correct market failures and provide desired public goods. They want the government to solve real-world problems without making things worse. What they *do not* want are public policies that benefit the few at the expense of the many.

THE PLAN OF THE BOOK

The following chapters explore the limits and possibilities of general-interest reform in American government. Chapter 2 examines general-interest reform as a political project. After providing a more complete definition of reform, the chapter summarizes what political scientists and economists have learned about the politics of reform adoption. It then identifies both the generic threats to reform sustainability and the structures and processes that can render the reforms durable over the long haul.

Chapters 3 thru 8, the empirical heart of the book, examine seven major domestic policy reforms in American national government: tax reform, agriculture reform, two attempts to recast the American public/private welfare state (ERISA and Medicare Catastrophic Insurance Coverage Act), procurement reform, airline deregulation, and the cap and trade program to curb acid rain emissions. I discuss the reforms roughly in ascending order of their sustainability, beginning with a relatively clear case of reform erosion (tax reform), and ending with two instances of successful reconfiguration (airline deregulation and emissions trading). *It must be stressed, however, that key parts of even the least sustainable reforms have endured, just as reforms that have largely stuck have failed to live up their expectations in some respects.* These are very complex cases that require careful scrutiny.

A small-N comparative case approach is appropriate for an inquiry into the factors that influence reform sustainability. It permits a nuanced examination of the relationship between distinct configurations of ideas, institutions, and interests on the one hand, and reform outcomes on the other. Such causal-process observations are valuable in making inferences into the sources of reform sustainability because they permit exploration of the specific mechanisms that generate positive or negative feedback. While the number of reforms examined is much too small to permit rigorous quantitative analysis, the comparative case element of the research design permits comparisons to be drawn across multiple reform experiences and ensures that the findings have at least some degree of generalizability. The case materials in fact offer more than seven opportunities to tease out the impact of key factors, because each of the major reforms under review has a number of components, and these components may each exhibit a different degree of sustainability. As Henry Brady, David Collier, and Jason Seawright emphasize, analytic leverage can derive from a close knowledge of cases and context because "subunits of a case may be very different from the overall case."[46] For example, we will find that some components of agricultural reform have been far more resilient than others, and that these patterns can only be understood by analyzing the complex impact of political institutions and policy feedback effects.

Each case-study chapter explores three sets of issues.[47] First, I interrogate the *pre-reform situation*. I examine the substance and dynamics of policymaking in each arena, identify the groups that were advantaged or disadvantaged under preexisting arrangements, and try to explain why policy reform got on the policy agenda. Next, I examine the *content of reform* itself. I examine the supporters and opponents of reform, the compensation mechanisms or other tactics used to neutralize the opposition, and the expectations of key actors at the time of the reforms' adoption.

The third and most important set of issues concerns the *evolution of the reforms* over time. I examine the extent to which each reform reconfigures policymaking dynamics. In particular, I examine whether the reforms generate changes in coalitional patterns, positive or negative feedback effects, and Schumpeterian "creative destruction." The analysis attends to the role of elected officials, clientele groups, and market actors after enactment. Do they maintain their commitment to reform in the face of foreseeable (or unforeseeable) shifts in political or economic conditions? Did the interest groups hurt by the reforms accommodate themselves to the altered policies? Or did they attempt to push the government into reversing course and, if so, were they successful? Did new interest groups emerge in the wake of the reforms? Did they approve or disapprove of the new policy direction? Finally, did the reforms gather momentum and become politically self-reinforcing? Did they (in Orren and Skowronek's formulation) successfully "preempt" skeptics, engage the opinions and values of the mass public, and cause policy elites to acknowledge "the rightness of what has occurred?"[48]

Chapter 9 generalizes about the politics of reform sustainability. It summarizes common themes from the cases, teases out broader lessons for the study of public policymaking, and offers some practical suggestions for promoting reform sustainability.

THE CASE STUDIES

Because the case studies provide the empirical material for the analysis of reform durability, it is important to select them with care. I chose the cases for several reasons. First, each of the cases is important in its own right. For example, procurement reform altered the way the federal government manages its relations with thousands of vendors and contractors who produce and sell the goods and services citizens receive in exchange for their tax payments, and airline deregulation profoundly changed how Americans travel for pleasure and business. The sample includes examples of reforms that have served as the basis for generalizations about the conditions under which American government can serve the interests of ordinary consumers and general taxpayers. If these reforms cannot endure, scholars may need to revise their beliefs about the performance of the American democratic polity.

Second, the cases were selected to represent a range of *tools* of government action, because it has been argued that different categories of tools create distinctive political and administrative consequences.[49] The cases thus feature attempts to change patterns of taxation (tax reform), direct government spending (farm subsidies, the MCAA), and administrative or economic regulation (procurement reform, ERISA, airline deregulation, and the cap-and-trade program).

Third, while I was largely unfamiliar with the details of the various reforms before I began the project—and the details turned out to be crucial—I included cases that a general awareness of current events suggested have had very different political fates. Thus, the sample includes both reforms that have been repealed (e.g., cost sharing for Medicare catastrophic coverage) and reforms that have persisted (airline deregulation).

Fourth, the sample was constructed to include cases that vary according to the *perceived costs of reform*. My analysis thus draws on James Q. Wilson's well-known typology for classifying policies.[50] Wilson divides the world into four kinds of policies, based on the perceived distribution of their costs and benefits: "majoritarian politics" (when both the costs and benefits of a policy are widely distributed over many citizens); "entrepreneurial politics" (when society as a whole or some large part of it benefits from a policy that imposes substantial costs on some small identifiable group); "client politics" (when benefits are concentrated on some narrow group, but a large part of society pays the costs); and "interest group politics," when a policy confers benefits on some relatively small identifiable group and imposes costs on another small equally identifiable group).

If the purpose of this book was to examine the development of public policies *in general*, the empirical analysis would have to examine clientele policies or interest group policies, which offer benefits to narrow groups. In fact, we *already know* that clientele policies (e.g., agricultural subsidies) tend to build powerful supportive constituencies and that interest group policies (e.g., OSHA regulations) can count on having the support of some organized lobby (though such policies will also typically draw protests from some other constituency). The central research question is whether policy reforms that are perceived not to *offer* concentrated benefits can become entrenched over time. The sample includes reforms whose costs were perceived to be narrowly concentrated (tax reform, agricultural reform, airline deregulation, and a cap-and-trade program for acid rain emissions) and broadly diffused (procurement reform, beneficiary cost-sharing for Medicare catastrophic insurance, and ERISA).

While attention to tools and perceived costs offers certain insights, these factors turn out to be less helpful in explaining differences across the cases than one might predict. My central argument is that political fate of general-interest reforms turns on the nature of the reactions, adaptations, coalitional patterns, and investments the reforms generate from social actors. What kinds of institutional changes and policy feedbacks promote sustainability and what kinds lead to reform erosions and reversals? Chapter 2 examines this question.

CHAPTER 2

Policy Reform as a Political Project

THE NEXT FIVE CHAPTERS provide a detailed examination of reform experiences in key arenas of American national government. To lay the theoretical foundation for this analysis, this chapter discusses the nature of general-interest reform as a political project. Reform is a formidable political task because it requires current officeholders to acknowledge that the current direction of policymaking is dysfunctional and to alter governing arrangements on which social actors have come to rely.[1]

After a brief review of the special conditions under which general-interest reform measures are enacted, the chapter discusses the post-adoption challenges to reform sustainability. I highlight the structural factors and political dynamics that promote the sustainability of reforms over time. My central argument is that sustainable reforms *reconfigure* political dynamics. They disrupt longstanding patterns of governance, recast institutions, upset existing power monopolies, and create policy feedback effects that render it difficult or unattractive for the government to reverse course. Reforms that do not accomplish these things, or that do so only superficially, can be expected to unravel.

As a preface, I discuss the meaning of general-interest reform itself. At the outset, it should be acknowledged that any definition of policy reform is bound to be controversial. Some experienced observers of the national political scene, weary from watching countless "reform" proposals either serve as vehicles for an individual officeholder's self-promotion or else produce results that fall far short of their expectations, suggest that it would be a good idea to expunge the word "reform" from our political dialogue.[2] Certainly politicians can abuse the word reform for parochial ends, and the fact that a proposal is labeled a "reform" does not mean it will promote general-interests. Accordingly, I focus on public policies that satisfy certain criteria. By providing an explicit definition of reform, I invite others to offer their own formulations.

THE MEANING OF GENERAL-INTEREST REFORM

As noted in chapter 1, general-interest reform or "policy reform" (I shall use the terms interchangeably) can be defined as a *conscious, non-incremental shift in a preexisting line of policymaking intended to produce general benefits*. This definition can be unpacked to distinguish policy reform from related concepts.

Conscious. All public policies undergo change over time due to the impact of exogenous economic, demographic, and social forces.[3] These changes do not indicate that policy reform has occurred, however. Reform involves the *purposive* recasting of existing policies through formal governmental action.

Non-incremental. In stable democracies like the United States, most policy-making involves small changes from the status quo due to reliance on incremental decision-making processes, path dependency, and so forth. While a series of incremental moves can gradually produce large-scale change, policy reform involves an effort to significantly alter the course of a policy within a fairly short period of time, often involving a change in policy instruments and not merely in decision outputs. For example, in the acid rain case, the government shifted from the use of command-and-control regulation to a system of tradable permits for sulfur dioxide emissions.

Shift in a preexisting line of policymaking. Reform involves a departure from an ongoing pattern of governmental activity and performance. The focus of my analysis is therefore not on what happens when the federal government adopts "breakthrough" policies and moves into a heretofore unoccupied field for the first time, as it did quite often during the Progressive and New Deal eras.[4] Rather, the focus is on whether U.S. policymakers can adopt and sustain efforts to reformulate in some comprehensive way a policy area in which many program commitments and vested interests are *already in place*. This is a difficult test for a democratic polity. As Hugh Heclo has pointed out, "Major reform in a policy field already well populated by public or private arrangements is bound to encourage resistance from powerful stakeholders already organized around prevailing approaches."[5]

Yet this is *precisely* the task that U.S. politicians increasingly face today. Whether Democrats or Republicans win office, "Big Government" is here to stay. As the size and scope of American national government has expanded, policymaking has increasingly become "its own cause."[6] Government programs and regulations create vested interests, but they also give rise to fiscal, administrative, and myriad other problems that elected officials must address. In the modern American state, governance typically involves the recasting of old programs and policies rather than the creation of new ones.[7]

While policy reform frequently involves the withdrawal of subsidies to narrow clientele groups and a greater reliance on free market forces, it does not imply the disappearance of government. Markets cannot function without property rights, a legal system, and other institutional auxiliaries supplied by the public sector. It is often not enough for government simply to "get out of the way."[8] Any analysis of the impact of reform on patterns of governance must be sensitive to these complexities.[9]

General benefits. Finally, reform seeks to promote benefits for diffuse groups like consumers, workers, or taxpayers. Hence, general-interest reforms (whether motivated by self-regarding, or other, preferences, or some combination thereof) can be distinguished from *special interest* policies. General-interest reforms are policies that would theoretically be adopted if information, organization, and transaction costs of the general polity were zero.[10]

Two generic categories of general-interest reform exist, as David R. Mayhew helpfully observes. The first consists of efforts to apply "universalistic distributive standards" on the activities of government or, more broadly, to "have the government venture forth and impose universalistic distributive standards on society."[11] Reforms in this vein (which, as Mayhew notes, may impinge on "particularism" or "servicing of the organized") include tax reform, farm subsidy reform, airline deregulation, Medicare Catastrophic Coverage Insurance, and ERISA. The second category of reform activity involves "efforts to impart instrumental rationality on governmental undertakings."[12] Examples include procurement reform and the emissions-trading program for acid rain. These are obviously broad categories. Each of these overarching reform styles encompasses a variety of more specific policy techniques, from deregulation and the creation of new markets to policy retrenchment.

The benefits of reforms show up in different guises. They include *fiscal benefits* (e.g., lower taxes or smaller future budget deficits). They also include administrative benefits (e.g., more effective public service delivery) and economic benefits (e.g., lower consumer prices). Whatever form the benefits take, it is critical to distinguish a reform's distributional effects (*who* receives a given supply of benefits) from its implications for social welfare and economic efficiency (*how many* benefits are available for distribution).

The distributional effects of reform are readily understood. They arise when a general-interest measure reallocates wealth, transferring it from a special-interest group to some broader constituency. One group wins, another loses. Such distributional effects will be highly salient in the political debates surrounding reform.

But policy reform, at times at least, may entail more than giving diffuse groups a larger slice of the existing economic pie. It may also *increase the size of the pie*. Reform may promote economic efficiency and growth in two ways. First, it may lower political "rent-seeking" costs—that is, the campaign contributions, lobbying expenses, and public relations efforts that narrow groups undertake in order to obtain pure profits, or what economists call "rents." Resources devoted to rent-seeking move "wealth around without increasing it."[13] Narrow groups will expend rent-seeking resources up to the amount they expect to gain from the transfers. All these expenditures constitute resources that are not going to create more socially productive activities. Since real costs are being incurred, "the economic pie shrinks in the process of being redivided."[14] Reform may also expand the economic pie by reducing "deadweight losses"—that is, losses in consumption or production not offset by gains to *anyone*. When deadweight losses can be mitigated, the winners from reform could theoretically compensate the losers and *still* come out ahead. Thus, policy reform is no longer a strictly zero-sum game.[15]

It is, of course, not unproblematic to identify *specific* general-interest reform policies, even if a generic definition of reform is accepted. Everyone claims that her preferred policies provide benefits for all; that is the nature of democratic politics. In this study, as in many others, the focus is on the claims of relatively disinterested policy analysis, as performed by academics, independent think tanks, and others. I also focus on policies that display the tell-tale signs of general-interest reform, including sponsorship by policy entrepreneurs, rationalization of public policy, and passage over the initial opposition of narrow group interests. Finally, I focus on policies that have received substantial attention in the political science, economics, and policy analysis literatures on reform enactments.

THE TWO PHASES OF REFORM

The policy reform process is composed of two phases, each of which requires attention.[16] The first involves getting reform proposals on the policy agenda, mobilizing key supporters, neutralizing the opposition, and building a winning political coalition for the passage of reform legislation. These are formidable tasks, given the inevitable existence of entrenched reform opponents. But they can be accomplished with the right mix of entrepreneurial energy, procedural manipulation, and political strategy.

The second phase of reform begins the moment *after* the curtain falls on the high drama of legislative enactments. It entails the recasting of interests, institutions, and ideas.[17] In the long run, this second phase is even more important than the first, because it is then that reform ideas meet the tough realities of democratic politics. All the political compromises and administrative complexities that were denied or papered over during the adoption phase will show themselves, sooner if not later.

THE POLITICAL LOGIC OF REFORM ADOPTION

The initial passage of general-interest reforms is a puzzle that requires a *political* explanation. This statement is not uncontroversial. On the contrary some "Chicago School" economists claim that the losses in potential economic output from inefficient arrangements naturally generate support for reforms that will preserve more value, so that more benefits are available for distribution to organized groups.[18] In other words, there will be continuing pressure to curb inefficiencies until none remain. But this is Panglossian.[19] Inefficient public policies and institutions can persist for very long periods of time.[20] The fact that the general public has a powerful stake in reform does not mean its diffuse interest will be represented. Organization, information, and transaction costs all intrude.

Indeed, the more one contemplates the forces at play in American politics, the more remarkable the passage of general-interest reforms seems. Yet general-interest reforms *do* occur. The special interests can be defeated, and policy inefficiencies and pathologies can be mitigated, if not everyday, then with sufficient frequency to suggest that reform is an integral, if not inevitable, part of the American political tradition. How do policy reformers manage to harness the latent power of diffuse interests to recast public policy?

A small but fascinating body of political science research addresses this important puzzle. This literature has not produced a formal model that can predict exactly when specific policies will be recast. However, it draws attention to the role of policy entrepreneurs who find ways to upset an old equilibrium to bring about positive change.[21] The literature suggests three strategic conditions that generally must be fulfilled for general-interest reform measures to be adopted. First, reform advocates must lower the *information costs* of mass publics by linking reform solutions to salient issues; second, reform proponents must use *procedural* strategies to render the organizational advantages of narrow groups relatively less potent; and finally, reform advocates must use *tactics* to neutralize the political opposition.

Raising the Awareness of Uninformed Citizens

Inefficiencies and policy distortions may persist because mass publics fail to recognize the costs of existing arrangements. Politics is an enormously complex matter that requires time and energy to follow and understand. Most ordinary citizens are occupied with their jobs, families, and personal lives. They do not spend their spare time reading *The Economist*, *Congressional Quarterly*, and *The New York Times*. If citizens are to grasp their stake in general-interest reform, they need someone to prompt them. A key role of entrepreneurial experts and public officials is to lower the information costs faced by ordinary citizens.[22]

In their powerfully argued book, *The Politics of Deregulation*, Martha Derthick and Paul Quirk state that deregulation of the airline and trucking industries would not have occurred if academic economists and well-placed executives like Alfred E. Kahn at the Civil Aeronautics Board had not made such a strong intellectual case for it. Yet the ideas of policy experts, by themselves, will not bring about the passage of reform measures. To be useful in an age of sound bites and thirty-second campaign commercials, expert advice must be responsive to the needs of officeholders for solutions to salient "problems." Such advice must be "graspable" to mass publics, meaning capable of being rendered by the media and other agenda-setting actors "in simple, symbolic, intuitively appealing terms."[23] In the airline deregulation case, for example, key politicians such as Senator Ted Kennedy (D-MA) reduced information costs by linking the deregulation to ordinary voters' fears of runaway inflation. By packaging policy information in a way that can be understood by ordinary voters, reform advocates can overcome the rational ignorance that shields inferior government policies from political criticism and revision.[24]

Manipulating the Procedural Context of Decisions

A second reason why reforms are hard to adopt is because the groups who profit from existing policies generally face lower organizational costs than the larger, more dispersed groups that are harmed by them. The politics of blame avoidance thus naturally encourages lawmakers to serve the better-organized.[25]

How then to neutralize the organizational advantages of clientele groups in reform debates? R. Douglas Arnold persuasively argues that the key step is for coalition leaders to frame the debate over reform measures in a way that compels lawmakers to consider not just the preferences of attentive well-organized clienteles, but also the *potential preferences* of ordinary citizens in future election contests.[26] This often requires skillful manipulation of the procedural setting in which policy decisions are made. If open meetings are filled with lobbyists, then meetings can be closed. If open rules during floor debates permit recorded votes on particularistic amendments, then rules can be closed. As chapter three discusses, tax reform coalition leaders adopted procedural strategies to mask legislators' individual responsibility for closing inefficient loopholes favored by powerful clientele groups. Leaders met in secret, avoided recorded votes, and adopted restrictive rules to prevent emasculating amendments, giving lawmakers the opportunity to vote for a major tax bill that offered significant rate reductions to average citizens. In a similar vein, when Congress wished to terminate a number of politically sensitive, but militarily obsolete, installations during the 1980s, it gave a bipartisan commission the authority to propose a list of base closures, which then had to be voted up or down without amendment, keeping members' attention focused on the package's overall reform goals. In sum, reform advocates can craft decision-making procedures that encourage lawmakers to respond to diffuse interests. Collective responsibility and the pursuit of individual self-interest can be mutually reinforcing.

Making Tactical Concessions to the Opposition

Finally, reformers must often make tactical concessions in order to build a winning political coalition. The concentrated costs associated with general-interest reform proposals may initially render them unfeasible. By modifying a reform's design, coalition leaders may be able to improve its chance of passage. Key tactics include the use of transition mechanisms, compensation schemes, and side payments.[27] In the tax reform case, for example, Senate Finance Committee chairman Bob Packwood (R-Oregon) doled out "transition rules"—special preferences that exempt certain groups from the new tax law—to hold the reform coalition together.[28] While fiscal constraints may limit the generosity of direct "buy out" packages, the scope of compensation payments can sometimes be masked though the use of complex payment schedules. Partial compensation can also be provided without any explicit payments to targeted groups by phasing-in the reforms gradually.

THE LIMITATIONS OF REFORM ADOPTION STRATEGIES

The use of informational, procedural, and compensation strategies is crucial to winning the adoption of general-interest reforms. They allow political entrepreneurs to reframe the debate in ways that encourage responsiveness to diffuse interests. *Unfortunately, these strategies do not guarantee a reform's long-term sustainability.* In part, this is because political forces gain and lose strength independently of decisions by political entrepreneurs. Economic developments, demographic changes, election outcomes and other exogenous factors affect reform outcomes. In addition, each reform strategy has inherent limitations (Table 2-1). Attention to these limitations offers insights into why some reforms have stuck and others have not. There is also a practical importance to these issues. Reformers who wish to see their creations last need to be aware of the strengths and weaknesses of various strategies.

TABLE 2-1
Distinctive Limitations of Reform Strategies

Reform Strategy	Key Post-Enactment Limitations
Information strategies	Limits of symbolism
	"Issue-attention cycle"
Procedural strategies	Declining collective payoff to hand-tying
Compensation tactics	Commitment problems (political uncertainty and time-inconsistency)
	Perverse incentives for constituencies

The Limitation of Information Strategies

Reform advocates often seek to lower the information costs of mass publics, allowing ordinary citizens to connect reform goals with salient problems. While it is possible to lower these information costs temporarily, it is not easy to do so indefinitely. Consider the use of political symbolism to make complex reform issues compelling to uninformed citizens. Symbols evoke emotional or intuitive responses from mass publics. They are easiest to deploy when officeholders must take a high-profile stand on some issue, such as casting a roll call vote on the passage of a comprehensive reform measure. The apparent finality of the vote provides the drama needed to cast the debate in clear, compelling terms, especially when powerful lobbyists are mobilized on the other side. When, however, general-interest reforms already on the books are threatened with the slow death of a thousand nicks—such as when politicians think about opening a new tax loophole after a base-broadening reform has been signed—it may be difficult for reform advocates to use symbols to good effect. The proposed change will not in and of itself destroy the reform, and its proponents can easily find some reason to claim that an "exception" to the existing policy framework is warranted. Only after an encompassing reform has been thoroughly gutted through the steady accumulation of particularistic modifications will most people begin to notice, and by then it is too late.

The dynamics of media attention also can serve to undermine reforms. During the initial debate over reform adoption, the media may gravitate toward a compelling issue definition that lowers information costs and advantages reform advocates. Unfortunately, it is in the nature of media coverage to shift attention over time. According to Anthony Downs, many public issues are subject to an identifiable "issue-attention" cycle.[29] An initial sense of the pressing need to mitigate a given problem can be lost when the sense of an impending crisis fades, the costs of resolving the problem become apparent, and other issues arise that compete for the attention of policy elites and mass publics. Over time, the spotlight of the media may shift either to alternative "framings" of an issue or to a completely different topic.[30] Such attention shifts may make it easier for the narrow interests who would profit from the unraveling or dilution of a preexisting reform to win new policy concessions.

Other available information cost-reducing mechanisms are also likely to be less effective during the post-enactment stage than during the more visible, earlier contest over a reform's passage. For example, information costs may be lowered though information provided by third parties, such as public watchdog groups. Citizens may not know what to make of a complex reform debate, but if a trusted group provides cues, they may be able to figure out their stand with relatively little effort. It is reasonable to expect, however, that watchdog groups will have a weaker incentive to monitor the post-adoption phase than they did to get involved in the pre-adoption politics. They do not receive as large a substantive or symbolic payoff from the hard work of ex-post-monitoring as they did from the pre-adoption advocacy. The battles over policy changes will tend to be far murkier and the "good guys" and "bad guys" harder to identify. Given these difficulties, and the probable lack of sustained media attention to the reform's post-enactment fate, the staff and volunteers of watchdog groups will tend to be less motivated.

The Limitation of Procedural Strategies

Procedural strategies, such as the use of restrictive legislative rules to prevent consideration of particularistic amendments, also have important limitations. Lawmakers are generally free to adopt whatever procedural rules they wish.[31] While general-interest reforms enacted by large majorities may enjoy some insulation from decay, the conditions that lead policymakers to "tie their hands" are unlikely to persist.[32] General-interest reforms involve an effort to recast an existing line of policymaking. Policymakers may be willing to limit their flexibility during the adoption stage because they are attacking an egregious problem. The comprehensive nature of the reform allows policymakers to deliver a large amount of benefits for the mass public, making the collective payoff from hand-tying high. The Tax Reform Act of 1986, for example, allowed members to vote for rate reductions for millions of individual taxpayers by closing hundreds of tax loopholes at once. Coalition leaders were able to convince back benchers that it was in everyone's interest to restrict the menu of options.

After reform adoption, however, the policy status quo changes, and the politics of incrementalism often returns. When lawmakers are considering minor modifications to a reform already on the books, they may be unwilling to restrict their options. For example, the creation of a new tax break allows policymakers to offer concentrated benefits to some constituencies at a relatively modest cost, but maintaining a clean tax code will not permit tax rates to be lowered any further without increasing the deficit; the cost savings are too small. Maintaining a commitment to a reform may not deliver enough benefits to make the continued use of restrictive procedures attractive.[33]

Lawmakers are unlikely to face pressure from diffuse publics to maintain reform-compatible decision rules. The media typically does not cover procedural votes, and it is hard to capture the interest of ordinary citizens who are busy with their work and personal lives. Procedural issues are just too arcane. These low-profile procedural issues are precisely the kind where narrow groups have their greatest advantage because of their lower costs of political mobilization. They can be expected to pressure lawmakers into considering decisions under procedures more favorable to their interests. For all these reasons, policymakers are far more likely to agree to "tie their hands" when major reforms are initially being considered than during the post-adoption stage.

The Limitations of Compensation Tactics

Finally, compensation strategies also have limitations. While the use of transition schemes may be essential to buying out the opposition, it will only promote the case of reform if opponents *stay bought*. Unless the reform process has permanently damaged or stigmatized them, however, the losers from reform will have every incentive to pursue their own parochial agendas as soon as the ink is dry on the page with the reform printed on it. As the composition of government changes over time, these clienteles may well find politicians sympathetic to their causes. Not only will new problems and solutions emerge on the agenda, and will objective conditions change, but the goals of today's officeholders are unlikely to be shared completely by the officeholders of tomorrow.[34]

Even policymakers who voted for the original reform may find it hard to turn a deaf ear to groups' particularistic demands, especially if the post-reform experience turns out worse than anticipated at the enactment stage (and narrow groups will have every incentive to highlight the reform's costs and to suppress any discussion of its general benefits). Policymakers may also struggle to avoid the temptations of symbolism when outcomes are bad or simply hard to defend before mass publics. In sum, the problem is not only that politicians may not be able to bind their successors. They may not even be able to *bind themselves*. While lawmakers may initially possess a strong incentive to agree to a buy-out scheme, they may have an equally strong incentive to reverse course later—even when sticking to the original schedule would be socially optimal.[35] This is the so-called "time-consistency" problem.[36] It can arise whenever there is a tension between the best general plan, and the preferred thing to do at a particular moment.[37]

The larger problem is that many general-interest reforms, especially those involving the unleashing of market forces, take time to consolidate themselves. Actors must learn about the new policies, information must be exchanged, and a new political equilibrium must be established. While policymakers and social actors need to give the reforms time to work, they may have very short time horizons. A key political challenge is therefore protecting the reforms during their initial years, when they may be most vulnerable to reversal.

MAKING REFORM LAST

The main lesson is that reform outcomes are never completely settled. Policy reform must be seen as a dynamic process in which forces seeking to protect a reform may be opposed by forces seeking to undo it.

Yet it is entirely possible for a reform to become so deeply rooted in political practice and culture over time that its dismantlement becomes all but unthinkable.[38] What accounts for the variance in reform trajectories? Because reform is best understood as an evolutionary process, attention must be directed to the factors that determine the willingness and capacity of policymakers to encourage, extend, or frustrate a reform's development.

As the politics of reform unfolds over time, three factors come into play. The first is the extent to which *political structures* propel a reform forward, supply necessary legal and administrative supports, and buffer the reform from pressures to change course. The second is whether the market forces unleashed by a reform induce *creative destructiveness*. The final factor is whether the reform generates positive *policy feedback effects*. I discuss each of these factors in the following pages. The order of this discussion is not accidental. While political structures clearly affect the long-term fates of reforms, market forces frequently matter more, and policy feedback matters most of all.

Political Structures

Scholars as diverse as Barry Weingast, Terry Moe, and Stephen Skowronek have discussed the role of institutions in promoting durable policy change. While current policymakers always retain the legal authority to revise existing laws, a reform has better odds of sticking, and of serving as a platform for reinforcing policy changes over time, if its passage occurs simultaneously with supportive shifts in its structural environment. Four kinds of shifts may be important.

First, reforms may strengthen governing capacities.[39] This may occur through changes in administrative authority to better align the incentives of bureaucrats, through the hiring of new staff with relevant policy expertise and through the elimination of "red tape" that frustrates the appropriate exercise of administrative discretion. Second, reforms may raze the structural foundations of "cozy policy subsystems" and "iron triangles." Their destruction may be necessary to prevent inefficient patterns of governance from reproducing themselves post-enactment. A reform may constrain future decision-making through administrative procedures or bureaucratic structures.[40] Or it may even bring about a bureau's termination.[41] Alternatively, reforms may weaken policy subsystems by empowering actors with broader perspectives on governance, such as executives or budget guardians in Congress. Third, political transaction costs can be raised or lowered to make a reform more sticky.[42] This might be done to promote credibility and give actors confidence that movement along a reform path will continue. Transaction costs might be raised, for example, to block the adoption of inefficient policies (e.g., budget rules that require a supermajority for the adoption of a tax expenditure benefiting a small number of people). Rather than making it harder to do the "wrong thing," rule changes can also make it easier to do the "right thing." For example, amendments that would accelerate future movement along an existing reform path can be placed on a legislative "fast track," allowing them to circumvent normal procedural roadblocks or veto points.[43]

Finally, control over a given policy arena can be shifted to a political venue in which reform coalitions enjoy privileged access.[44] For example, reformers may seek to relocate policymaking authority from one congressional committee to another or from the regulatory process back into Congress or even into the courts. In the fragmented U.S. political system, official policy decisions concerning a particular set of government activities can typically be made through multiple venues. As Frank Baumgartner and Bryan Jones observe, each venue is generally associated with a prevailing understanding of the core issues. This policy image, in turn, determines which client groups are considered politically legitimate and which groups are viewed as unwelcome outsiders.[45] In a world of multiple equilibria, shifting authority over an issue from one venue to another may determine which equilibria are actually brought about.[46]

Some long-lasting reforms have been reinforced through multiple structural mechanisms. An illustrative example is the Reciprocal Trade Agreements Act (RTAA) of 1934, a landmark trade policy reform that successfully collapsed logrolling coalitions supportive of high tariffs. The reform shifted the locus of trade decisions from the tax arena (in which Congress considered each tariff separately) to treaty negotiation (in which the president negotiated comprehensive tariff packages with other nations); "bundled" foreign tariff reductions and domestic tariff reductions into one legislative package (which legislators had to vote up or down on without amendment); and created special voting rules that avoided the need to obtain supermajority support for tariff reductions in Congress.[47]

Yet if the development of a reform is shaped by its structural environment, future policy outcomes rarely can be "locked in."[48] One reason is that political structures are not infrequently the products of political compromise. They may be little more than "common carriers" of multiple interests.[49] Tensions and contradictions among these goals may limit any clear sense of purpose or mission. Second, efforts to "stack the deck" can backfire, even when institutional designers have shared goals. Institutional design is an inexact science. Even the cleverest and most farsighted reformers cannot wholly escape the law of unintended consequences. Finally, it is hard to compel outcomes in a free society in which sustaining a reform and implementing it successfully typically requires the support—or at least the acquiescence—of private actors, who possess some capacity to withdraw their support.

Consider the case of ERISA. As we shall see, this reform was designed to universalize and raise the funding standards for defined-pension benefits, yet the Pension Benefit Guaranty Corporation was crafted without the authority to impose market-based insurance premiums. At the same time, however, ERISA funding rules proved unacceptably stringent to many sponsors of defined-benefit pensions. The largely unplanned result was to accelerate a movement among private firms toward defined-contribution plans.

Creative Destruction

Before a reform can create a new order, it must break up the existing one. Joseph A. Schumpeter famously described a process of "creative destruction," which occurs when entrepreneurs introduce new products, create new markets, or invent new methods of production.[50] In the first case, this requires the conscious disequilibration of the status quo. In the second, it is the product of the "impersonal forces of the market."[51] While Schumpeter was writing about the cultivation of new consumer demands for economic innovations, his ideas have clear affinities to policy reform. Political reformers attack power monopolies and invest in the development of new policy ideas. Sometimes political entrepreneurs are able to bring about the total destruction of their targets. More often, their reform victories are partial and incomplete. As Adam Sheingate observes in an excellent essay on political entrepreneurship, reform advocates rarely can dislodge their political rivals altogether.[52] The lawmakers who lose in one round of reform may return to fight another day.[53]

But what is true about the *political* losers from reform may not be true of the *economic* losers. Here, competitive market forces may come into play.[54] Markets can be harsh, fickle, and unpredictable. Yet markets may well be in an excellent position to have the last word on policy reform. While market forces possess a particularly large influence on policy outcomes when reforms mediate or deregulate economic behavior or create new marketable goods, they in fact matter anytime the targets of reform possess a degree of exit power. Unlike politicians who voted against reform (who can hang on as long as their constituents are willing to tolerate their losing positions) market actors who lose market share in the post-reform environment can easily disappear.[55] The market forces unleashed by airline deregulation, for example, led to the demise of many existing air carriers and also destroyed the political cohesion of the regulated industry.

The powerful shaping role of autonomous market forces (as against the political influence of business corporations) is somewhat downplayed in the APD literature. Most historically oriented political scientists focus on durable changes in *formal* authority. But the uncoordinated and often unpredictable choices of producers and millions of consumers arguably often have a greater influence over social outcomes in many policy sectors than do elected officials, lobbyists, or voters. The influence of markets must be brought into the foreground in studies of policy development over time. While markets are underpinned by public authority, they have a major influence on the menu of sustainable reform options.

Policy Feedback

Sustaining a reform is a *constructive* process as well as a destructive one. Once enacted, reforms may create new political facts on the ground. Here, I draw upon the literature on "policy feedback," the study of how policies, once passed, influence political dynamics going forward.[56] This literature has demonstrated that policies are not only the result of ongoing political struggles. They also reshape the identities, interests, and goals of individuals and constituency groups, allocate political resources, encourage or discourage political mobilization, and create—or fail to create—expectations among individuals and groups that make it difficult or unattractive for leaders to reverse course.

The literature on policy feedback effects traces its origins to E. E. Schattschneider's observation that "new policies create a new politics."[57] It also has antecedents in the policy typologies offered by Theodore Lowi and James Q. Wilson, which attempted to show how different kinds of policies stimulated different political dynamics.[58] In more recent years, scholars such as Theda Skocpol, Paul Pierson, Andrea Campbell, Jacob Hacker, Suzanne Mettler, and Joe Soss have investigated policy feedback in fine-grained detail.[59] I draw extensively on this literature but seek to broaden its scope of application to general-interest reforms, including market-oriented policies. My analysis covers several distinct types of interest-group feedback. I also suggest a new framework for thinking systematically about the conditions under which reforms are most sustainable.

Nearly all of the recent work on policy feedback has focused on welfare state programs. There are two reasons for this. First, the policy feedback in this arena is often extremely strong because the relevant programs have a massive tangible impact on citizens' lives on a daily basis.[60] Andrea Campbell has demonstrated, for example, that Social Security transformed senior citizens from the most beleaguered to the most politically active age group.[61] In a similar vein, Suzanne Mettler has shown that the G.I. Bill's educational benefits increased veterans' subsequent membership in civic organizations and political activity.[62] These programs define the meaning of democratic citizenship in America. The second reason why scholars have focused on feedback from welfare state programs is that they offer clues as to the historical causes of American exceptionalism. Jacob Hacker has argued, for example, that the creation of a tax-subsidized employer-based private insurance system created peculiar obstacles to the enactment of universal health insurance in the United States.[63]

In contrast, almost no scholarship has explored the possible feedback from general-interest reform laws. Yet the sustainability of these reforms hinges on the reactions, expectations, and behavioral change they generate over time. To be sure, one should not expect such reforms to stimulate significant feedback *in the mass public.* Compared to programs like Social Security or Medicare, the benefits of politics like airline deregulation, farm subsidy reform, tax reform, and procurement reform are just too diffuse, invisible, and distant.[64] But the reforms can potentially generate crucial feedback on policy elites, especially interest groups.[65]

Several types of interest-group feedback should be distinguished (Table 2-2). The first is *creating constituencies.* The primary intended beneficiaries of reforms, such as taxpayers and consumers, typically are too dispersed to constitute an effective organizational force, except where there is the continuing involvement of a policy entrepreneur to lower information and mobilization costs. However, producers who receive the "spoils" from reform, such as low-cost air carriers post-deregulation, may become vested in the new system.[66] Second, reforms may also increase or decrease the *political cohesion* of a previously regulated or subsidized industry or sector. All things being equal, less cohesive sectors (e.g., industries in which individual firms have different cost structures, strategies, and business plans) are more costly to mobilize. Rather than being a pure negative for sustainability, the generation of such collective action problems *among reform enemies* may reduce pressure on government to renege on its reform promises. Multiple clientele groups may counteract one another, just like classical pluralist theory predicts.

Third, reforms may alter the *cognitive mindsets* of preexisting groups.[67] A key challenge after reform is to convince narrow clientele groups that their long-term economic fate depends upon their own productive efforts, rather than on their success at winning favors and advantages through political lobbying efforts.[68] Whether a group in fact alters its political behavior after reform, however, depends in part on its exceptions. If the credibility of a reform is high, the interest group may conclude that future rent seeking is not profitable. In contrast, if the reform lacks credibility, the group may rationally continue to look to the government for sustenance.[69]

Finally, the debate surrounding the enactment of a reform may *tarnish the public image* of a group formerly held in high regard.[70] This may occur through a process of stigmatization, in which a group with a previously favorable image becomes associated with greedy or parochial behavior. An example would be the change in the image of the tobacco industry from the producer of a sexy revenue-producing product to a mass killer.[71] Alternatively, it may occur through "unmasking," which happens when reforms strip narrow clientele groups of their subsequent ability to camouflage their agendas (e.g., huge agribusinesses somehow losing their ability to hide behind the symbolism of the family farmer). In sum, potential interest-group feedback from reform includes both the generation of reliable allies *and* the weakening of enemies.

A fair number of moving parts exist here. Unfortunately, a full understanding of the aftermath of policy reforms requires attention to all of them. It is nonetheless possible to suggest hypotheses about the *general* conditions under which reforms will be most sustainable and about the specific kinds of post-re-

TABLE 2-2
Varieties of Interest-Group Feedback

Mechanism	Feedback Effect
Material stakes / investments	Countervailing constituencies
Costs of collective action	Change in diversity and political cohesion of group interests
Policy learning	Shift in "cognitive mindsets" Tarnishing of group images

form dynamics that should be expected to arise under different circumstances.[72] Two overarching feedback effects are crucial. The first is the way reform affects the *identities and political affiliations of relevant group actors*.[73] After reform, the scope and composition of the interest-group environment may be generally stable, and the identities and alliances of preexisting interests may undergo relatively little change. Because the sector is not being continually penetrated by new groups with diverse preferences and incentives, interest-group cohesion in the sector will be relatively high. There may still be areas of conflict on particular issues, but the fact that group memberships and patterns of interaction are reasonably stable facilitates the emergence of a sector-wide consensus on major counter-reform efforts. Alternatively, group dynamics may change dramatically after reform enactments. A sector may see the entry of an ever-changing constellation of groups, each of which finds itself in a somewhat different economic and strategic situation. Lobbying in the sector will be characterized by rapidly changing coalitions, as allies on one issue become adversaries on the next. The fragmentation of the emerging "issue network" will tend to inhibit organizational mobilization around a common anti-reform agenda, leaving each group to pursue its own narrow goals.[74] Such dynamics are more likely to emerge in very broad policy sectors like taxation.[75]

A second important feedback process is the effect of the reform on actors' *investments*. After the reforms, relevant societal interests can make extensive commitments based on the expectation that the reform will be maintained. This suggests an increasing returns process in which groups develop assets that are specific to the new policy regime.[76] There is no guarantee that reforms will induce complementary public or private investments, however. In sum, reforms potentially *may* generate path dependence, but it is an empirical question whether they actually do so.[77] This implies a simple two-by-two matrix in which both the stability and cohesion of group identities and the level of investments vary (Figure 2-1). Four post-reform paths can be specified.

In the upper-left quadrant, where affected groups fail to make significant investments and the interest group environment is stable and cohesive, there is a high probability of *reform reversal*, meaning an implicit or explicit repeal of

Group Investments	Group Identities and Affiliations	
	Stable (Identities and group affiliations remain stable, many clienteles have common policy preferences)	**Fluid** (New groups emerge, coalitional alignments undergo rapid change, interest group cohesion is low)
Modest (Social actors fail to make large scale investments; organizational adaptations to the reform are minimal)	*REVERSAL OF REFORM* "The Empire Strikes Back," "Never mind!"	*EROSION OF REFORM* "Death by a thousand cuts," "Smothering"
Extensive (Groups make large scale, often highly specific investments based on the expectation that the reform will continue)	*ENTRENCHMENT OF REFORM* "Dug in"	*RECONFIGURATION* "Whole new ball game"

Figure 2-1. Policy Feedback and Post-Reform Dynamics.

the reform, leading to a return to the status quo ante. Two variants of the reversal dynamic may appear. The first is "The Empire Strikes Back."[78] Here, the previously dominant coalition that lost the prior battle over reform adoption is able to regroup and to exert strong pressure to restore the status quo ante. The other variant is "Never Mind!," which occurs when politicians *themselves* take the lead in reversing a reform. (Of course, it is possible for both clientele groups and politicians to be culpable in a reform reversal, as we shall see in the agricultural reform case. The key point is that both governmental and nongovernmental actors can play important roles.)

In the upper-right quadrant, where passage of a reform fails to promote significant clientele investments but the interest-group environment is very fluid, the erosion of reform should be anticipated. This is a more subtle and usually more gradual process than outright reversal. The reform statute itself remains on the books, and some of its substantive policy achievements may even stick, but the logic of the reform is not extended over time. Continual micro-level pressures are applied by various rent seekers to erode the reform after enactment because the policy sector features a diversity of unvested interests. The erosion dynamic has two variants, which may occur separately or in tandem. The first is "Death by a Thousand Cuts." This occurs when policymakers repeatedly adopt incremental amendments that undercut the reform. While each amendment constitutes only a marginal departure from the status quo, and might be justified by the need to make a "special exception" to the reform's overarching rules, the cumulative effect is very large. The reform gradually loses its coherence and integrity, and its particularistic exceptions swallow its more general rules. The second erosion dynamic is "Smothering." In this scenario, a reform law is not formally amended, but policymakers enact subsequent laws with antithetical policy goals. The original reform remains "good law" but gets buried so deeply under a maze of conflicting statutes or rules that it all but disappears from view.[79]

In the bottom-left quadrant, patterns of interaction among relevant groups remain stable, and the organizational cohesion of the sector is fairly high, but actors make large-scale investments based on the reform's expected maintenance. Here, the *entrenchment* of a reform is predicted. Reform gains are consolidated because group actors adapt to the new facts on the ground—they are "Dug in." But the constellation of actors in the sector does not significantly change. Preexisting coalitional alignments remain in tact, but the reform is now something that groups must deal with.[80]

Finally, in the lower-right quadrant, political dynamics experience a *reconfiguration*. The creative destructiveness of the market or other powerful forces causes new producer or consumer groups to join or replace preexisting interests in the sector. The diversity of interests raises the transaction costs of organizing a sectorwide counter-reform effort. Coalitional patterns undergo rapid change, upsetting previous alliances and patterns of political mobilization. Each group actor faces a different strategic situation, but is nonetheless stimulated to invest heavily in ways complementary to the reform's maintenance. The old rules of political behavior no longer apply, and there may be considerable uncertainty about how the "whole new ball game" is to be played. The defining feature of reconfiguration is the impossibility of going back to the pre-reform status quo, even if some actors wish to do so. Political dynamics can no more easily be reversed than "scrambled eggs" can be unscrambled (an image that politicians sometimes invoke to describe the vast societal transformations wrought by airline deregulation).

· · ·

This chapter has argued that the enactment of general-interest reforms is theoretically possible but far from inevitable. Concentrated groups have organizational advantages over more diffuse ones, and blame-avoiding politicians are often reluctant to challenge longstanding governing arrangements. Yet unorganized, diffuse interests *can* be politically influential. And the societal benefits of instrumentally rational policy can carry the day over symbolism. The adoption of reform legislation becomes feasible when political entrepreneurs connect reform ideas to salient public issues, employ decision-making procedures to keep the focus on the general benefits of reform, and use compensation tactics to buy out the losers. After reform adoption, new political challenges arise. The enactment of a reform is no guarantee of its long-term sustainability. Reforms may have many enemies, and their supporters may be too dispersed to mobilize.

All is not lost, however. The reforms may generate creative destruction, tossing aside old forms to make space for new ones. Political structures and policy feedback effects can help protect the reforms from inhospitable policy change, creating a self-reinforcing dynamic in which social actors adapt themselves to the new policy regime. In sum, reforms *can* endure. What has been the experience with major general-interest reforms in the United States? Why have some reforms been more sustainable than others? To answer these questions, and to understand the political, historical, and institutional contexts in which reforms stick or fall apart, it is necessary to turn to a detailed examination of actual cases.

CHAPTER 3

Expert Ideas Meet Politics: Reforming the Tax Code

MAJOR POLICY REFORMS CAN BE unraveled without ever being repealed. A leading example has been the gradual erosion of the Tax Reform Act of 1986 (TRA), which has been justly described as "one of the most extraordinary economic policy initiatives of the 20th century."[1] TRA lowered tax rates, eliminated hundreds of special-interest tax credits and deductions, broadened the tax base, and shut down mass-marketed tax shelters for high-income individuals. Promoting the goals of the reform required politicians to restrain themselves from using the federal tax code as a vehicle for credit claiming and particularistic favor provision, but they did not. In the late 1980s, President George H.W. Bush pushed hard for new tax preferences for capital gains, reneging on the promise that all income would be taxed alike. A few years after, President Bill Clinton and a Democratic Congress raised marginal tax rates on upper-income families. President George W. Bush and a Republican Congress then lowered tax rates and created new tax breaks. The TRA remains on the statute books, and a number of its policy achievements live on. Nonetheless, the 1986 reform has been eroded by the subsequent changes that have narrowed the tax base and created new opportunities for sheltering taxable income. As Yale law professor and former Treasury Department official Michael Graetz writes, "Tax experts now regard the 1986 act as a promise failed."[2]

The TRA's unraveling was predictable because the reform was built upon weak political foundations. While some hoped the reform's passage would initiate a new era of tax policymaking, the TRA failed to change political incentives. It did not recast institutions to constrain future rent-seekers. Lobbyists retained easy access to the tax-writing panels in Congress, which continued to collect campaign contributions from interested parties. The TRA also did not generate positive policy feedbacks. In general, the TRA had only a transitory impact on economic investment decisions, and there were no significant changes in clientele expectations. In sum, the TRA represented a stunning victory of general interests over narrow ones that was driven by elite ideas about good tax policy, but the reform failed to durably reconfigure the political dynamic. The erosion of the TRA is not as happy a story as its initial passage. As a window into how American national government works, however, it is no less significant.

THE PRE-REFORM SITUATION

During the post-war era, elected officials became increasingly attracted to special tax provisions as a way to deliver benefits to particular regions, economic sectors, or constituency groups. Federal tax rates were then based on nominal income levels, causing tax revenues to rise automatically during periods of rapid inflation as taxpayers became subject to higher marginal rates. Defense cutbacks and economic growth also generated healthy revenue growth. With so much "free money" on the table, policymakers were eager to distribute some to the many interest groups pressing for special benefits within the tax code. The concentrated benefits of tax preferences allowed lawmakers to claim credit with recipients and lobbyists, while the diffuse costs ensured indifference from mass publics. Expanding tax preferences also enabled the government to grow without the appearance of a larger bureaucracy.[3] The members of the tax writing committees in Congress also had a stake in the steady creation of tax breaks: it enhanced their power, and made them attractive targets for lobbying and campaign contributions.[4]

Beginning in the early 1960s, tax policy economists and lawyers argued that tax preferences created complexities and gross inequities across taxpayers with similar incomes. Stanley Surrey, a Harvard professor who served as Assistant Secretary of the Treasury under President Kennedy, compiled a list of loopholes in the income tax that were functionally equivalent to the simultaneous collection of revenue and direct budget outlay to beneficiaries. By drawing attention to these "tax expenditures," Surrey hoped to create momentum for comprehensive tax reform.[5] Joseph Pechman and colleagues at the Brookings Institution argued that tax rates could be much lower if the government maintained a broad tax base, and that the proliferation of special tax preferences harmed the economy.

Some conservatives have argued that no "normal" tax base exists and that the government is not granting a privilege when it chooses not to tax something. While there has been a degree of ideological or partisan conflict on the legitimacy of the tax expenditure concept, historically a much more important pattern has been the inconsistency between politicians' rhetoric and behavior. Democrats and Republicans alike have embraced tax reform in theory, even as they demonstrated an eagerness to expand the tax expenditure system to create new benefits. As John F. Witte argues in his definitive study of the political development of the income tax over the post-war era, "rhetorical calls for tax reform coexist with a persistent stream of policy decisions that make a shambles of any conception of a simplified broad-based tax."[6] In his 1962 economic message, for example, President Kennedy called for simplification of the tax structure and the equal treatment of equally situated persons. Yet Kennedy simultaneously proposed the creation of an expensive investment tax credit to subsidize the purchase of business equipment. When the House Ways and Means and Senate Finance Committees marked up the Administration's bill, the tax breaks were retained but the loophole-closing provisions were gutted or eliminated. The result was the Revenue Act of 1962, a ramshackle bill that followed "no coherent plan or pattern other than to spread around the tax pork barrel."[7]

Most tax laws enacted in the 1960s and 1970s followed a similar pattern.[8] The closest Congress came during this period to passing a comprehensive tax reform measure was in 1969. The reform tightened a number of tax preferences, including the investment credit, the tax benefits granted to corporate mergers, and the oil depletion allowance. But the reform victory was short-lived. In 1971, for example, Congress reinstated the investment credit and created new tax preferences for export companies.[9] By 1982, tax expenditures accounted for 8.2 percent of GDP, up from 4.4 percent in 1967. Measured as a percentage of income tax receipts, tax breaks grew from 38.0 to 73.5 percent over this period.[10]

While much of the expansion of the tax-break system was due to high rates and the automatic growth of tax preferences already on the books, such as the home mortgage interest deduction, it also reflected the weakening of political constraints on the creation of new tax loopholes. During the post-war era, the tax writing panels in Congress exercised a measure of collective responsibility. Wilbur D. Mills (D-AK), chairman of the House Ways and Means Committee between 1957 and 1975, accepted the inevitability, and indeed desirability, of tax expenditures, yet he also believed in tax equity, efficiency, and simplicity. Mills tried to constrain the growth of the tax-break system. He often closed meetings to insulate Ways and Means from the demands of clientele groups and other lawmakers and he used special rules to protect carefully crafted tax packages from particularistic amendments on the floor. But Mills was thrown from power in 1974 after a sex scandal, and Watergate-era congressional reforms weakened the power of subsequent committee chairmen. The effect was to open the tax writing system to broader public participation and political influences.[11] The immediate winners from these changes were lobbyists, who found it easier to obtain special tax benefits for their clients. Another set of winners were tax accountants and lawyers, who advised doctors, lawyers, and other high-income professionals on how to exploit the differential tax treatment of different sources of income to obtain "tax arbitrage profits." The best-known form of arbitrage was the use of "tax shelters"—passively managed investments structured to create paper losses and reduce tax liabilities.[12] By the mid-1970s, tax shelters were proliferating at a rapid rate, leading President Jimmy Carter to call the U.S. tax system a "disgrace to the human race" throughout his 1976 campaign.[13]

Yet the general public was not clamoring for sweeping tax reform. Opinion surveys in the late 1970s showed that while base broadening and lower rates were attractive to citizens in the abstract, specific reform proposals failed to generate majority support.[14] While the analytic case for sweeping tax reform was extremely powerful, most knowledgeable observers believed the prospects for its adoption were exceedingly dim.[15]

THE POLITICS OF REFORM ADOPTION

Yet the Tax Reform Act of 1986 (P.L. 99-514) passed Congress by wide margins (292-136 in the House and 74-23 in the Senate) despite overwhelming opposition from some of the most powerful interests on Capitol Hill.[16] An army of well-heeled business groups, led by realtors and the oil-and-gas industry, worked feverishly to defeat the measure at every stage of the legislative process. The only significant organizational players on the pro-reform side, beyond public-interest lobbies such as Common Cause, were a limited number of highly taxed firms, including some wholesalers and electronics firms, which received few benefits from the existing tax-break system. These pro-reform business groups joined with consumers' unions and other supporters to form the Tax Reform Action Coalition. As Timothy J. Conlan, David R. Beam, and Margaret Wrightson argue in their insightful study of the passage of the 1986 Act, the presence of this coalition clearly helped protect legislative supporters from being labeled "antibusiness," but it simply "did not equal the strength of the multiplicity of groups opposing tax reform. Had Congress been a mere referee [among contending economic interests], the TRA would have lost in a lopsided game."[17]

Several factors were key to the stunning reform victory. First, skilled political entrepreneurs invested their time and energy in the reform cause. While most citizens were uninterested in tax reform, post-Watergate shifts in the political environment made it easier for strategically placed elites like Senator Bill Bradley (D-NJ) to push policy ideas that challenged longstanding arrangements. Bradley, along with Representatives Dick Gephardt and Jack Kemp, mediated between tax policy experts and the wider political arena.[18] A former New York Knicks basketball star who also had been a Rhodes scholar, Bradley knew from personal experience that high marginal tax rates created perverse incentives for tax-avoidance behavior.[19] With the technical assistance of Joe Minarik, the Congressional Budget Office economist and the support of organizations such as Citizens for Tax Justice, Bradley laid the political groundwork for a comprehensive tax reform plan. In August 1982, Bradley and Gephardt introduced the Fair Tax Act. The bill anticipated many of the principles that would be contained in the TRA, including substantial rate reduction and the curbing of many tax deductions, exclusions, and credits.[20] The most valuable resource of entrepreneurs like Bradley was the ability to get noticed, and the media offered a huge amount of publicity. *The New York*

Times placed tax reform on its front page fifteen times in 1984 and fifty-three times in 1985.[21] Most of this coverage was favorable to the tax reform cause, framing it as a symbolic battle between special interests and the public good.

Second, influential political leaders decided to endorse tax reform. After tax reform was put on the policy agenda, lawmakers had to take a stand. House Ways and Means Committee chairman Dan Rostenskowski (D-IL) was a supporter almost from the beginning. Senate Finance Committee chairman Robert Packwood (R-OR), in contrast, converted to the cause only after he realized that the media would portray him as an impotent pawn of the business lobby if he used his position to block reform. But Packwood never would have felt the pressure to support tax reform in the first place if President Ronald Reagan had not chosen to make the issue his own. In his January 1984 State of the Union address, Reagan asked the Department of Treasury to prepare a "plan for action to simplify the entire tax code."[22] Treasury I, the initial plan developed by C. Eugene Steuerle and other Reagan Treasury Department economists, was brutally tough. It concluded that business taxation was "deeply flawed." Subsidies to industry "distorted choices," and tax shelters for the affluent "undermined confidence in the tax system."[23] As Joseph White and Aaron Wildavsky observe, "If one picked a bunch of tax economists and lawyers at random, gave them the constraint of revenue neutrality, and told them to come up with a large-scale reform, Treasury I... would be it."[24]

A third key factor was a willingness of reformers to make political concessions. Ultimately, Treasury I proved too "pure" a reform, and many of its most far-reaching proposals, including curbs on tax breaks for employer-paid fringe benefits, were scrapped before the plan was sent to the Hill. Nonetheless, the striking thing—relative to prior patterns of tax policymaking—is how much of the academic experts' tax reform vision made its way into the final law.[25]

Despite President Reagan's support, tax reform's legislative fate was very much up for grabs. As R. Douglas Arnold observes, leaders such as Rostenkowski and Packwood, "employed virtually every strategy in the book" to hold the reform coalition together in Congress.[26] They targeted a large number of tax preferences for repeal, rather than chiseling at only a few at time, in order to generate the savings needed to permit dramatically lower tax rates, which were integral to the measure's public appeal. They insisted that the whole bill be revenue and geographically neutral to avoid exacerbating ideological or regional conflicts. They manipulated legislative procedures to protect lawmakers from narrow group pressures. Lawmakers met in secret, avoided recorded votes, and used restrictive rules to keep the bill from being picked apart on the floor. Finally, coalition leaders strategically used side-payments to lubricate the package's adoption. The bill included almost 700 so-called "transition rules" to exempt specific taxpaying entitles, such as General Motors, Pan Am, and the University of Delaware, from the general provisions of the reform. The stated objective was to ease the adjustment to the new tax system. The real purpose was to offer fence-sitting members some particularistic benefits for which they could claim credit with companies and organizations in their districts. The five-year cost of the transition rules was estimated at $10.6 billion.[27]

Major Provisions of the TRA

The TRA was projected to reduce the tax burden on individuals by $121.9 billion over five years while increasing corporate taxes by $120.3 billion and other taxes by $1.4 billion. Four out of five individual tax payers were expected to receive cuts, despite the elimination of many tax breaks and deductions. The reform replaced the existing 14 tax breaks for families (15 for single taxpayers), which ranged from 11 to 50 percent, with a two-bracket system, with rates of 15 and 28 percent, for 1988 and later years.[28] The standard deduction was increased to $5,000 for married couples and the personal exemption was raised to $2,000.

The reform eliminated deductions for state and local sales taxes, consumer interest, and two-earner couples. Caps were placed on deductions for business meals, entertainment, and medical expenses. Tax rates on long-term capital gains were increased to match rates on other income. The reform also shut down a number of tax shelters. For example, it eliminated, over a five-year phase-out period, provisions allowing so-called passive losses generated by investments in limited real estate partnerships, in which investors took no active managerial role. Under prior law, such losses could be used to reduce income for tax purposes. At the corporate level, TRA reduced the top corporate rate from 46 to 34 percent while tightening the corporate minimum tax. It broadened the corporate tax base by eliminating the investment tax break and scaling back depreciation deductions for machinery and equipment. All told, the bill closed about $500 billion in tax loopholes over five years.[29]

EROSION, *NOT* OUTRIGHT REVERSAL

Two decades after the 1986 Act, the federal tax code still bears vestiges of reform. For instance, a meaningful zero-bracket amount has been retained for individuals, and consumer interest, business meal, and medical expense rules are the same. But if the 1986 Act has not been reversed, its accomplishments nonetheless have been eroded. During the 1990s, Congress narrowed the tax base, raised tax rates, and created a host of new tax breaks for social purposes. While there has been no return to 1970s and 1980s-style *individual* tax shelters, new *corporate* tax shelters have popped up that have proved even harder for the government to shut down. The federal tax arena has featured policy *movement* over the past twenty years, but not sustainable progress along the 1986 reform path, especially with respect to tax neutrality and base-broadening.

THE LEGISLATIVE AFTERMATH OF TAX REFORM

On the eve of the bill signing ceremony for the TRA, the reform's sponsors proclaimed the dawning of a new era of federal tax policy. Chairman Rostenkowski announced that he would resist further substantive changes to the tax code over the next few years, telling a reporter that he had hung a "Gone Fishing" sign on the Ways and Means Committee door.[30] But tax policymakers were back in business almost as soon as the ink on the 1986 Act was dry. The core bargain underlying the TRA was that lower tax rates for all, including upper-income families, would be retained in exchange for a substantial reduction in special tax breaks and privileges. This commitment, however, was not hardwired in changes in rules or institutions.

In 1994, Rostenkowski was indicted on political corruption charges and resigned as Ways and Means chairman. Shifts in economic and political conditions gave successor politicians strong incentives to renegotiate the reform bargain. The presidents who followed Reagan, including his own vice president, George H. W. Bush, were uncommitted to tax neutrality and base-broadening. Bush was a traditional advocate of business tax preferences as a tonic for the economy. Indeed, he may well have invested more political capital in capital gains tax cuts than he did on any other domestic issue. For President Bill Clinton, tax expenditures were a valuable tool not only for economic stimulus but also for activist social policymaking in a conservative age. The Clinton Administration was not "about to forgo use of special provisions in the tax code to promote its domestic agenda if it couldn't make headway by increasing direct expenditures."[31] Bush and Clinton also shared a willingness to accept some tax rate increases to reduce the budget deficit. That fiscal policy position, however, was not embraced by George W. Bush, who successfully reversed many of the tax hikes of the 1990s, even while pushing tax break proposals of his own.

Fluctuating Marginal Tax Rates. . .

The 1986 Act, Graetz observes, was a marriage of "Democratic tax reformers who wanted to eliminate tax preferences and treat all income alike regardless of its source," and Republican supply-siders and deregulators who were "principally interested in lowering tax rates."[32] But this political marriage had tensions from the start. In March 1987, House Speaker Jim Wright (D-TX) announced his intention to raise taxes on the wealthy to reduce the budget deficit—a looming fiscal problem the 1986 Act had failed to confront. Some congressional Democrats, Rostenkowski included, believed that curbing tax privileges for powerful corporate interests would increase the public's confidence in the fairness of the tax system, making taxes easier to raise in the future.[33] In contrast, most congressional Republicans believed the deficit should be reduced through spending reductions. In sum, the bipartisan TRA coalition papered over a deep ideological conflict "regarding fairness" and the future of activist government.[34] Even if TRA's enacting coalition had remained intact, conflicts were bound to emerge.

To be sure, the bipartisan compromise held together for a few years. In 1988, Congress enacted a revenue-neutral bill that made technical corrections to the 1986 Act. The tax measures of 1987 and 1989 raised a modest amount of revenue to meet deficit-reduction targets, but Congress preserved the spirit of TRA by relying on base-broadeners instead of rate hikes.[35] But the conflict over tax rates, vertical equity, and deficit spending boiled over during the negotiations that preceded the passage of the 1990 Budget Agreement (OBRA90).[36] Liberal Democrats were increasingly distressed about growing income inequality. Fairness, they contended, required the rich to bear a greater share of the federal tax burden. To win the congressional Democrats' support for cuts in government spending, President Bush reluctantly agreed to break the "no new taxes" pledge he had made in the 1988 election campaign. Bush's "betrayal" on tax rates sparked a rebellion among conservatives in the House, led by minority whip Newt Gingrich. A majority of House Republicans voted against the 1990 omnibus budget package on final passage. The 1990 budget deal raised the top income tax rate from 28 to 31 percent and also removed the wage ceiling on payroll taxes for the Medicare program, further increasing the effective marginal tax rate on high-income taxpayers. Many pundits attributed Bush's defeat at the polls in 1992 in part to his reversal on taxes, helping make support for lower taxes a defining party test for Republican candidates and incumbents thereafter.

Shortly after the election of Bill Clinton, Congress passed OBRA93, which raised the top marginal income tax rate to 39.6 percent. The measure passed without a single Republican vote in either chamber.[37] Combined with the Medicare tax increase and phase-out provisions of OBRA90, these new "tax rate increases translated into top marginal tax rates that approached "the 50 percent top marginal tax rate" that had prevailed before the 1986 Act.[38] When Republicans accused Clinton of "breaking faith" with the 1986 reform bargain, the Administration argued that Clinton was not a party to the deal and that he had his own economic agenda. "The President campaigned on a promise to restore some of the progressivity to the tax system," said Laura D'Andrea Tyson, chairwoman of the Council of Economic Advisers. "That may be different from what was decided in 1986, but that's what he was elected to do."[39]

By the mid 1990s, the GOP had adopted a strong anti-tax position. President George W. Bush, working with slim but unusually cohesive and disciplined Republican legislative majorities, pushed through a series of major tax cuts during his first three years in office, ratcheting the top marginal tax rate back down to 35 percent and repealing or modifying many other tax provisions enacted under Clinton. In all, the top marginal tax rate changed five times between 1987 and 2003. Many of the Bush tax cuts were subject to sunset provisions and therefore likely to fluctuate in the future, "undermining the durability of the tax code and the certainty that taxpayers need for planning."[40]

Creation of New Tax Breaks

While 1986 was a moment of unusual vulnerability for tax expenditures, the TRA did not quite represent the political earthquake that it seemed. According to a careful empirical study by Alison E. Post and Paul Pierson, the tax breaks eliminated in 1986 were broadly similar in terms of their political character to the tax breaks repealed in other years.[41] What made the TRA *seem* different from prior tax laws was the sheer *number* of credits and deductions scrapped in 1986. But the TRA did not penetrate into legislative routines any more deeply than other tax laws. After the dust settled, breaks began creeping back into the tax code, shredding the principles of base broadening and horizontal equity almost beyond recognition.

A key test of the durability of a reform is whether subsequent politicians who were not official parties to the bargain feel constrained by it. In the case of the TRA, politicians essentially acted as if the reform had never been enacted. President George Herbert Walker Bush had never been a committed tax reformer, even though he had been vice president at the moment of reform enactment. During the debate over the Tax Reform Act of 1969, then Congressman Bush expressed his support for tax breaks as a non-intrusive method for the government to encourage investment. "I favor tax credits and tax incentives as the way to answer many of our problems as opposed to direct government subsidy or starting some new bureau on the Potomac to try to solve all the Nation's problems," he said.[42] During the 1988 presidential election campaign, Bush called for restoration of a lower tax rate for capital gains, claiming it would boost investment and economic growth. While he pushed relentlessly for its adoption, Bush failed to win congressional support for his capital gains proposal in 1989. Rostenkowski argued that the measure would only serve to encourage other special interests to seek narrow tax breaks, and Senate Majority leader George Mitchell blocked Bush's capital gains tax plan from coming up on the Senate floor.[43] But Bush continued to press the capital gains issue over the remainder of his presidency. The President also called for new tax preferences for child care, oil exploration, and enterprise zones, signaling to lobbyists that his Administration was in the tax-break business.[44]

Bill Clinton was also very enthusiastic about using special tax provisions as an instrument of economic policy. In his first presidential news conference, Clinton boasted that his proposal to restore the investment tax credit would create "over a half a million private sector jobs in the first year alone."[45] Clinton's business tax proposals came under fire from many legislative supporters of the 1986 Act. Senator Bill Bradley called some of the proposals a "rejection of the principle of tax reform."[46] "In 1986, we tried to clear up the tax code to make it as neutral as it could be to reflect economic decisions. And we want to keep it that way," stated Senator Daniel Patrick Moynihan (D-NY).[47]

No doubt these protests were sincere. Yet even as Bradley and Moynihan were coming to the reform's defense, pressure was intensifying on Capitol Hill for the TRA's unraveling. Between 1987 and 1998, more than 700 tax bills were introduced in Congress. Nearly all of these measures would have restored or added particularistic tax breaks.[48] According to a 1989 *Business Week* survey, nine in ten members of the Ways and Means and Senate Finance committees said they would use the tax code to encourage saving and investment. Five in ten favored tax incentives for specific industries, and eight in ten sponsored or cosponsored legislation in the previous two years to provide such incentives.[49] While Rostenkowski urged lawmakers to leave the tax code alone for a few years, other reform supporters were abandoning ship. Senator Packwood in October 1989, for example, introduced a bill to cut capital gains rates and promote IRAs.[50]

Budget legislation enacted in both 1990 and 1993 expanded some existing tax preferences (including the Earned Income Tax Credit) and created a few new ones. The Taxpayer Relief Act of 1997 opened the floodgates. The new tax breaks contained in the 1997 bill were expected to cost the Treasury $275 billion over the first decade and "vastly higher amounts" in the out years.[51] Since 1986, Congress has passed more than 100 different laws changing provisions of the tax code.[52] The number of major tax expenditures on the books of the Treasury grew from 115 in 1986 to 161 in 2006 (Figure 3-1). The total estimated revenue loss to the Treasury from tax expenditures in 1986 was $598 billion (in 2004 dollars). Over the next two years, the estimated revenue loss fell by 28 percent. From 1989 to 2006, however, revenue losses from tax expenditures climbed to $810 billion (in 2004 dollars), an increase of 76 percent over this period (Figure 3-2).[53]

Rather than reversing TRA outright, the tax policy changes made by Congress since 1986 have mainly caused the reform's *erosion*. To be sure, recent tax legislation has created or expanded some tax breaks for business interests. The American Jobs Creation Act of 2004 (P.L. 108-357), for example, established tax incentives for tackle box makers, Native Alaskan whaling captains, restaurant owners, Hollywood producers, makers of bows and arrows, NASCAR track owners, and importers of Chinese ceiling fans.[54] With the significant exception of a preferential tax rate for capital gains, however, the major business

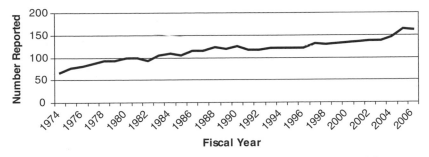

Figure 3-1. Number of Tax Expenditures Reported by Treasury, 1974–2006. *Source:* GAO analysis of OMB budget reports on tax expenditures, fiscal years, 1976–2006.

tax expenditures attacked in 1986 have not been resurrected. Instead, politicians have created a bevy of major new tax expenditures for *social purposes.* The Clinton Administration learned it could generate far more political support for new social tax breaks than for increases in direct expenditures.

After declining in value immediately after the TRA due to the lowering of marginal tax rates, tax breaks for individuals and families climbed from $363 billion (in 2004 dollars) in 1988 to $717 billion in 2006.[55] Revenue losses attributable to corporate tax breaks, in contrast, have risen only slightly over the 1987–2002 period (Figure 3-3). Measured as a share of the economy, social tax expenditures increased from 4.1 percent to 5.3 percent of GDP between 1990 and 2003 while corporate tax breaks (including capital gains preferences) declined from 1.6 to 1.2 percent of GDP over this period (Figure 3-4).

Some of the social tax breaks created in the 1990s were targeted at fairly narrow groups. Others were aimed at broad swaths of middle-class voters. Besides reducing capital gains tax rates from 28 and 15 percent to 20 and 10 percent, respectively, the Taxpayer Relief Act of 1997 (P.L. 105-34) introduced a tax break for a new individual retirement account (Roth IRA) and created many new provisions, such as the child, HOPE, and Lifetime Learning educa-

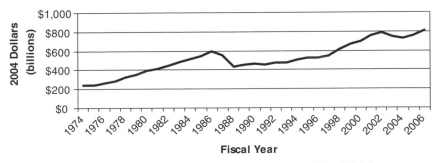

Figure 3-2. Sum of Tax Expenditure Revenue Loss Estimates, 1974–2006. *Source:* GAO analysis of OMB budget reports on tax expenditures, fiscal years, 1976–2006.

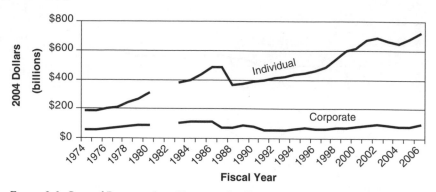

Figure 3-3. Sum of Revenue Loss Estimates by Taxpayer Group, 1974–2006. *Source:* GAO analysis of OMB budget reports on tax expenditures, fiscal years 1976–2006. The Treasury did not report separate estimates for the individual and corporate income tax expenditures for 1981 and 1982.

tion credits. The Economic Growth and Tax Relief Reconciliation Act of 2001 (P.L. 1907-16) continued the trend toward expanding social tax incentives by enlarging the child credit, softening the impact of the "marriage penalty," and creating additional tax breaks for retirement savings and education. The Job Creation and Worker Assistance Act of 2002 (P.L. 107-147) extended many credits, including those for the purchase of electric vehicles. The Jobs and Growth Tax Relief Reconciliation Act of 2003 (P.L. 108-27) expanded child care credits to $1,000 per child. Many policy experts doubted these new tax breaks would effectively achieve their social policy goals. For

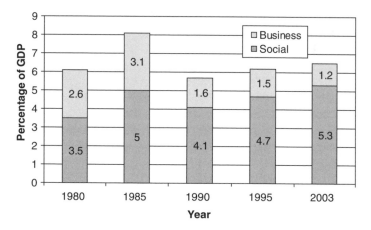

Figure 3-4. Tax Expenditures as a Share of the Economy, 1980–2003. *Sources:* Eric J. Toder, "The Changing Composition of Tax Incentives—1980–1999," The Urban Institute, http://www.urban.org/url.cfm?ID=410329; Eugene Steuerle, (Washington, D.C.: The Urban Institute Press, 2004), 43.

example, economists pointed out that poorly designed tax credits, intended to make college more affordable, might only lead colleges to raise their tuition.[56] The proliferation of social tax breaks also increased the tax code's complexity. Given the large number of overlapping tax incentives for higher education and retirement savings, for example, many ordinary taxpayers did not know which ones to take.

Public Skepticism

Policy elites applauded wildly when tax reform passed in 1986, but ordinary citizens greeted the reform with indifference. A Gallup poll taken on the eve of the measure's adoption found that less than one in three respondents expected it to improve the nation's economy, make the tax system less complicated, or promote a fairer distribution of the tax burden. A follow-up poll conducted four years later revealed that the public's relatively low expectations were not met. Only 15 percent of respondents thought the reform had had a positive effect on the economy while just 12 percent thought it had made the tax system less complicated. The public's assessment of the reform's impact on tax fairness was especially harsh. Almost four in ten (37 percent) of those surveyed stated the reform had made for a *less* fair distribution of the tax code (Table 3-1). There is little evidence that TRA boosted public confidence in the federal tax system.[57]

It is impossible to know for certain why public reactions to tax reform were negative, but several factors seem to be important. First, as explained in the next section of the chapter, the macroeconomic achievements of tax reform were not nearly so large as some prominent reform advocates had promised. Second, many ordinary citizens were upset about the complexity of the tax code, and the TRA fell far short of its tax-simplification aspirations. It is difficult to directly measure tax complexity, but proxy measures leave no doubt that the tax code has only grown more convoluted over time. The number of words in the IRS code and the number of pages in the 1040 instruction book have both mushroomed since the mid 1980s, contributing to the growth in the percentage of Americans who are willing to pay someone else to prepare their tax forms (Table 3-2). In a 1988 poll, 67 percent of respondents found the new tax law more confusing than the old one, with an 85 percent overall agreement that the tax law was too complicated.[58]

Third, many citizens may not have realized that the reform lowered their tax rates. Indeed, in one early 1988 ABC News/ Washington Post survey, 58 percent of respondents said they paid more taxes under the new law, while only 22 percent said they paid less.[59] The heated political debate over the tax rates of upper-income households received considerable media attention. Even middle-class taxpayers who had not seen their own tax rates rise may have thought they were next in line. There is also anecdotal evidence that many upper income people

TABLE 3-1
Public Opinion on the Tax Reform Act of 1986

1. All things considered, do you think TRA86 has had a positive effect on the nation's economy, a negative effect, or hasn't it made much difference one way or the other?

	Positive effect	Not much effect either way	Negative effect	No opinion
1986*	28	41	15	16
1990	15	56	20	9

2. Do you think TRA86 has made it less complicated for you to pay your taxes, more complicated, or about the same as the previous system?

	Less complicated	About the same	More complicated	No opinion
1986*	19	51	17	13
1990	12	48	31	9

3. Do you think TRA86 has made for a fairer distribution of the tax load among all taxpayers, one that's less fair, or is it not much different than the previous system?

	Fairer	Not much different	Less fair	No opinion
1986*	27	36	20	17
1990	9	40	37	14

* These questions were asked in the context of the public's expectations of the changes the Tax Reform Act of 1986 would bring about.

Sources: Alan J. Auerbach and Joel Slemrod, "The Economic Effects of the Tax Reform Act of 1986," Journal of Economic Literature (June 1997): 618; The Gallup Poll Monthly (March 1990, pp. 6-8).

tended to think they were worse off under the new system because of their lost deductions. Many of these people, however, were paying higher taxes because their income had gone up. They likely did not realize that their tax liabilities would have been even higher if the reform had not been adopted.[60] Most citizens are not accustomed to counter-factual public-policy reasoning.

A final explanation for the public's tepid reactions focuses on the politics of the reform's adoption. As previously mentioned, coalition leaders doled out billions in transition schemes to build a winning majority for the reform's enactment. While the reform effort almost certainly would have failed without it, the strategic use of side-payments may have reinforced citizens' cynicism

TABLE 3-2
Measures of Tax Complexity, Pre- and Post-Reform

Proxy	Pre-reform (Year)	Post-reform (Year)
IRS Code (thousands of words, income taxes only)	776 (1985)	1,286 (2005)
Percentage of individual returns signed by paid preparers	46 (1986)	57 (2001)
Instruction booklet pages, Form 1040	52 (1985)	128 (2004)

Sources: David Keating, "A Taxing Trend: The Rise in Complexity, Forms, and Paperwork Burdens," National Taxpayers Union, April 14, 2005, www.ntu.org/main/press_papers.php?Press ID=711; National Center for Policy Analysis, "Tax Preparation: A Growth Industry," June 6, 2002, www.ncpa.org/iss/tax/2002/pd060602b.html; and John S. Irons and Michael Powers, "Tax Complexity: By the Numbers," Center for American Progress, October 28, 2005, www.american progress.org.

about the tax system.[61] The special tax provisions included in the final bill were widely publicized in the media along with the tens of millions of dollars in campaign contributions that members of the key tax-writing panels received in exchange for these favors.[62] In one late 1980s survey, 78 percent of Americans agreed that the reform benefited special interests.[63] Ordinary citizens—who certainly had reason to be cynical about the credibility of politicians' tax reform promises given the long history of interest-group dominance in the sector—were probably mystified about why a tax reform bill had to create a bunch of new tax loopholes in order to close other ones. In sum, the coalition-building efforts needed to pass this general-interest reform may have played into public doubts about whether the reform constituted a break from politics as usual.

Economic Accomplishments and Limitations

Any change in the tax code is bound to affect the behavior of some economic actors, but these behavioral effects may be transitory or insignificant from the standpoint of the larger economy. If, for example, the government enacted a tax break for circus clowns who wear red wigs when they perform, it is likely that clowns who previously had worn blue or green wigs would immediately switch to red. The total number of employed circus clowns, or the number of circus performances annually in the U.S., would be unlikely to change, however. Alternatively, an increase in the capital gains rate effective in two months may affect the *timing* of stock market transactions, without permanently changing stock market behavior. An actor who intended to sell a stock in three months may decide to do so a month early, in order to complete the sale before tax rates change. But if there was no change in the equilibrium level of stock market investing, the effect of the rate hike would only be transitory. In sum, changes in tax law do not automatically produce significant and durable effects on the economy.

The promise of the TRA, however, was that it would lead to real improvements in efficiency, equity, and simplicity. Did the tax reform deliver on these economic promises? The best available evidence, marshaled by public economists Alan J. Auerbach and Joel Slemrod, suggests it did not.[64] This is not because the IRS failed to implement the TRA properly. Rather, the severe political constraints that tax reformers faced in 1985–86 when writing the law—including a commitment to revenue neutrality—virtually guaranteed that the TRA's economic impact would be relatively muted.[65]

There is solid evidence that the TRA affected the *timing* of economic transactions. Foreign direct investment in the U.S., for example, more than doubled in the fourth quarter of 1986.[66] The reform also generated a very large, albeit transitory, increase in the realizations of long-term capital gains as wealthy individuals scrambled to take their profits before rates climbed.[67] The TRA also had a major impact on how firms organized themselves for tax-reporting purposes. For example, there was a significant shift by small and medium business from C to S corporation status. Individuals reorganized their portfolios, shifting their personal debt from personal loans (which were no longer deductible) into mortgages (which were).[68]

As for *permanently* changing the economic behavior of American individuals or firms, however, the TRA's impact was decidedly mixed. On the one hand, there is some evidence that the reform generated an increase in housing starts and investment in equipment. On the other hand, the reform did not induce major changes in labor supply or the savings rate. Americans kept working about the same number of hours and saving about the same amount of money.[69] The reform also accomplished only a limited amount of base broadening for individuals because most middle-class tax breaks remained on the books. The growth of the tax preparation industry temporarily slowed, but accelerated beginning in the 1990s. Between 2001 and 2005 alone, the number of H&R Block offices in the U.S. grew 22 percent, from 9,133 to 11,161.[70] Some of this growth reflected a diversification of the giant tax preparation firm into related financial services business, but much of it also reflects the growing complexity of the tax system. In sum, the TRA was clearly an improvement over the policy status quo ante, but it was not a "policy watershed."[71]

Political Dynamics

Even more importantly for its sustainability, the law failed to generate a self-reinforcing political dynamic. Policy feedbacks were generally negative or non-existent, preventing the reform from becoming increasingly attractive to stakeholders over time. Influential political constituencies freely blamed the reform for all manner of economic and social ills. The banking industry, for example, claimed that the TRA contributed to the collapse of the savings and loan industry. The argument had a logical basis. To combat abusive tax shelters, the reform tightened rules governing depreciation and passive losses, which made owning commercial real estate less attractive than it had been. When the tax policy–induced real estate bubble burst, savings and loans found themselves stuck with overvalued properties. While many other factors contributed to the S&L crisis of the late 1980s, the TRA did play a role (although the real policy mistake surely was artificially subsidizing real estate through tax preferences in the first place). Far more questionable were complaints by financial planners and Wall Street brokers that TRA had curbed the tax shelter industry (that was the whole point!), or that it harmed retirement savings by tightening the rules on IRAs (the evidence suggests IRAs do little to encourage new savings, mostly shifting existing savings from other investment vehicles).[72]

These criticisms would have carried less political weight with members of Congress if the TRA had generated even a moderate level of political support from organized groups, but virtually no important clientele came to the reform's defense. Even group actors that had been quite enthusiastic about the law's rate cuts in 1986 had no compunction about abandoning its base-broadening framework. For example, The National Association of Wholesaler-Distributors, a key member of the Tax Reform Action Coalition in 1986, began lobbying just three years after the reform's passage for cuts in the estate tax for family business owners. The TRAC itself continued to exist, but didn't make a peep when Congress approved bills to restore preferential tax treatment of capital gains and reopen loopholes for farmers and timber growers. The group's president, Dirk Van Dongen, acknowledged that these policy shifts could undermine the bargain of lower rates in exchange for the curbing of tax preferences, but said the prevailing attitude among business tax lobbyists was, "If you can have your cake and eat it, too, and have no change in the rates and get goodies . . . well, why not?"[73]

Tax reform also failed to alter legislative dynamics. If the TRA established a credible commitment to the maintenance of a broad, less particularistic tax code, the value to members of serving on the tax writing panels might be expected to decline since one of the central issues the committee handles would have been rendered less important. Yet a seat on the Ways and Means and Senate Finance committees continued to be highly prized by lawmakers.[74] One reason is because a seat on these committees virtually guarantees ready access to campaign contributions from actors interested in changing the tax code. When the TRA was being developed, interest groups gave huge sums to members of the tax panels in hopes of preserving their privileges. Ways and Means members on average received a 24 percent increase in donations during 1985–86 over the previous election cycle.[75] But the fundraising bonanza didn't end when the reform was passed. Chairman Rostenkowski, for example, collected $1.3 million in contributions in the 1991–92 election cycle, almost as much as he received during the entire decade of the 1980s.[76]

Only one important political factor served to promote the durability of tax reform, and even its importance soon faded: the commitment in the 1990s to controlling the budget deficit. This commitment was institutionalized in the paygo rules of the 1990 Budget Enforcement Act, which required that new tax breaks be paid for either through revenue increases or reductions in entitlement spending.[77] Under the rules, if members wanted to create a new tax loophole, they had to close another one, or find some other source of the required savings. The rules played a key role in the liquidation of the budget deficit during the second Clinton Administration.[78] By 1997, however, the fiscal situation had brightened considerably. By taking advantage of this economic improvement, and by using accounting gimmicks such as sunset provisions and phase-outs, lawmakers were able to enact a number of major tax expenditures while technically conforming to the paygo rules. Following the election of George W. Bush and the September 11, 2001 terrorist attacks, the political climate changed markedly. The budget deficit became a much less salient issue, even though the nation's long-term fiscal situation continued to deteriorate. Congress permitted the paygo rules to expire, giving lawmakers a license to propose new tax loopholes without identifying offsetting budget savings.

The Reemergence of Tax Shelters—in a Different Guise

The TRA slowed the proliferation of tax shelters by *individuals*. This accomplishment has been eroded, however, by the recent growth of *corporate* tax shelters. In the 1970s and early 1980s, tax advisers, investment bankers, and others mass marketed tax shelters to high-income individuals. The 1986 TRA effectively put an end to these types of tax shelters by imposing limits on passive losses.[79]

Since the early 1990s, however, a new corporate tax shelter industry has emerged that is far more "sophisticated and complex than its 1980s predecessor."[80] Corporate tax shelters may involve tangible assets but often "have no nontax economic substance at all. One common technique is to create a financial transaction with offsetting gains and losses, and have the losses allocated to a U.S. corporation while the gains are allocated to a taxpayer not subject to U.S. income taxation," such as a foreign financial institution.[81] Between 1990 and 2000, the gap between book income and taxable corporate income more than doubled, in real terms, to more than $90 billion. These shelters narrowed the tax base, reduced voluntary tax compliance, and complicated "the tax code by forcing legislators to take remedial action."[82] While exogenous factors clearly played a role in the recent growth of corporate tax shelters, including shifts in capital markets, it has also resulted from the entrepreneurial activities of clever attorneys who lost tax practice after 1986 and were actively looking to create a new market.[83] In sum, the "creative destruction" from the TRA was limited. The service industries that help sustain an inefficient tax code were largely able to reconstitute themselves. As one tax expert observes, "If the Tax Reform Act of 1986 put any tax professionals out of business, it was only a short layoff, because if the Tax Reform Act of 1986 fixed things, they didn't stay fixed for very long."[84]

Failure to Change the Terms of Debate

Durable reforms do not merely change the decisions actors make. They shift the terms of the policy debate. As Karen Orren and Stephen Skowronek argue, a critical test of the durability of shifts in governance arrangements is therefore whether the changes preempt opponents, engage ideologies, and force relevant actors to "declare the rightness of what has occurred."[85] On these crucial dimensions, the TRA's lack of durability is painfully apparent. Policy actors over the past decade have advanced rival conceptions of tax reform that explicitly or implicitly repudiate the traditional principles of efficiency, simplicity, and tax neutrality. These principles have come in for harshest criticism from conservatives who seek to radically transform the income tax into a de facto consumption or wage tax, rendering nearly all investment income tax-free.[86] According to advocates, such as Robert E. Hall of the Hoover Institution, the tax code currently discourages investment and savings.[87] Economists associated with Democratic think tanks such as the Brookings Institution, however, question whether any proposed changes in tax policy would in practice strengthen incentives for Americans to save and invest.[88]

This tension among alternative conceptions of "tax reform" is to some degree a reflection of the growing political polarization in Washington. As the two parties have drifted apart since 1986, the bipartisan consensus on what constitutes "good tax policy" has frayed. As Graetz argues, liberals and conservatives today both seem to want a narrow tax base—just not the same one.[89] The result of this political dissensus is that the government has been unable to advance, let alone stick with, *any* coherent definition of tax policy, whether based on consumption, income, or wages.[90]

In November 2005, a high profile advisory panel on tax reform, appointed by President Bush and chaired by a prominent former Republican Senator (Connie Mack III, Florida), took a stab at developing a comprehensive solution. Noting that "constant legislative tinkering" had led to more than 15,000 changes in the tax code since 1986, the panel lamented that federal tax policy was currently distorting the economic decisions of American families and businesses and that the significant reform achievements of the TRA have been undone.[91] The panel proposed lower rates and the elimination or reduction of most tax expenditures, including popular provisions largely untouched in 1986, such as deductions for home mortgage interest and employer-provided health insurance.[92] Predictably, realtors, life insurance firms, and other well-heeled interests immediately mobilized against the suggestions.[93] A month after the release of the commission report, however, President Bush announced that a tax overhaul would not be a priority in the near future.[94]

CONCLUSIONS

On the day President Reagan signed the TRA into law, *The New York Times* warned that the reform might not stick. "As sure as there will be a new Congress in January, it will feel heavy pressure to undo major accomplishments that don't sit well with influential taxpayers. Just as reform wasn't written overnight, today's signing doesn't end it."[95] After the reform's passage, the question among seasoned Washington observers was not *whether* the principles of base broadening, simplicity, and tax neutrality would be eroded, but rather "how far and how fast the erosion will take place."[96]

While the TRA was a stunning piece of reform legislation, it did not successfully reconfigure the political economy of tax policymaking. Its failures as breakthrough policy are both multiple and mutually reinforcing. The TRA did nothing to disempower tax lobbyists or slow the proliferation of new groups seeking privileged tax treatment. The reform did not raise the political transaction costs to the government of creating or expanding tax loopholes. There were no institutional or procedural reforms to insulate rational tax policymaking from intensifying partisan and ideological polarization on fiscal matters, thereby discouraging the emergence of new bipartisan coalitions in support of base broadening. Positive policy feedback—self-reinforcing shifts in ideas, group identities, and political dynamics—has been notable for its absence. Finally, policy venues were unchanged. Authority to shape tax legislation—and thereby to deliver particularistic tax benefits to favored groups—remained firmly in the hands of Congress. More radical shifts in jurisdictional authority, such as the delegation of tax policymaking to an independent technocratic agency comparable to the Federal Reserve Board, were never seriously considered.[97] The distributive benefits from tax policy are apparently too important to members of Congress for them to relinquish political control.

The improvement in tax policy "will turn out to be temporary," free market economist Milton Friedman predicted shortly after the TRA's adoption. "Nothing has changed to prevent the process that produced our present tax system from starting over. As lobbyists get back into action, and as members of Congress try to raise campaign funds, old loopholes will be reintroduced and new ones invented."[98] History has largely borne out Friedman's predictions.

CHAPTER 4

Reforming the Agricultural Welfare State: The Mixed Case of the Freedom to Farm Act

ON MAY 13, 2002, President George W. Bush signed into law a farm bill with an estimated ten-year price tag of $190 billion despite declining federal revenues and pressing national security spending priorities. The agriculture bill featured large government payments to farmers who produce wheat and corn and new crop subsidies for wool, mohair, and honey. Signing the bill represented a personal defeat for President Bush, who came to office rhetorically praising the virtues of free markets. During the 2000 election campaign, Bush had extolled a landmark 1996 agricultural reform that had sought to wean farmers off federal subsidies while lifting most government restrictions on planting decisions.[1] "Freedom to Farm," as the 1996 reform is known, was the most market-friendly agriculture measure of the past half-century and a crowning achievement of the new Republican congressional majority. But Congress failed to stick to the seven-year schedule of declining market-transition payments contained in the law. When crop prices plummeted in 1998, critics began calling the 1996 bill "Freedom to Fail."

Between 1998 and 2002, Congress increased the payments established in the 1996 measure by 50 percent and doled out tens of billions annually in "emergency" farm assistance.[2] With an eye to the upcoming midterm elections, President Bush in May 2002 signed a multiyear farm bill that replaced this discretionary aid with new counter-cyclical support payments. The media portrayed the 2002 farm bill as an election year boondoggle. "Mr. Bush signed a farm bill that represents a low point in his presidency—a wasteful corporate welfare measure that penalizes taxpayers and the world's poorest people in order to bribe a few voters," editorialized *The Washington Post*.[3]

The 2002 farm bill does not merit praise, but its economic effects—and larger political implications—are more complex than have been advertised.[4] An understanding of these nuances requires careful attention to the policy design of the Freedom to Farm reform law itself. Many general-interest reforms involve multiple parts, each of which can give rise to negative or positive feedback effects. The 1996 reform bill is a case in point. The most visible and easily understood part of the reform—the subsidy cuts—has indeed been significantly *reversed*. But agricultural reform has not been a complete failure. The elimination of market-distorting restrictions on planting decisions—the other major reform thrust—has thus far stuck. Farmers have retained, with some exceptions, the flexibility to choose what to plant. There has been no return to pre-1996 acreage set-asides. Agricultural special interests are still gaining at the expense of general interests, but society as a whole is losing less from these special-interest transfers than it once did. Understanding these complex patterns requires careful attention to the mediating role of political institutions and policy feedback effects.

THE POLITICAL ORIGINS OF U.S. FARM PROGRAMS

Modern farm safety-net programs in the United States originated in the New Deal.[5] Commodity prices plummeted during the early years of the Great Depression, when about a quarter of the American population lived on farms. During FDR's first 100 days in office, Congress passed the Agricultural Adjustment Act (AAA) of 1933 to support farm income. The AAA established a voluntary program in which farmers who agreed to cut their production of stable crops such as wheat received cash "rental" payments from the government, financed through processing taxes on the specific commodities. In addition, a new agency, the Commodity Credit Corporation (CCC), was established to give farmers loans on favorable terms. Farmers who received the loans placed their crops in storage after harvest. If prices rose by a high enough amount to cover interest charges and other costs, farmers paid back their loans in cash. If the market price was below that level, farmers simply forfeited their crops to the government.[6] The effect was to place a marketwide floor, the CCC loan rate, under the price of these commodities.[7]

In 1936, the Supreme Court overturned the 1933 Act on the grounds that the federal government's authority to impose processing taxes was not recognized in the Constitution, but Congress two years later passed a second AAA that provided for price support payments funded through general revenues. The AAA of 1938 featured four main policy mechanisms to maintain farmers' income: payments for shifting land into conservation uses; crop acreage allotments to restrict production of farmers who wanted to participate in the price-support program; marketing quotas (implemented by a two-thirds referendum vote of eligible growers) to limit the amount of a crop any individual farmer could bring to market; and, finally, CCC loans to set a floor on commodity prices.[8] In 1949, Congress amended the AAA to give the Secretary of Agriculture more flexibility in setting price support levels. Over the next half century, Congress would pass many farm bills, but the underlying 1938 and 1949 Acts still remain on the books.

After World War II, the two political parties clashed on how to respond to the problem of excess crop production, brought about by vast technological improvements in farming methods. In general, Democratic administrations favored high subsidies and tight production controls while Republican administrations supported lower subsidies and more planting flexibility. The debate split farm interest groups and rural state legislators, but the high subsidy / supply management framework largely prevailed. While agriculture executives in both Democratic and Republican administrations sought to rationalize farm policy, Congress jealously guarded its authority to determine the marketing rules for individual commodities. Farm policy became increasingly particularistic over the 1960s as the politics of credit claiming emerged. As Graham Wilson has observed, some crops were subsidized more generously than others, partisan divisions over farm policy were blurred, and broad-based agricultural lobby associations, such as the Farm Bureau and National Farmers' Union, lost influence to commodity-specific interest groups, like the sugar and wheat lobbies.[9] Relative to farm lobbies in other wealthy nations, "U.S. agricultural interest groups developed in a highly fractured manner."[10] Rather than a single farm policy iron triangle, multiple agricultural policy subsystems emerged in which various commodity organizations enjoyed privileged access to government. But the practical consequences of this growing fragmentation were limited. While there was a degree of competition among farm organizations, virtually all of them supported some form of market subsidy, and they enjoyed huge informational, political, and organizational advantages in policy debates. Ordinary citizens, in their roles as taxpayers and consumers, had far less at stake and had much weaker influence on key decision makers.

Changes in the larger political and economic environment during the 1960s and 1970s threatened the agricultural welfare state, but farm interests managed to retain most of their benefits. One key threat was a decline in the level of farm representation in Congress because of economic shifts and legislative reapportionment. John Mark Hansen has estimated that in 1930, 55 percent of all House members represented districts in which at least one in five residents lived on farms. By 1980, less than 1 percent of all House districts satisfied that criterion.[11] These changes in the representational bases of agricultural interests made it increasingly difficult to pass stand-alone farm bills in Congress. But rural members sustained political support for farm programs by entering into "logrolls" with members from urban districts who favored higher spending on the food stamp program. Reform-minded agriculture secretaries tried to break up this rural-urban coalition by shifting authority over the food stamp program to the Department of Health, Education, and Welfare, but the Agriculture Committee of Congress blocked the move.[12]

A second important threat was high price inflation, which focused public attention on the costs of farm programs for consumers. Market prices for grains climbed rapidly during the early 1970s because of macroeconomic conditions and a surge in demand from the Soviet Union. A crop shortfall then occurred. The Nixon Administration tried to exploit high commodity prices by proposing a phase-out of farmers' cash support payments over three years. But the system of direct payments and acreage set-asides proved impossible to uproot. Nixon acquiesced to a modified system of "deficiency payments" to make up the difference between the market price for major field crops (wheat, corn, cotton, rice, grain sorghum, and barley) and a "target price" legislated by Congress. Farmers would be paid for their base acreage in each crop, which they would have to produce if they wanted to obtain the full subsidy.[13]

While target prices were initially set well below market levels, the commodity price boom ended in the mid 1970s, generating intense pressure on Congress to make the deficiency payments even more generous. The 1977 farm bill raised target prices and loan rates and tied future rates to increases in farm production costs. In 1985, the Reagan Administration tried to retrench farm subsidies, proposing to cut direct payments by 30 to 50 percent from existing levels. The Administration also called for the repeal of the permanent 1949 farm legislation. But the attempt to restructure farm policy came at a time when the agricultural sector was experiencing its worst financial crisis since the Depression. Music stars like Willie Nelson organized "farm aid" concerts to focus media attention on the situation. With tremendous public sympathy for the plight of "family farmers," Reagan's retrenchment proposal was summarily rejected by both Republicans and Democrats in Congress.[14]

In the end, the Reagan Administration did achieve some of its reform goals, but at a steep budgetary cost. The 1985 farm bill lowered loan rates for export crops and took some key initial steps toward "decoupling" cash payments to farmers from planting decisions, thereby reducing market inefficiencies. But target prices remained high and direct cash payments skyrocketed. To limit crop surpluses, the government was forced to impose new supply controls, including a new unpaid acreage reduction program. In addition, a new Conservation Reserve Program (CRP) was created that gave farmers annual rental payments to retire erodable or other "environmentally sensitive" land for at least ten years.[15] By the late 1980s, over 75 million acres—almost 25 percent of the acreage used for the major crops—was being idled under government programs.[16]

The Case for Farm Policy Reform

New Deal farm programs became increasingly vulnerable to criticism as the agricultural sector modernized and farmers became more prosperous. First, they transferred resources from large diffuse groups (taxpayers, voters, consumers) to narrow ones (commodity producers). The accumulated budgetary costs of farm payments were quite high, leaving less money for other federal spending priorities. Deficiency payments alone cost American taxpayers more than $100 billion between 1985 and 1995.[17] Farm payments could not be justified on equity grounds. Farmers were not an impoverished group. In the

1930s, farm family income was one-third that of urban residents.[18] By the early 1990s, the average farmer had an income slightly *above* the average for all U.S. households, and the cost-of-living in rural areas is cheaper than in most cities and suburbs. Farmer payments were not targeted efficiently to reduce poverty. The bulk of farm subsidies went to recipients, including owners of large agribusinesses, with the highest incomes. According to one study, 80 percent of farm subsides in the 1990s went to farm operators with a net worth of over $500,000.[19] In sum, farm subsidies redistributed little if any wealth from the rich to the poor.

Other publicly expressed justifications for farm programs were also dubious. While farm subsidies are often claimed to play a key role in preserving a traditional rural lifestyle, massive government subsidies failed to prevent the disappearance of the family farm. While 30 percent of the U.S. population resided on farms in 1920, that figure had fallen to 1.8 percent by 1992.[20]

Finally, and most importantly, farm programs have created massive market distortions. The government imposed restrictions and import controls on items such as sugar and milk, enriching producers at the expense of American consumers. Until recently, restrictions on planting flexibility prevented farmers from making the most efficient selection of crops. Acreage reduction programs—the most wasteful aspect of the system—caused good farmland to go unused and forced the government to monitor farmers' behavior to ensure compliance with the law. Acreage controls also reduce employment opportunities for workers who supply inputs such as farm machinery, transport, and marketing.

According to a careful study by Bruce L. Gardner, a leading agricultural economist, the net losses to the nation from commodity programs was approximately $5 billion in 1987 (Table 4-1). While producers gained $17.5 billion in higher prices and direct payments, consumers paid about $5 billion more on sugar and other products than they would have in the absence of government interventions, and taxpayers spent almost $18 billion. In sum, farm programs transferred resources from the many to a privileged few in a highly inefficient manner. *The losers (consumers and taxpayers) lost more than the winners (producers) gained.*

Farm policy reformers have faced two major challenges. The first is to eliminate or reduce farm subsidies in order to provide diffuse benefits for taxpayers and consumers. If agricultural-sector income stabilization remains a priority objective for the federal government, risk management tools such as futures markets and forward contracting are far more appropriate mechanisms than direct subsidies.[21] The second challenge is to reduce the market distortions from agricultural programs. If U.S. farm interests are simply too powerful to be denied government benefits, they should be subsidized in a manner that imposes the fewest costs on the national economy.

By the 1960s, blue-ribbon panels such as the Committee on Economic De-

Table 4-1
Costs and Benefits of Commodity Programs (billions of dollars, 1987 fiscal year)

Commodity	Producers	Consumers	Taxpayers
Feed grains	8.9	0	−10.3
Wheat	2.4	0	−3.7
Rice	0.5	0	−0.6
Cotton	0.9	0	−1.5
Sugar	2.7	−3.1	0
Milk	1.3	−1.2	−1.4
Tobacco, peanuts, wool	0.8	−0.5	−0.2
Column totals	17.5	−4.8	−17.7

Grand total   −5.0

Source: Bruce L. Gardner, *American Agriculture in the Twentieth Century* (Cambridge, MA.: Harvard University Press, 2002), 239.

velopment were calling for the elimination of farm support programs. Yet efforts to scrap the New Deal–era framework of agricultural subsidies and acreage controls met with fierce opposition. The limited farm policy reforms that occurred prior to the 1990s were "incremental, incomplete, and often costly."[22] Why did agricultural policy reformers make so little progress even after the New Deal–era farm programs lost their original justifications? Several factors discouraged policy reform.

First, farm interests enjoyed tremendous clout. While the number of farmers fell rapidly over the post-war era, their political influence did not decline in tandem. If anything, the consolidation of agricultural production ensured that the surviving farmers would have more interests in common (including the preservation of subsidies), thereby lowing the costs of collective action. The larger public bore no animosity toward farmers whatsoever. In addition, government programs to support farmers induced massive policy feedback effects. The benefits of federal farm programs were largely captured by owners of fixed sector-specific assets. USDA economists estimated that land values would fall 20 percent in the Midwest, for example, if subsidies were scrapped.[23] Finally, inherited institutional configurations, including the delegation of agricultural policymaking to the USDA and congressional subcommittees with narrow jurisdictions, suppressed attention to the social costs of farm programs while restricting access to potential critics. The farm lobby contributed heavily to congressional campaigns to maintain its subsidies. In the mid 1990s, dairy cooperatives were donating almost $2 million a year to congressmen, and grain lobbies were providing over $500,000 a year.[24]

Yet despite these barriers to reform, Congress passed the landmark Federal Agriculture Improvement and Reform Act in 1996. Instead of getting deficiency payments when market prices fell, eligible farmers of wheat, corn, cotton, rice, sorghum, barley, or oats would receive fixed annual "market transition payments" over seven years. The transition payments would begin at $5.7 billion in 1996 and decline to $4.0 billion in 2002. This approach followed economists' reform prescription. Because the transition payments were "decoupled" from market prices, they would not distort farmers' incentives to produce. In addition to subsidy reductions, the reform featured deregulatory measures to reduce the scope of government's agricultural market interventions and give farmers more control over their land. Farmers would no longer have to idle land to receive subsidies, and they would have the flexibility to plant a variety of crops (except fruits and vegetables) to take advantage of market prices. "Farmers will be producing for the market, rather than [being] restricted by federal government supply controls, for the first time since the Great Depression," said Senate Agriculture Committee chairman Richard G. Lugar (R-IN).[25]

PASSAGE OF "FREEDOM TO FARM"

"Freedom to Farm" passed Congress by solid margins (the Senate passed the legislation on March 28, 1996, 74-26, and the House cleared it the following day, 318-89). Yet the reform victory did not come easily.[26] Some rural legislators were slow to embrace reform. A majority of Senate Democrats opposed the bill on final passage, and the proposal initially could not even get out of the House Agriculture Committee. Ultimately, however, the momentum for farm reform proved strong, and President Clinton agreed to sign the legislation despite misgivings about the measure's shift away from traditional farm safety-net programs.[27] Three factors propelled the reform's eventual passage: high commodity prices in 1995–96; Republican control of Congress; and the willingness of reform proponents to make strategic accommodations to farm interests.[28]

The most important factor—a necessary if not sufficient condition for reform enactment—was rising commodity prices. While many experts had predicted that farm prices would fall in 1995, they increased dramatically. Export demand for U.S. commodities was strong, but domestic farm yields were very low due to late frosts in the Midwest, flooding during the planting season, and an extremely dry summer.[29] If commodity prices had not been soaring, lowering scheduled payments to farm constituencies under existing arrangements, policymakers would have been unwilling to cut traditional farm safety-net programs.

Macropolitical configurations also contributed to the reform climate. While partisan differences on farm policy faded after World War II, Republicans remained far more committed than Democrats to market-oriented reform.

When the GOP took over Congress in 1994, Speaker Newt Gingrich and other top party leaders were intent on cutting Medicaid and welfare to reduce the budget deficit. The Republican majority recognized that politically it could not be seen as only targeting benefits for the poor, it also had to go after unnecessary middle-class supports like farm subsidies. House Agriculture Committee chairman Pat Roberts (R-KA), although a representative from a wheat-growing district and a strong advocate of farm support programs, knew that the political winds had shifted and that agricultural subsidies would be a key target for retrenchment. Roberts faced the delicate political task of protecting the economic interests of farm organizations while crafting a new farm bill that was broadly responsive to the House leadership's demand for sweeping reform. Roberts settled on a strategy of offering farmers an end to unpaid acreage set-asides and planting restrictions in exchange for lower direct support payments. The initial reception of this market-oriented framework among Agriculture Committee members was unenthusiastic. In a strong rebuke to the party leadership, four Republicans from cotton or rice districts joined with Democrats to defeat the legislation.[30]

But Roberts successfully played the party leadership off his committee backbenchers. With the support of Speaker Newt Gingrich (R-GA), Roberts temporarily ceded control over his proposal to the leadership-dominated budget committee, which quickly folded the proposal into its mammoth budget reconciliation bill.[31] As Sheingate notes, "This move placed farm legislation in the hands of a committee with little rural representation."[32] Under the reconciliation process, lawmakers could not oppose farm reform without voting against tax cuts, welfare reform, and other important elements of the new Republican majority's "Contract for America." While Clinton vetoed the budget reconciliation proposal because of his opposition to proposed cutbacks in Medicare and Medicaid, Republicans had been forced to go on record in support of agricultural reform. When Freedom to Farm was taken up as a standalone measure in early 1996, Republican opposition disappeared.

Finally, reform advocates made strategic concessions to neutralize the opposition. Some of the most sensitive farm programs, such as price supports for sugar and peanuts, were barely touched. In general, commodities supported by price supports were less vulnerable to "budget-driven retrenchment" than those supported by direct payments.[33] While unpaid acreage set-asides were abandoned, the law retained a $2 billion environmental conservation reserve program that pays farmers to keep millions of acres of farmland as wildlife habitats. Generous marketing loan programs also were continued. In addition, the permanent farm laws of 1938 and 1949 were left on the books, ensuring that generous pre-war-level farm subsidies would return after 2002 if the reform were not reauthorized.

The most important accommodation was the provision of generous compensation to commodity groups harmed by the elimination of deficiency payments. The market transition payments for 1996 and 1997 were actually *higher*

than the payments that farmers would have received in the absence of the reform, although the Congressional Budget Office's official estimates—which
media coverage used to frame the issue—made them appear smaller. The CBO
baseline was several months out of date at the time Congress debated the reform. Because the baseline had not yet been revised to reflect the recent improvement in commodity prices, it overstated the level of deficiency payments
that farmers were owed. Indeed, farmers faced the prospect of having to *repay*
$2 billion in subsidy checks that the government had distributed when weaker
market conditions had been forecast.

Freedom to Farm thus gave farmers an immediate fiscal windfall, with the
cuts pushed into the "out years." "We're basically buying the farmers out in the
short term to get rid of the price-support mechanism in the long run," said the
Senate Budget Committee's staff director.[34] Chairman Roberts convinced
farm interest groups that the best way for them to "capture the baseline" was
to accept the shift to decoupled payments before the CBO updated its estimates to reflect higher commodity prices.[35]

Although Freedom to Farm was not a pristine law, it was the most significant reform in farm policy since the 1930s. Policy experts justifiably hailed the
reform as a triumph for the common good. According to one leading agricultural economist, what was striking about the reform is "how exactly the approach follows what standard welfare economics has promoted for decades—
the replacement of market distorting interventions by lump-sum payments."[36]
As chairman Roberts accurately stated on the House floor, "Never before had
a farm program proposal enjoyed such broad and diverse support as this one.
From the Ivory Towers of academia and the think tanks to the editorial board
rooms of our nation's newspapers to a broad spectrum of farm, commodity, and
agribusiness groups, support for this proposal is strong."[37]

The $64,000 Question

The question left unanswered when Freedom to Farm was signed into law was
whether the government would keep its promise to wean farmers off subsidies
if agricultural market conditions changed for the worse. It did not take long to
discover the answer. When agriculture market income fell in 1997–98, politicians of both parties were quick to come to the farmers' rescue, doling out billions in new transfer payments. Yet Freedom to Farm has not unraveled completely. The major deregulatory aspects of the reform have endured, reinforced
by dramatic shifts in farmers' market behavior.

Lower Prices, Higher Subsidies

The immediate experience with Freedom to Farm was extremely positive.
Agricultural exports reached a record high of almost $60 billion in 1996 and
farm crop cash income climbed to a record $112 billion in 1997.[38] But in 1998

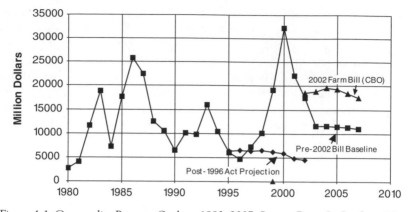

Figure 4-1. Commodity Program Outlays, 1980–2007. *Source:* Bruce L. Gardner, "Commodity Support, Investment and Productivity," Prepared for the Conference on Economics of Water and Infrastructure, Rehovat, Israel, December 18–20, 2002.

the bottom fell out. A collapse of key export markets due to the Asian financial crisis, along with surging production worldwide, caused commodity prices to plummet.[39] U.S. farmers were partially insulated from the effects of this sharp market decline because they retained access to lucrative federal loan programs. But farm interests pushed for increased federal aid to protect their income streams. Democrats in Congress, less invested in the reform than many Republicans, signaled their eagerness to respond. Some Republican lawmakers initially tried to stand firm, arguing that the 1996 reform was fundamentally sound, and that agriculture was an inherently cyclical business, meaning good economic times for farmers would soon return. But eventually the pressure became impossible for GOP lawmakers to resist.

Congress approved more than $25 billion in "emergency" payments to farmers between 1998 and 2000. In addition, the Freedom to Farm market transition payments were doubled and then raised again.[40] Rather than declining steadily after 1996 as called for in the FAIR payment schedule, federal farm aid increased (Figure 4-1). By 2000, nearly half of all farm income was coming from American taxpayers (Figure 4-2).

Reform advocates like Pat Roberts, who gave up his chair of the House Agriculture Committee upon his election to the Senate in 1996, blamed the predicament on a peculiar series of events that could not have been expected. "We've been hit with unprecedented circumstances," Roberts said. "Nobody would have ever thought you would have local depressions in our markets to the extent we had. Nobody would have thought the value of the dollar would work to our detriment. Nobody would have predicted three record world crop years."[41]

While this exact constellation of events was obviously not foreseeable, some observers predicted that farm subsidy reform would not stick. "The farmer is a self-reliant independent creature—on Mars. In America, if the farm economy

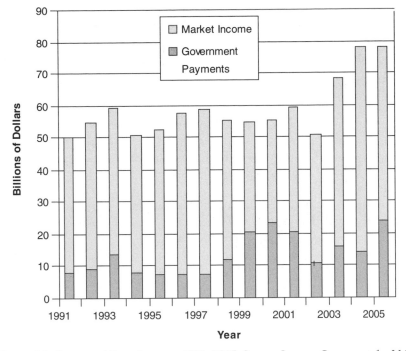

Figure 4-2. Sources of Farm Income, 1991–2005. *Source:* Income Statement for U.S. Farm Sector, Economic Research Service, USDA, www.ers.usdagov/Briefing/Farm Income/Data/nf_t2.htm.

crashes and crop prices collapse, look for farmers and their friends in Congress to seek old-style price-sensitive subsidies on top of the new ones," wrote political analyst Jonathan Rauch shortly after the reform's passage.[42]

Once the subsidy spigot had been turned on, farm advocates were eager to use the emergency payments made between 1998 and 2001 as the template for a new multiyear farm bill. The agricultural lobby won a major victory in April 2001, when Congress passed a budget resolution that permitted a 75 percent increase in baseline spending under the FAIR Act and allowed the reform to be rewritten a year before its authorization had expired.[43]

THE 2002 FARM BILL: A PARTIAL RETREAT

As ultimately passed, the 2002 farm bill was estimated to cost $83 billion more than the cost of continuing the 1996 programs over ten years. It replaced the yearly aid Congress had been authorizing since 1996 with a new counter-cyclical payment program based on crop prices. Payments for grain and cotton farmers were increased by two thirds; price supports for wool, mohair, and honey were restored; and a new dairy program was established.[44] The House adopted the conference report by a vote of 280-141 on May 2. The Senate cleared the bill 64-35 on May 8. Senate Republicans voted 20-28 against the measure. The margin of victory in the upper chamber was supplied by GOP Senators from farm states.

Republican opponents strongly urged President Bush to veto the measure, reminding him that he had earlier praised the Freedom to Farm law for encouraging farmers to reduce their reliance on government. But the Bush Administration ultimately concluded it could not risk a veto of the farm bill in an election year in which partisan control of the Congress would be determined by the outcome of tight races in farm states such as South Dakota, Montana, Minnesota, and Iowa.

The Administration publicly denied that the law was a retreat from the party's free market principles.[45] White House economic adviser Lawrence Lindsay argued that the bill, while imperfect, "protects the fundamental reforms in the 1996 Freedom to Farm legislation."[46] By contrast, many legislative supporters portrayed the bill as a sharp—and overdue—turn away from the market-oriented approach in Freedom to Farm. "The bill reforms our farm programs in a way that will not require the emergency expenditures of the past few years. The 1996 farm bill was a philosophical document written by the House committee leadership. It was an utter failure. It failed our farmers," said Charles Stenholm (D-TX).[47] Opponents were equally adamant about the significance of the new law, arguing that it was a throwback to New Deal–era government support policies. "We know better than to do this... We are in danger of systematically turning farmers into dependent serfs of the federal government," complained Rep. Patrick J. Toomey (R-PA).[48]

In reality, the 2002 farm bill was a mixed affair. It unmistakably signaled the failure of Congress's effort to wean farmers off direct government supports. The level of federal spending on farm subsidies was extremely high in cost compared to both the $10 to $12 billion average annual cost of 1988–97 and to the level of spending anticipated when Congress adopted Freedom to Farm in 1996 (Figure 4-1).[49] Yet the Administration's insistence that the 2002 bill protected core achievements of the 1996 reform was not groundless, because the former measure maintained the fundamental commitment to planting flexibility. In sum, Freedom to Farm unraveled in part, and stuck in part. *These patterns require scrutiny.*

Why Subsidy Reform Didn't Last . . .

The reversal on subsidy reform reflected the failure to alter legislative incentives, political transaction costs, or the public image of the farm lobby. Members of Congress continued to reap electoral benefits by delivering farm subsidies. With control of government hanging in the balance, farm policy became the object of expensive bidding wars between the two parties.[50] In 1999, for example, the Republicans started the bidding at an "emergency" aid package of $6.5 billion. The Democrats countered at $11 billion, and the two parties ultimately compromised on $10 billion.[51]

Significantly, Freedom to Farm left the favor-provision capacity of lawmakers undiminished. The reform imposed no new procedural barriers on subsidy distribution and actually expanded the number of subsidy recipients to some farmers that had previously not filed for benefits. Reform advocates acknowledged as much when the bill was passed. Agriculture committee chairman Pat Roberts told farm groups that if the reform did not work out, Congress itself was the long-term safety net.[52] The Agriculture committee's loss of control over farm legislation during 1995–96 was not a permanent venue shift. Committee property rights were not reallocated.[53] To be sure, the budget reconciliation process continued to be a potential institutional locus for loss imposition. Yet any discipline from the budget process collapsed following the emergence of budget surpluses in 1998. The agricultural committees largely preserved their historic dominance over the farm policy agenda.

Reform advocates did make efforts to bind future Congresses. Early versions of the Freedom to Farm law included a provision that would have ended all traditional commodity programs once and for all. The permanent 1949 farm program law and related legislation would have been repealed. But key farm state Democrats such as Senator Kent Conrad (D-ND) made retention of permanent law a key priority. In a roll call vote, Senate conferees in 1995 voted 9-2 to retain permanent law.[54] As ultimately enacted, Freedom to Farm mandated that if Congress failed to enact a new farm bill after 2002, policy would reverse to the commodity policies of the 1940s. The USDA would have been forced to impose severe production limits and boost price supports for major crops by 50 percent or more. This made it more likely that some sort of farm-subsidy system would be retained after Freedom to Farm expired.

Finally, subsidy reform was rolled back because farmers were not really stigmatized or organizationally incapacitated. Unlike some general-interest reforms that portray target constituencies in an unflattering light, such as anti-smoking laws that cast tobacco companies as killers, Freedom to Farm was largely unaccompanied by a shift in policy images. To be sure, some environmental groups tried to dispel the myth of the "family farmer" by pointing out that subsidies largely benefited agribusinesses and the wealthy. The main rhetorical emphasis during the reform debate, however, was on empowering farmers and expanding their freedom to plant for the market—not on withdrawing benefits from the morally undeserving.

While Planting Flexibility Persisted . . .

While the effort to retrench farm subsidies was largely reversed, the deregulation of farmers' market activities has stuck. Historically, farmers were required to plant certain crops in order to keep getting subsidies, constraining their ability to move back and forth between different crops in response to market

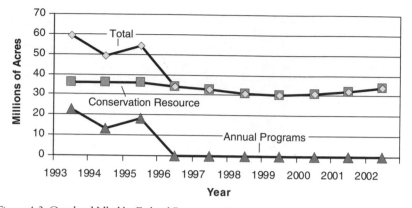

Figure 4-3. Cropland Idled by Federal Programs, 1993–2002. *Sources:* Economic Research Service, USDA, http://www.ers.usda.gov/Briefing/LandUse/majorlandusechapter.htm.

conditions. Additionally, as earlier noted, the government imposed a mandatory annual acreage reduction program that require subsidized farmers to idle portions of their land, thereby reducing commodity supplies and raising consumer prices. While these opportunity costs received little media attention, they seriously distorted the marketplace. The termination of the USDA's acreage reduction authority in 1996 resulted in major efficiency improvements. Some 20 to 30 million more acres were in production due to the 1995 reform, causing annual deadweight losses from farm programs to fall to approximately $1.1 billion in 1999 from roughly $5.0 billion in 1987 (Figure 4-3).[55]

Two factors have reinforced the durability of this change. First, the USDA was stripped of its legal authority to idle cropland. It is rare that a venerable Washington agency like the USDA loses power. The effect of this change was to signal the credibility of the government's new regulatory posture.

Second, and just as important, agricultural deregulation had massive effects on private-sector investment decisions. Freed from government planting restrictions, wheat and barley growers in the northern plain states converted millions of acres to higher-value soybeans, a crop that was ineligible for assistance under farm programs of earlier years (Figure 4-4).[56] Others were using their new operational freedom to plant peas, safflowers, and lentils on acreage formerly devoted to wheat. Other farmers did not change their crops but simply planted more. Such planting decisions, in turn, created huge ripple effects throughout the farm economy. Because farmers were devoting their land to more diverse crops and using their acreage more intensively, agricultural suppliers had to adjust their inventories. "That will require more inputs [fertilizer, pesticides, and herbicides], more transportation and storage, and more trickle-down economic activity," said one farm expert.[57] These investment responses created new alignments of groups with a stake in the continuation of the reform. Even lob-

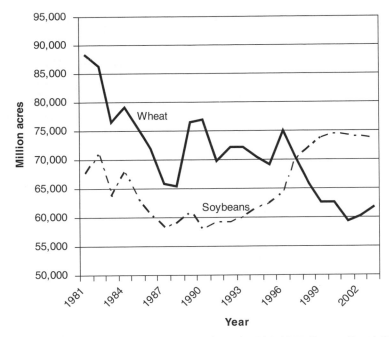

Figure 4-4. Acres of Wheat and Soybean Planted, 1981–2003. *Source:* David Orden, "U.S. Agricultural Policy: The 2002 Farm Bill and WTO DOHA Round Proposal," International Food Policy Research Institute, February 2003.

byists who pressed Congress to fund new counter-cyclical farm payments in 2002 pleaded with Congress not to bring back inflexible supply controls. "We appreciate the fact that the [House Agriculture] committee maintained a planting flexibility that was the hallmark of the 1996 farm bill," testified the president of the National Association of Wheat Growers in 2001. "Planting flexibility has revolutionized many of our growers' operations, allowing them to plant to the market and maximize returns on every planted acre."[58]

The Freedom to Farm Act created a Commission on 21st Century Production Agriculture to assess the reform and recommend future legislation. The Commission held hearings around the nation at which it received testimony. It learned that farmers liked the freedom to choose what to plant, and the commission ultimately recommended expanding production flexibly to all crops.[59]

Aftermath

Although unapologetic about its actions, the Bush Administration was never deeply enamored by the 2002 farm bill. Once the 2002 midterms were behind them, with Republicans retaining their majority status, the Administration began trying to scale back some of the law's generosity. In its fiscal 2006 budget submission, the Administration proposed a 5-percent across-the-board cut in agricultural spending, in part by limiting annual subsidies per farm to $250,000, down from $360,000. The Administration also promised closing loopholes in payment rules to make it harder for farmers to exceed these limits. These proposals were estimated to save almost $6 billion over 10 years.[60]

Less than three months later, the Administration was forced to back off these proposals, despite enthusiastic support from environmental groups, deficit hawks, and some foreign governments. The proposed cuts hit cotton and rice farmers in the South and California particularly hard, engendering the opposition of Senate Agricultural Chairman Saxby Chambliss (R-GA). While some small farmers endorsed the proposal because they believed high subsidies drive up land prices, key farm interest groups, including the National Farmers Union and the National Corn Growers Association, also opposed the plan.[61] While the Bush Administration continued to call for subsidy reductions, it did not reveal a willingness to spend any political capital to achieve them.[62]

CONCLUSION

The embarrassing failure of the drive to curb farm subsidies over the past decade demonstrates how difficult it is to reconfigure the government's role in a policy domain when the affected clientele is perceived as a crucial actor in the electoral process and enjoys a highly favorable public image. Groups can lose benefits temporarily only to recoup them subsequently. In the case of Freedom to Farm, the losses were more apparent than real, because the transition payments were actually more generous over the medium run than what existing law provided. For those who believe that scarce federal resources should be allocated to strong claims, rather than to strong claimants, the recent history of federal farm policy is a cautionary tale of what happens when reform principles intersect with politics.

However, it would be a mistake to draw too pessimistic a conclusion from this episode. To some degree, Freedom to Farm was the victim of bad luck. Its passage was horrendously timed. If the farm economy had improved instead of tanked after 1996, the law would have had a much better chance of sticking, just as welfare reform has endured in part because the economy performed well during the years immediately after its adoption. Before farmers were forced to adapt themselves to the new policy regime, their cash incomes declined as a result of an exogenous change in export market conditions.[63]

While the generous farm aid packages of 1998–2002 were made possible in part by the improvement in the nation's fiscal condition, the return of budget deficits may make the costs of farm subsidies a retrenchment target in future years. Bills have been introduced for fundamental farm subsidy reform, and a skillful political entrepreneur may yet find a way to reframe the debate. The next time farm subsidy reform gets on the agenda—and there will be a next time—reformers may push harder for the procedural changes that were not won in 1996, such as the repeal of permanent farm program legislation. Agricultural subsidy reform is an extremely difficult task for American polity, but it is not an impossible one.

However, the main reason why pessimism should be tempered is because agricultural reform is not only about reducing the costs of subsidies to taxpayers. An equally important objective has been to make U.S. farm policies more efficient, reducing deadweight losses—the pure waste that benefits nobody. Because traditional farm programs were so inefficient, they created huge unrealized gains—the equivalent of $20 bills on the ground. Farmers could profit from deregulation of planting decisions, without even the need for politically troublesome compensation mechanisms. Most of the farm subsidies allocated under the 2002 bill are not directly tied to current market conditions. And the termination of annual unpaid idling programs puts more of the nation's fertile land to work. These policy changes have been reinforced by changes in institutional configurations and the farmers' own behavior, making them even more likely to persist. Serious problems in U.S. farm policy remain to be addressed, but sustainable progress has been made.

Reforming the American Welfare State: ERISA and the Medicare Catastrophic Coverage Act

SOCIAL POLICY reform is a special case of general-interest reform. While many of the reform episodes examined in this book involve the withdrawal of particularistic subsidies from relatively narrow clienteles (e.g., agricultural reform, airline deregulation) or the rationalization of public administration (e.g., procurement reform), social policy reform involves attempts to improve social insurance mechanisms or to impose distributive standards on the wider society. Social policy reforms that change the flow of benefits or allocation of risks in the name of some broad interest like fiscal control or economic security will necessarily have a tangible impact on the lives of millions of citizens. This makes social policy reform an especially treacherous project for blame-avoiding politicians.

The exceptional design of the American welfare state adds further complications.[1] Compared to the welfare states of other advanced democracies, the U.S. welfare state relies heavily on the private sector. Many Americans receive health and pension benefits from their employers, rather than from public bureaucracies. Welfare state reform in the United States therefore often entails attempts to encourage or compel business corporations to serve public purposes. Reformers can write their social goals into the law, but business managers—and impersonal market forces—usually get the last word. In addition, the U.S. social safety net, while massive in size and expense, has big holes. Many population subgroups and social risks are covered poorly or not at all. The upshot is that welfare state reformers not only have to satisfy or placate private interests, they must worry about managing rising costs *and* addressing unmet social needs.

These differences notwithstanding, welfare state reforms share key features with other general-interest reform projects. First, welfare state reformers, like their counterparts in other arenas, seldom have the luxury of writing on a blank slate. They must navigate around the interests of preexisting stakeholders and respond to popular expectations about government's role as guarantor of social welfare. Another similarity is that the prime movers behind the reforms are often policy entrepreneurs who use their media access and political marketing skills to get reforms on the agenda. Such entrepreneurial actors, however, seldom do the hard follow-up work required to sustain their reform visions over the long haul.

The two instances of social policy reform examined in this chapter—the Employee Retirement Income Security Act (ERISA) and the Medicare Catastrophic Coverage Act (MCCA)—illustrate these complexities. A response to concerns about lost pension benefits arising from bankruptcies, mergers, and corporate scandals, ERISA established national corporate pension standards to promote the economic security of workers and retirees. ERISA was strongly opposed by most employer groups and had only "wavering support" from much of organized labor, making it a "minor miracle" that the reform passed at all.[2] Over the past thirty-five years, ERISA has recast the American social welfare landscape. About 55 percent of full-time workers in the United States today participate in a retirement plan governed by ERISA.[3] An even larger share of the workforce participates in an ERISA-covered health plan. ERISA has durably reconfigured interest group alignments, corporate governance, and the institutional and legal context of social policymaking. There is no going back to a pre-ERISA world.

This ERISA case also has a larger significance for understanding the sustainability of policy reforms. Its development illustrates that the political fate of reforms depends not only upon the benefits and costs they directly create, but upon how they shape the incentives of economic actors and public policymakers over the long haul. This is a far more complicated—and interesting—story than ex-ante "lock in." While ERISA was designed to protect workers who participate in defined benefit pension plans, employers, for a host of reasons, including the regulatory burdens imposed by ERISA itself, have increasingly not vested their employees in such plans in the first place. In addition, ERISA's preemption of state regulation of self-insured health plans, in conjunction with court decisions and unforeseen changes in corporate financing of employee insurance benefits, has had profound consequences for the provision of health care. ERISA's legal requirements and prohibitions can be circumvented to some extent, but their embodiment in court decisions, business practices, and organizational expectations makes them virtually impossible to repeal.

The second reform, the MCCA (P.L. 100-360), expanded Medicare's limited benefit package to offer a measure of social protection against the rising out-of-pocket costs of covered hospital and physician services, as well as the expense of prescription drugs. To avoid adding to the budget deficit, the new benefits were funded solely from beneficiary premiums—a fiscally responsible approach, yet one that constituted a sharp departure from the tradition of using payroll taxes on current workers and general revenues to cover most of the costs of seniors' health benefits. Congress overwhelmingly passed the MCAA in 1988. In a stunning reversal of public policy, however, Congress repealed the measure just over a year later because of a harsh backlash over the measure's self-financing mechanism among segments of the elderly population, giving the MCAA the dubious honor of being one of the "shortest-lived pieces of social legislation" in American history.[4] The political embarrassment over the collapse of the MCCA has set in motion negative reactions against social policymaking along similar lines. These reactions can be detected in the design of the Medicare prescription drug benefit enacted in 2003.

In short, ERISA and the MCCA have had contrasting fates, but the two reforms have each cast long shadows on American social policymaking.

EMPLOYEE RETIREMENT INCOME SECURITY ACT

Enactment of the Employee Retirement Income Security Act of 1974 (P.L. 93-406) was a landmark in the development of the American public/private welfare state. As James A. Wooten argues in his superb detailed history, ERISA "redefined the government's role by making security of pension promises a basic goal of federal policy."[5] While the Act did not require companies to establish pension plans, it stated that those that did so had to meet minimum standards to ensure workers would receive at least some of their defined benefits, even if the company later faced bad times. In so doing, ERISA transformed the U.S. occupational pension from a "personnel instrument of private employers into an instrument of national public welfare."[6] ERISA has had far-reaching impacts on employee rights, ensuing patterns of social policymaking, and the organization of American business.

Pre-reform Situation

The first private pensions in the U.S. were established by the railroad industry in the 1870s to prevent labor unrest and provide an incentive for the retirement of superannuated workers.[7] By the 1920s, pensions had begun to diffuse into the banking and insurance industries, public utilities, and institutions of higher education. The growth of private pension plans surged in the 1940s and 1950s. Public policy encouraged this expansion, primarily through tax relief. The Revenue Act of 1921 allowed corporations to contribute tax-free to profit-sharing plans established for a firm's workers. The Internal Revenue Act of 1942 provided stricter participation standards, imposed some disclosure requirements, and permitted integration of corporate pensions with Social Security. Wage stabilization programs during World War II and the Korean War also contributed to the growth of pensions. Since firms were barred from offering pay raises, business managers used the promise of future pension benefits to retain workers. Participation increased from 19 to 45 percent of private sector workers between 1945 and 1970.[8]

While the government subsidized the growth of industrial pensions, employers and unions retained almost complete discretion over the operation of their pension plans. Many plans were unsound actuarially, and there was "no requirement for vesting or preservation of benefits for workers who terminated their employment before they were eligible for retirement."[9]

Media coverage of pension failures brought these problems to national attention. The most notorious incident was the financial collapse of the Studebaker auto company. When the firm closed its South Bend, Indiana plant in 1964, it possessed only enough cash on hand to cover the accrued benefits of retirees and fully vested workers who were over age 60. Vested employees under age 60, including some who had spent their entire careers with the firm, received "a lump sum payment worth only about 15 percent of the value of their pension. Employees whose benefit accruals had not vested—including all employees under age forty—got nothing."[10]

The Politics of Adoption

Even before Sudebaker's collapse in 1964 served as a focusing event, experts had begun to lay the groundwork for major pension reform legislation. In 1962, John F. Kennedy appointed a President's Committee on Corporate Pension Funds. The committee's final report was not publicly released until 1965 and not transmitted to Congress due to the intense opposition of business leaders like Henry Ford.[11] The report recommended that qualifying plans cover eligible employers after no more than three years of service and that workers receive half vesting after 15 years. It also recommended mandatory funding of current accruals and amortization of unfunded past-service liabilities.[12] These recommendations subsequently formed the model for Senator Jacob Javits's comprehensive pension bill and for a proposal developed by the Department of Labor in May 1968 under President Johnson.[13] Both Javits's bill and the DOL bill contained many of the elements that ultimately would be contained in ERISA. Yet it took another six years for these provisions to become law. The extended delay reflected the opposition to pension reform from employers, the insurance and banking industries, and most of organized labor. Indeed, President Johnson himself was skittish about pension reform. Despite Johnson's strenuous attempts to distance himself from the Labor Department proposal, the media portrayed it as his bill, and Johnson ended up stirring up a conflict with the business lobby.[14]

The opposition of the corporate sector to pension reform is not too surprising. Most executives viewed pensions as a personnel administration tool for building worker loyalty and motivating good job performance. They rejected mandatory vesting and funding standards as an unwelcome intrusion on business autonomy. More interesting is the lack of support from much of organized labor. To be sure, the United Auto Workers and steelworkers unions supported pension termination insurance because many of their workers had underfunded pensions. But craft and garment unions feared that strict funding standards would force plans to cut benefits or shut down completely. They remained steadfastly opposed to reform until ERISA's enactment was assured.[15]

The task of building the case for pension reform initially fell to policy experts like Stanley Surrey, Assistant Treasury Secretary under Presidents Kennedy and Johnson.[16] The research of Surrey and other Treasury analysts during the mid-1960s on the revenue costs of federal "tax expenditures" signaled that corporate pensions enjoyed generous federal subsidies. Since eliminating favorable tax treatment of pensions was considered "politically impossible," experts believed the government had an obligation to ensure that the pension system served a public purpose.[17] As Jacob Hacker observes, "Ultimately, [ERISA] must be viewed as an outgrowth of the pressures created by federal intervention itself—a legislative response to the forces unleashed by previous public policies."[18]

Expert ideas normally are no match for well-organized clienteles, but policy entrepreneurs skillfully built a winning coalition. The key political actor between 1967 and 1974 was Senator Jacob K. Javits (R-NY). Javits was able to call upon the expertise of Frank Cummings, a labor lawyer who previously worked for the firm that represented Studebaker before joining Javits's staff to help draft Javits's 1967 pension reform legislation. Javits in 1971 organized several hearings in cities around the nation to publicize horror stories about loyal employees who had worked for the same firm for thirty or forty years only to see their pensions vanish.[19] The hearings drew extensive sympathetic coverage from the media. Seeing a window opening for policy reform, other entrepreneurs got involved in the issue. In May 1972, Ralph Nader launched an aggressive attack on the corporate pension system, calling it "one of the most comprehensive consumer frauds that many Americans will encounter in their lifetime."[20] Nader's solution was a vast expansion of the Social Security program, but his proposal failed to win the support of Republicans in Congress, who were already nervous about the rapid growth of Social Security spending. (Congress had just passed the largest Social Security benefit hike in the nation's history.) As Christopher Howard argues, Republicans began to see pension reform "as a way to solidify company pensions and curb demand for future expansions of Social Security."[21]

In 1970, Javits gained a key reform ally in Senate Labor and Public Welfare Committee chairman Harrison (Pete) Williams (D-NJ). Two years later, Javits and Williams introduced a new pension bill that included financial and disclosure reforms, vesting and funding standards, termination insurance, and a voluntary portability program. But members with close ties to the business lobby remained wary. The Senate Finance Committee took up the Javits-Williams bill in September 1972 and "totally gutted the measure."[22] Public pressure for pension reform was steadily mounting, however, as members discovered when they went back to their districts to campaign for the November 1972 midterm elections.[23] Still, Javits's marketing campaign might well have failed. A key turning point, Wooten observes, came when many state legislatures began responding to the call of newspapers and other media outlets for pension reform legislation. In 1973, several states considered far-reaching pension reform laws. Anxious to avoid a maze of conflicting state mandates, the business community and the AFL-CIO "reversed their position and endorsed federal legislation in order to prevent the states from regulating."[24]

Pension reformers also benefited from external forces. The Nixon Administration had hoped to satisfy the demand for pension reform with an incremental bill, but the Watergate scandal eroded its influence on the Hill. Still, ERISA's legislative journey proceeded at a glacial pace in 1973-74. Four committees—the House and Senate labor committees, House Ways and Means, and Senate Finance—had jurisdiction over the mammoth legislation. The bill was stuck in conference in the spring and summer of 1974 and overshadowed by the Watergate hearings. Nixon's resignation on August 9, however, cleared the decks for the bill's enactment. ERISA passed with overwhelming bipartisan support in both chambers (407-2 in the House and 85-0 in the Senate).[25] President Gerald Ford signed ERISA into law on Labor Day.[26]

ERISA contained six sets of reforms.[27] First, were fiduciary reforms (to ensure that plans and plan assets were managed responsibly). Second, were participation and vesting rules (to address the risk of forfeiture as a result of layoff, quit, or job change). Third, were funding requirements (to increase the likelihood that assets were available to pay pension obligations). Fourth, was termination insurance (to pay pensions if assets were not sufficient). The Act established a new agency, the Pension Benefit Guaranty Cooperation (PBGC), to cover benefits (subject to certain limits) in the event plan sponsors could not. The PBGC was authorized to collect revenues of $1 per year per participant in each plan. Fifth, were increased discourse requirements (to give plan participants accurate and comprehensive information about their plans). Finally, ERISA contained tax reforms, which included IRAs (to make tax-favored retirement saving more widely available) and rollovers (to increase portability).[28]

A Surprising Reconfiguration

Since 1974, ERISA has become a permanent fixture of the American economic landscape. It has transformed the internal organization of business firms, recast patterns of political representation, and constrained the direction of subsequent health care reform efforts. This has been a remarkable reconfiguration.

Yet it has also been in many ways a surprising, even ironic, reconfiguration. A declining percentage of workers today are enrolled in the very type of pension plan (defined benefit) that ERISA was meant to secure.[29] While ERISA is not wholly responsible for the shift to defined contribution plans, it did little to counteract the trend, and in certain respects even contributed to it.[30] ERISA has also "powerfully shaped the evolution of health provision in the United States."[31] Its expansive preemption of state law, coupled with the failure of Congress and the courts to provide federal remedies, created a "regulatory vacuum" during the 1980s and 1990s. Many workers were left unprotected from the erosion of employer health coverage. Recently, state policymakers have attempted to fill the ERISA regulatory vacuum, but the very strategy they have selected to address the health insurance crisis (individual coverage mandates) demonstrates the powerful policy feedback from ERISA's original design.

Securing Pension Rights

Most pension experts agree that "ERISA has succeeded in meeting its stated objective of strengthening workers' claims on benefits."[32] ERISA was designed to protect individual pension rights and it has. While thousands of small employers abandoned their pension plans shortly after enactment because of high compliance costs, most large firms rewrote their plans to confirm with ERISA.[33] A 1976 survey of firms employing more than two million workers found that about half liberalized their vesting requirements.[34] Some improvement also occurred in corporate funding of defined benefit plans.[35]

The Transformation of Corporate Governance

These policy successes have been rooted in profound shifts in patterns of corporate governance.[36] After ERISA, firms were stimulated to rewrite their pension plans to comply with the new regulations, to set up centralized benefit offices, and to hire benefit experts who could redesign benefit plans. As sociologists Frank Dobbin and Frank R. Sutton point out in their insightful study "The Strength of a Weak State," the modern Human Resources industry owes itself in no small part to ERISA and to the adoption of equal employment opportunity rules in the 1960s and 1970s.[37] Key features of ERISA's policy design engendered this remarkable reconfiguration of corporate governance. First, ERISA was the product of political compromise, and compromise is the mother of complexity. The Act regulated pensions and benefit plans in mind-numbing detail. Indeed, ERISA is widely regarded as one of the most convoluted and esoteric laws ever passed by Congress.[38] Yet central features of the Act were also essentially ambiguous. For instance, pension plan managers were required to exercise "fiduciary responsibility," but ERISA did not define what this meant or how funds were to be invested. ERISA allowed managers to select from three different sets of pension vesting guidelines. As Dobbin and Sutton observe, "Compliance [under ERISA] was not simply a matter of following a blueprint—it required accountants and tax attorneys who could weigh a dizzying mix of options."[39]

While ERISA did not set out clear litmus tests for compliance, the penalties for noncompliance were very high. Employers that did not follow ERISA's rules risked "losing tax deductions for their contributions, having their plans terminated by the PBGC, and being sued by current and former employees."[40] Many firms found they needed to hire experts and consultants to protect themselves against these risks. In sum, ERISA contributed to the rise of human resource divisions in the private sector. Management of employee fringe benefits was bureaucratized, legalized, formalized, and made to service corporate efficiency goals. If a core purpose of ERISA was to make pensions more than a discretionary tool of individual managers, it was in the operations of corporate human resource bureaucracies that this objective was achieved.

The Fragmentation of Public Authority

While changes in corporate governance helped institutionalize private pensions as an instrument of national social welfare, the authority of public agencies over employee pensions remained fragmented and weak. Jurisdiction over ERISA was split among four congressional committees, and administrative powers over the Act's implementation were divided among the Treasury Department, Labor Department, and the PBGC. In contrast to pure punctuated equilibrium accounts of policy change, ERISA did not permanently shift control over pension benefits to a new decision-making venue. Rather, it layered multiple centers of governance atop one another. The predictable result has been policy incoherence: "Each arena favored certain kinds of interests over others," Christopher Howard observes, "and these interests often worked at cross-purposes."[41] Congress has responded to these cross pressures in its usual way, by favoring one set of preferences and then another.[42]

PBGC Funding Problems

The pension termination insurance program at the heart of ERISA has had persistent funding problems.[43] The agency has managed to stay afloat through premiums and the money it inherits from failed plans, but its liabilities have regularly threatened to outstrip its assets. (Private pensions were thought to be underfunded by more than $450 billion in 2004.)[44] The PBGC's problems largely reflect weaknesses and tensions embedded in its institutional design.[45] While government corporations like the FDIC have the independent authority to raise fees, Congress refused to give the PBGC such authority, retaining that control for itself.[46] There is an inherent tension between the goals of pension security and broad coverage.[47] Stringent funding standards offer greater protection to plan participants, but if the cost of offering a defined benefit plan gets too steep, plan sponsors will abandon them.[48]

The fundamental problem is that PBGC's design gives the agency little protection from "moral hazard"—that is, the risk that pension plan sponsors will engage in risky behavior (e.g., increasing pension liabilities rather than current wages) knowing the government will bail them out if things go awry.[49] If the PBGC ever runs out of money, Congress will almost certainly step in to safeguard the benefits of pension plan participants (who would comprise a sympathetic political constituency), just as it bailed out S&L depositors in the 1980s.[50] Any statements that the PBGC is the "pension guarantor of last resort" are simply not credible. The risks of an underfunded PBGC are ultimately borne not by the sponsors of defined benefit plans that pay premiums into the PBGC, but rather by *general taxpayers*. The business community therefore has relatively little stake in improving the PBGC's funding.[51]

Unsurprisingly, Congressional attempts to increase these PBGC premiums have been subject to ongoing pressures from business and labor groups opposed to making the system self-sufficient.[52] Pension plan sponsors have been permitted to increase benefits (and thus future PBGC liabilities) even when the plans are in dire financial shape. The PBGC's premium structure also does not properly reflect market risks. Historically, the PBGC's income has come mostly from flat-rate premiums. While variable-rate premiums were added in 1987 to give firms an incentive to better fund plans, they do not take into account key factors such as plan asset investment strategies or its demographic profile. Finally, the sponsors of underfunded pension plans have been able to avoid minimum funding contributions if they have earned funding "credits" as a result of contributing more than minimum amounts in past years. These credits can be carried to future years, even if the value of the earlier payment has declined.

Congress recently enacted legislation to address some of these problems.[53] As signed into law by President Bush, the Pension Protection Act of 2006 limits, but still allows, some use of credit balances.[54] It requires managers to fund 100 percent of their defined benefit plan liabilities, up from 90 percent, and it forces firms that underfund their plans to payer higher premiums to the PBGC. But the reform did not go as far as some hoped. The funding provisions of the law will not take effect for two years to ease the transition. It also gave special breaks on the rules to financially troubled legacy air carriers. Delta and Northwest, for example, were given as much as seventeen years to fully fund their plans.[55]

The Shift Toward Defined Contribution Plans

The major problem today is no longer the protection of defined pension promises, but rather the "absence of promised pensions in the first place."[56] One of the most important developments over the past four decades has been the massive decline of defined benefit plans, relative to defined contribution plans (Table 5-1). Between 1975 and 2004, the total number of private pensions more than doubled, from 311,000 to 683,000. Most of this net growth, however, has occurred among defined contribution plans, especially 401(k) plans. In 2004, there were 635,000 defined contribution plans, up from 208,000 in 1975. The number of defined pension plans declined by more than 50 percent over this period, dropping to 48,000 in 2004.

Participation has skewed even more heavily toward defined contribution plans. In 1975, just after ERISA's enactment, about three workers in four (74 percent) who had a private pension had a defined benefit plan. By 2004, less than four in ten (39 percent) of workers with pensions had such plans. This figure actually understates the movement toward defined contribution plans because the overall participation rate counts retirees. Among active employees, the shift away from defined benefit plans has been stark. In 1973, only 13 percent of active employees were enrolled in defined contribution plans. By 2004, that figure had climbed to 71 percent. Defined benefit plans today are the exception rather than the rule.

There is no shortage of reasons why defined benefit plans have been losing ground as the preferred private pension vehicle. Some of the factors have clearly been beyond government's control, including changes in firm size, the decline of unionized manufacturing jobs, aggressive marketing efforts by the financial services industry, shifts in employee preferences due to greater job mobility, and increased global competition.[57] But ERISA, especially in synergistic interaction with the adoption of 401(k)s shortly thereafter, fueled this trend in several ways.[58]

First, ERISA and its subsequent amendments imposed a much heavier regulatory burden on defined benefit plans than on defined contribution ones, including minimum funding rules. The associated compliance costs were quite significant, especially for smaller employers that could not mitigate them through economies of scale. Second, ERISA capped the amount of the sponsoring employer's stock that could be held for a defined benefit plan at 10 percent of total plan assets. A third way ERISA decreased the attractiveness of defined benefit plans was by requiring participating firms to pay fees to the PBGC. In contrast, defined contribution plans were not subject to similar insurance premiums.[59]

Finally, ERISA established the tax-deductible IRA to allow workers not covered by pensions in their current jobs to contribute money toward their own retirements. In 1974, the IRA was crafted as a partial solution to the problems of portability and universal coverage in a defined benefit world. But this world was crumbling, in part because the IRA created a political opening during the early 1980s to the enactment of scores of costly new tax breaks for 401(k)s and other individualized savings accounts that in turn generated pos-

TABLE 5-1
Decline of Defined Benefit Plans Since 1975

	1975	1980	1990	1995	1998	2004
			(rounded, in thousands)			
Total Plans[a]	311	489	712	693	730	683
Defined benefit	103	148	170	69	56	48
Defined contribution	208	341	462	599	674	635
Defined contribution as percentage of total	67	70	73	84	92	93
			(rounded, in millions)			
Total Participants[b]	45	58	77	87	99	106
Defined benefit	33	38	39	40	42	41
Defined contribution	12	20	38	48	58	65
Defined contribution as percentage of total	26	34	50	55	58	61
Active Participants	31	36	40	47	52	73
Defined benefit	27	30	29	24	23	21
Defined contribution	4	6	12	23	29	52
Defined contribution as percentage of total	13	16	30	49	56	71

[a]Excludes single-participants plans.

[b]Includes active, retired, and separated vested participants not yet in pay status. Not adjusted for double counting of individuals participating in more than one plan.

Source: U.S. Department of Labor, Pension and Welfare Benefits Administration, *Private Pension Plan Bulletin*, various years.

itive feedback effects that allowed them over time to grow into a huge component of the American public/private welfare state.[60] As one expert concludes, "In short, ERISA, without anyone intending it that way, laid the grounding for the defined contribution society . . . "[61]

The Consequences for Health Policy

ERISA has not only contributed to the decline of defined benefit pensions. It has also shaped the politics of health care policy. An obscure provision of ERISA (Section 514) states that "The provisions of this title shall supersede any and all State laws insofar as they may now or hereafter relate to any employee benefit plan." The so-called preemption clause played an important, if contested, role in ERISA's passage. Employers and many union leaders were not enthusiastic about national pension reform, but they vastly preferred it to the prospect of dealing with a patchwork of state and local mandates. When state legislatures began threatening to regulate private pension and welfare plans if Congress did not act, the business community and the AFL-CIO had little choice but to accommodate themselves to ERISA.[62]

There is a fascinating scholarly debate over whether the consequences of ERISA's preemption provision on state efforts to regulate health plans were intended by Congress. The evidence suggests that a few very knowledgeable actors, such as Senator Javits, understood and were "exceedingly troubled by the implications of ERISA's broad preemptive scope."[63] Other scholars argue that the "full effects" of the preemption provision were "unforeseen because the target of ERISA was pensions, not health insurance."[64] The safest conclusion is that preemption was adopted "neither by accident nor quite by design."[65]

But there is no denying the importance of the preemption provision for health politics and policy.[66] ERISA preemption became increasingly consequential over time—an illustration of how obscure technical policy changes can have massive subsequent consequences.[67] At the time of ERISA's enactment, most firms contracted with commercial insurers to pay for their employees' health benefits.[68] Only a small minority of large firms opted to finance their employees' health plans themselves. By the early 1990s, however, more than two-thirds of American companies, and nearly all the big ones, chose to self-insure in order to escape growing tax and regulatory burdens.[69] As Hacker persuasively argues, "By the time pro-government liberals realized that the movement toward self-funded insurance would hurt their cause, the movement was largely irreversible and a formidable coalition of defenders had arisen to stymie efforts at reversal."[70]

ERISA's preemption of state regulations of pensions has a logical basis, since ERISA sets detailed federal standards for pensions. Yet ERISA also preempted state regulations of self-insured health plans, even though it was virtually silent on how such plans should be run.[71] Self-funded health plans were not subject to federal rules concerning coverage, funding, or vesting requirements. The result was a "regulatory vacuum" in which Congress prohibited the states from offering legal remedies to workers, but failed to offer any of its own.[72] Early Supreme Court rulings interpreted the preemption clause expansively, striking down a host of state laws intended to regulate health care delivery or coverage, such as a New York law mandating that employers provide pregnancy disability benefits to employees.[73] The courts have since retreated a bit, but ERISA preemption continues to sharply constrain what actions states can take to improve health care coverage, further balkanizing the U.S. health insurance market.[74]

Recently, the courts overturned a 2006 Maryland law that would have effectively forced the largest employers, such as Wal-Mart, to expand health benefits to their workers.[75] Massachusetts then attempted to circumvent ERISA by passing a law that requires employers with more than ten employees to contribute a "fair share" to employee health coverage.[76] It is too soon to know whether the Massachusetts law and similar "pay or play" reforms will survive an ERISA challenge. Even if they do, though, ERISA will have had a profound influence on the politics of U.S. health policymaking over the past several decades by shaping the menu of feasible reform options. Rather than trying to develop the reforms that make the most technical sense, health care reformers have spent the last several decades searching for ever-more indirect and "clever ways to skirt the limitations imposed by ERISA."[77] The United States would doubtless still face a national health insurance crisis today if ERISA had never been enacted, but policymakers would likely have had a much wider scope in crafting new solutions.

The Representation of Interests

ERISA has reshaped the representation of political interests.[78] A number of new business lobbies focused on pension and health issues formed shortly after the reform's passage. One of the most visible and active groups has been the ERISA Industry Committee (ERIC), founded in 1976 to represent the interests of larger employers.[79] ERIC maintains a Washington, D.C. lobbying office and a network of some 1,500 human resource experts across the nation. At the top of its political agenda has been the preservation of the ERISA preemption clause, a priority shared by a number of other business groups.[80] Other business associations that formed in the wake of ERISA include the National Employee Benefits Institute (1977) and the Employee Benefits Research Institute (1978). The latter is a major research organization sponsored by employers, unions, banks, insurance companies, and consultants. The business community has not simply accommodated itself to ERISA, it has become in many ways the reform's main defender. As one corporate executive stated on the occasion of ERISA's twenty-fifth anniversary, "I can't help but be struck by the fact that legislation that was described at the time of its passage in certain [business] quarters as standing for every ridiculous idea since Adam is now celebrated and protected."[81]

The political representation of labor also evolved after ERISA. Unions created several new groups, including the National Coordinating Committee for Multiemployer Plans (1975). During the 1980s and 1990s, portions of organized labor joined with business groups to defend ERISA preemption for self-insured health plans, even as employers were withdrawing health insurance benefits form some workers. As political scientist Marie Gottschalk observes, "ERISA helped reconfigure the constellation of interest groups and their preferences in unanticipated ways and bolstered organized labor's attachment to private-sector solutions for health-care reform."[82] Of course, labor and business continue to battle over employee benefit issues. The big change since ERISA is that many of these conflicts now play out through actual or threatened litigation. The courts ruled more than 4,000 times on the preemption clause between 1989 and 1999 alone.[83] Unsurprisingly, a cottage industry of lawyers has emerged in each state whose practices consist of efforts to lead or defend ERISA class actions, such as multiplaintiff and representative lawsuits on issues like fiduciary duties, plan terminations, spousal benefits, and federal preemptions.[84]

In sum, ERISA has not resolved or eliminated the conflict between labor and business over employee fringe benefits. Workers and unions still would like to get more, and employers would prefer to give less. But ERISA has fundamentally altered the terms of the policy debate. It has had profound, and largely unexpected, effects on the trajectory of the American public/private welfare state.

THE MEDICARE CATASTROPHIC COVERAGE ACT

If the political development of ERISA shows that reforms can last even when they have unforeseen downstream consequences, the MCCA case demonstrates that reforms can collapse even when they promise benefits to a large majority. It is insufficient for reforms to be well-intentioned. Sustainability requires reforms to create constituencies and defang opponents. The reform consolidation process hinges on group perceptions, reactions, and expectations, and there is no guarantee that such responses will be self-reinforcing.

Pre-reform Situation

The adoption of the MCCA in 1988 grew out of concerns that the Medicare benefit package had failed to keep pace with medical costs and evolving norms of private-sector health insurance. Medicare did not cover most long-term nursing home care, even though seniors were living much longer. Nor did it cover outpatient prescription drugs, which were increasingly the first line of treatment for myriad health conditions. In addition, Medicare Part A paid the full costs of hospital stays only up to sixty days, after which participants were subject to expensive copayments. By the mid-1980s, the elderly were spending nearly as much of their income on health care as they did before Medicare's enactment.[85] Both political parties, for different reasons, had incentives to address this issue in the mid-1980s.[86]

The Politics of Adoption

Catastrophic health insurance might not have gotten on the policy agenda under President Ronald Reagan but for the entrepreneurial efforts of Health and Human Services Secretary Otis R. Bowen, who had chaired a 1984 advisory council on Social Security that recommended the creation of a voluntary program that would cap out-of-pocket expenses for physician services.[87] "Without Bowen, there would have been no advocate in the administration willing to push catastrophic health insurance, and without such an advocate, Medicare expansion would not have received presidential sponsorship," writes Jonathan Oberlander.[88] At Bowen's urging, President Reagan signaled his support for the concept of catastrophic insurance in his 1986 State of the Union Address. Some of Reagan's closest advisors strongly opposed the initiative on both ideological and fiscal grounds, but Bowen ultimately won Reagan's support for a plan that would cover unlimited hospital stays and cap beneficiaries' out-of-pocket payments for Medicare-covered services at $2,000 a year. The new benefits would be paid from a flat $4.92 increase in monthly Part B premiums. Reagan described Bowen's plan as a lifeline for people who had to "make a choice between financial ruin and death."[89]

It is impossible to know whether Bowen's relatively modest catastrophic insurance plan—which covered neither long-term care nor prescription drugs—would have stuck if it had been enacted. Before the bill reached President Reagan's desk, its benefit and financing provisions were modified in ways that helped bring about the reform's ultimate collapse.[90]

Reagan's endorsement of the Bowen plan was warmly received on Capitol Hill, but the president imposed two conditions for his support. First, any catastrophic health insurance bill had to be budget neutral, meaning the program could not add to the deficit.[91] Second, the costs of the program had to be covered by seniors themselves. Democrats reluctantly accepted these conditions because they were unwilling to raise general taxes heading into the 1988 presidential election. Many Democrats felt that the benefits offered under the Bowen plan were too meager to justify the shift away from Medicare's traditional reliance on payroll taxes and general fund subsidies. If seniors were going to be asked to pay for their own benefits, the benefits had to be worth it. Congress liberally added sweeteners to the Bowen package, including new or expanded coverage for respite care, protection against spousal impoverishment caused by the medical bills of one partner, and, most importantly, a prescription drug benefit.

The final bill imposed a flat $4 increase in premiums of the optional Part B program. This charge was estimated to cover about one-third of the program's costs. To cover the remaining two-thirds, higher-income Medicare recipients were also required to pay a supplemental premium (which critics labeled a "surtax") that climbed with the individual federal income tax liabilities. While the supplemental premium was technically a user fee, not a tax, it was to be administered through the Internal Revenue Service using the 1040 form. The AARP preferred a broader financing mechanism, but realized it "just wasn't in the cards."[92]

Proponents of the MCAA recognized that the "elderly only" financing mechanism was a controversial departure from past methods of funding Medicare benefit expansions, made necessary by budget constraints, but argued that the seniors would ultimately appreciate the new law.[93] "As the [catastrophic health] benefits become clear to people over time, the program will become widely accepted," predicted Sen. George Mitchell (D-ME), chairman of the Finance Subcommittee on Health.[94] There was good reason to think Mitchell would be proved right. About 60 percent of seniors stood to receive net benefits under the program. Proponents like Congressman Fortney H. "Pete" Stark (D-CA) pointed out that savings on Medigap policies would more than offset the costs of higher Medicare premiums. "The idea that it's going to be expensive is correct, but what most seniors are carrying now is even more expensive," observed Stark. An AARP poll taken two months before the bill's passage found that 91 percent of seniors (age sixty-five and older) supported the bill. Just 6 percent were opposed, and 4 percent had no opinion.[95]

The MCAA passed overwhelmingly in both chambers despite strong opposition from the pharmaceutical lobby.[96] The final Senate vote on the conference report was 86-11 and the final House vote was 328-72.[97] President Reagan signed the bill in a Rose Garden ceremony on July 1, 1988. Supporters of the new law basked in their accomplishment. Senator David F. Durenberger (R-MN) called the MCCA "the most far-reaching, sensible, and compassion extension to Medicare in the twenty-three years" since the program's enactment.[98]

Backlash

It did not take long for this legislative achievement to become a political debacle. As political scientist Richard Himelfarb points out in his excellent book *Catastrophic Politics*, "By November 1988, a mere five months after passage of the MCAA, seniors were in open revolt against the program, particularly its supplemental premium . . . The virulence of the reaction surprised even congressional veterans who had supported the legislation."[99] How did a bill with overwhelming support collapse?

Several factors played a role. While redistribution in social insurance programs was hardly unknown in the American welfare state—low-income workers receive a higher return than upper-income recipients on the taxes they pay into Social Security, for instance—the redistributive mechanisms of the MCCA were unusually transparent. The wealthiest seniors could not miss that they were bearing the bulk of the program's costs (even though they continued to receive a subsidy of $400 from general tax revenues for their Medicare benefit package as a whole). While "only" 40 percent of the elderly may have been scheduled to pay the supplemental premiums, "for those paying the premium at higher rates, the costs were considerable."[100]

Yet public opposition to the MCCA was not confined to the affluent elderly. After enactment, support plummeted even among low income seniors who stood to gain the most from the program (Table 5-2).

Public confusion and doubt was actively fomented by interest groups that

TABLE 5-2
Support and Opposition to MCAA Among Seniors over Age 65, by Income

	December 1988	February–March 1989	August 1989
High Income			
Support	70%	52%	47%
Oppose	13	23	27
Difference	+57	+29	+20
Moderate Income			
Support	62	49	38
Oppose	23	33	45
Difference	29	16	−7
Low Income			
Support	67	43	38
Oppose	31	43	57
Difference	+32	+5	−19

Source: Richard Himelfarb, *Catastrophic Politics: The Rise and Fall of the Medicare Catastrophic Coverage Act of 1988* (University Park: Pennsylvania State University Press), 63, using AARP survey data.

had tried to block the reform's passage. The most visible opposition group was the National Committee to Preserve Social Security and Medicare, a direct mail and advocacy group. In January 1989, the National Committee announced that it was sending three million letters to its members to encourage them to complain to elected officials about the law's financing. The National Committee was joined in opposition by forty other organizations, including unions and groups representing retired federal workers. The political campaign against the MCCA evidently confused many seniors into believing that they would pay the full $800 surtax, despite the fact that only a tiny fraction of seniors would face the maximum charge and even those that did would have faced charges less than the insurance value of the new benefits. A number of firms that sold Medigap policies ran ads that attacked the surtax as an unfair tax on seniors who saved for their own retirements. Attacks by the bill's opponents might have been less effective if seniors understood what was in the law, but the government failed to launch a major information campaign or run media ads to explain it.[101] Seniors were inclined to think the worst about the law, especially because it failed to address the problem they feared the most: the high cost of nursing home stays. The most prevalent misconception about the MCCA was that all seniors were subject to the maximum $800 surtax. "I can't tell you how many calls I've gotten from people who said, 'I live on my Social Security and a small pension and I can't afford $800,'" the AARP's John

Rother later reflected.[102] While conservative Republicans were the first to abandon the program, liberals soon joined them. A critical threshold was crossed in the spring of 1989 when a number of labor unions abandoned their support of the law.[103] Members of Congress who went back to their districts over the 1989 summer recess were hounded by constituents upset about the program.[104] A crowd of senior citizens furious about the new premiums blocked the car of Ways and Means Chairman Dan Rostenkowski (D-IL), hitting it with picket signs.[105]

Important decisions made in conference committee to promote the general-interest purposes of the bill helped bring about the reform's demise. For example, conferees agreed to phase-in the new benefits slowly but collect the premiums up-front in order to create a trust fund in case the program's costs exceed initial estimates. This front-loaded design was fiscally responsible, but it meant that only a tiny fraction of Medicare beneficiaries would see an immediate benefit from the program.[106] Another decision that made technical but not political sense was making the surtax mandatory for upper income seniors even though the flat premium could be avoided (because enrollment in Part B was voluntary). This fed into the impression among wealthy seniors that they were being coerced into supporting others who had not had the foresight to save for their retirements.[107]

Congress Says "Never Mind!"

Sixteen months after the reform's enactment, Congress voted overwhelmingly to repeal virtually all of the MCAA. President George H. W. Bush signed the repeal measure on December 13, 1989. The House voted 360-66 on October 4 to scrap the measure and waive the 1990 budget enforcement rules that would otherwise have made it impossible to eliminate taxes without offsetting the lost revenues. Two days later, the Senate voted 99-0 for a plan offered by Republican John McCain of Arizona to repeal the surtax but to keep the flat premium and several of the new Medicare benefits, including unlimited hospital coverage.[108] But the House position prevailed after even ardent supporters such as Henry Waxman conceded the program was unsustainable.[109] On November 21, the House voted again for repeal, 352-63. The Senate voted for repeal by unanimous consensus. The final repeal measure eliminated the premiums and scrapped all the new Medicare benefits, including the prescription drug benefit.[110] "There's no public support for this program," conceded one House Democrat.[111]

Negative Policy Feedback

Although it is not uncommon for policy reform achievements in the United States to be eroded, politicians usually do not terminate the underlying reform statue itself. The MCCA is the exception to the rule. Given its tax structure, sustaining the measure was so politically risky for Congress that the only thing worse than the embarrassment of voting for repeal was voting against it.

Yet the striking thing about the MCCA's collapse is how large its impact has been on subsequent health policy dynamics. Even as the MCCA was being repealed, supporters continued to assert that significant gaps in Medicare's benefit package remained, particularly the lack of a prescription drug benefit. Negative cognitive and interest-group feedback from the repeal of the MCCA, however, ensured that any future prescription drug bill would reflect the insights gleaned in this searing experience.[112]

These insights can be detected in the design of the Medicare Prescription Drug Improvement and Modernization Act (MMA) of 2003. One of the messages politicians took from the MCCA experience is that seniors resent being forced to pay for coverage they believe they do not need. Hence, participation in the new prescription drug program is voluntary.[113] Strong incentives exist to enroll, but Medicare beneficiaries who are happy with their existing private supplemental insurance plans may stay in them. Politicians also concluded from the MCCA repeal that seniors will balk at paying the costs of their prescription drug benefits themselves. The new prescription drug plan is thus financed largely through general revenues at a cost of around $400 billion dollars to taxpayers.[114] Finally, the MCAA experience convinced politicians that they must phase-in some social benefits quickly in order to cultivate a constituency. The MMA almost immediately gave beneficiaries a discount card for prescription drugs and a lower deductible.[115] These differences—along with greater support from pharmaceutical companies eager to receive the highly generous subsidies—help explain the sustainability of the MMA, despite some major political vulnerabilities, including the bizarre gap in coverage known as the "donut hole."[116]

Interestingly, the MMA revived the most detested aspect of the MCCA—income-related premiums. Individuals with incomes over $80,000 and couples with incomes over $160,000 must now pay a higher Part B premium than individuals with lesser incomes. Estimates are that the supplemental premium will initially affect about 3 percent of beneficiaries.[117] One reason why the supplemental premiums in the MMA did not spark a backlash is because they did not go into effect immediately. While the MCAA premiums were frontloaded to safeguard the budget, the MMA's income-related premiums did not take effect until 2007—more than three years after the Act's passage. By then, millions of Americans were receiving tangible benefits from the program. Early on, some predicted that the MMA might suffer the same fate as the MCCA.[118] But it appears the new program will endure, albeit at a substantial cost to the American taxpayer.[119]

CHAPTER 6

Uncle Sam Goes Shopping: Reinventing Government Procurement

A CORE TASK OF AMERICAN national government is to purchase goods and services from the private sector for government use. This sounds like a trivial activity. It is not. The federal government today spends more than $375 billion a year, almost 40 percent of its discretionary budget, on purchases of goods and services.[1] Only sixteen countries in the world have economies as big as the federal procurement budget.[2] The government buys military equipment for combat operations, computers to run the Social Security and tax collection systems, and office supplies for virtually every federal agency. The government "contracts out" extensively in part because politicians like to keep the federal bureaucracy relatively lean, but mostly to economize on transaction costs. Just as automobile manufacturers typically do not produce their own tires or car stereo systems and universities do not make the light fixtures that illuminate their libraries, it is efficient for the federal government to buy many of the items it needs from private suppliers.

For many years, outside experts and government officials agreed that the federal procurement system was an irrational mess. Excessive red tape prevented agencies from delivering the best value to taxpayers. The General Services Administration, for example, could not purchase an ashtray unless it first issued a nine-page document that described what an ashtray is and specified the number of pieces it may break into should it be hit with a hammer.[3] When government workers needed pens or manila folders, they couldn't go to the nearest supply outlet to pick up more.[4] More importantly, the government was prohibited from punishing a contractor for poor performance. When bids were weighed, all contractors had to be treated equally, even if they were known to provide horrendous service. The government often got stuck buying defective goods from unreliable suppliers. Many of the inefficiencies in the traditional procurement system were not accidental. They had been deliberately created to avoid fraud and abuse, and to promote social goals, such as assisting small business. While some of these rules may have made perfect sense on their own terms, the collective result was a cumbersome, overregulated system with excessive costs. In the early 1990s, a major effort was made to reform and improve the federal procurement system as part of the larger "Reinventing Government" initiative led by Vice President Al Gore. The thrust of the changes was to curb red tape to allow procurement officers to use common sense and good judgment when making purchasing decisions. Despite the myriad obstacles to organizational transformation in the bureaucracy, procurement reform has improved government performance along many dimensions. While important problems remain, the federal acquisition system is far more efficient than it was.[5] Many federal employees felt trapped by the traditional procurement system and have embraced their new flexibility.[6]

The question is whether the reforms will be sustainable. A mixed forecast seems appropriate. On the one hand, the government is not going to stop contracting out. Washington today relies so heavily on the private sector that it would be impossible for it to do everything "in house" even if it wished to do so. It also seems unlikely that the federal procurement system will again be as grossly inefficient as it was in the 1980s. The procurement reforms of the 1990s have strong defenders, not the least of which is the politically well-connected government contractor community. Meanwhile, the perceived losers from reform, such as public sector unions and procurement attorneys who might prefer a more litigious process, currently lack the strength to force a "counter reformation." Organizational inertia also helps protect the new system.

On the other hand, a result-oriented procurement system for the 21st century—which must increasingly manage the nonroutine purchase of government-specific goods and services—requires a large and well-trained set of contracting officers. Yet the federal acquisition work force has atrophied significantly since the 1990s due to retirements and deliberate personnel reductions. The contracting system has been under tremendous stress since the Katrina hurricane recovery effort and the Iraq War. At some point, the federal procurement workforce could collapse under the sheer weight of its administrative burden.

The most direct threat to the sustainability of a high-flexibility acquisition system is a hostile political environment in which the incentives for Congress and Inspectors General to cast blame are often far stronger than they are to offer neutral assistance to public managers who have to deal with tenacious administrative problems.[7] The risk is that future contracting abuses, real or perceived, will be attributed to the reforms of the 1990s, prompting a return to heavy-handed legislative attempts to dictate front-line purchasing decisions. The kinds of institutional shifts and positive policy feedback effects needed to foreclose this scenario have to some degree occurred inside the executive bureaucracy, but they have not occurred on Capitol Hill. The broader "reinventing government" spirit of the procurement reform project therefore remains vulnerable to downstream erosion, if not reversal.

THE PRE-REFORM SITUATION

This is not the place for a comprehensive history of the federal purchasing system. Suffice it to say that the federal government has purchased goods and services for its operations from private vendors ever since General Washington struggled to supply the Continental Army.[8] The use of contracting has expanded with the scope of the American state and has especially grown in times of war. Over time, the range of goods and services purchased by the government has grown more and more complex, taxing the ability of managers to obtain the best value for the federal taxpayer.

In theory, the traditional federal procurement regulatory system was simple, logical, and economical. Government agencies were usually required (or strongly encouraged) to award contracts to the lowest qualified bidder who met elaborate government specifications. Procurements were to be widely advertised, and the winning bid would be selected only after "full and open" competition. The stated goals were to keep costs low and to prevent favoritism and corruption. Since procurement officers possessed little discretion, bribery was discouraged.

In practice, the procurement system was rigid, slow, and often expensive. One cause of the problem was structural. As Donald F. Kettl has shown, government often has specialized purchasing needs, and many of the markets it operates in are less than perfectly competitive.[9] Legislative politics, however, also contributed to the problem. Congress has a "fondness for procedural safeguards against fraud, waste, and abuse. Congress may want simpler and more economic purchasing, but it also cherishes using the procurement process to serve nonprocurement goals," including helping small business, American manufacturers, and organized labor.[10]

Procurement officers had to comply with thousands of pages of regulations contained in the Federal Acquisition Regulation (FAR), statutes, and countless agency-specific mandates. These rules sometimes required the government to specify what it wanted to an absurd extent. For example, the Department of Defense's procurement rules ("MIL-SPECs") just for purchasing chocolate chip cookie mix were twenty pages long.[11] Because the rules were so detailed, it frequently took months or even years to award contracts. Many commercial suppliers refused to do business with the federal government rather than upset their normal operations. As a result, agencies often had to buy from government-only suppliers, even when their products were more expensive than those widely available from commercial vendors. The federal procurement system was thus not merely cumbersome, slow, and expensive, it was also *ineffective*. The emphasis on avoiding the appearance of corruption caused many procurement professionals to become hidebound and skittish. They were so intent on avoiding risk, they frequently lost sight of their responsibility to obtain the best value for the citizenry.

A core problem is that contract officers were generally prohibited from using information about a contractor's performance on previous contracts when deciding whom to buy from. The ostensible purpose of the prohibition against backward evaluations was to limit favoritism. Just because a vendor had received a contract in the past should not mean she receives one in the future. The practical result, however, was that bidders often promised too much and delivered too little, knowing that their underperformance would not be penalized. Unsurprisingly, this is not how contracting works in the private sector. When private firms purchase goods, they do not write up detailed specifications and then award the contract to the lowest bidder who meets the specifications. Rather, they develop long-term, often asset-specific relationships with reliable suppliers, who know their performance will determine whether they get more contracts in the future.[12] Government, by contrast, had to treat all companies alike, even though some were notoriously poor performers.

During the 1980s, Congress further tightened controls over the federal procurement system in response to perceived contracting abuses.[13] The most notorious scandal involved the alleged purchase of a $435 hammer by the navy. In fact, the $435 hammer was a myth. Under the government's accounting rules then in effect, suppliers were required to distribute overhead costs in equal percentages to each item. The idea was to simplify matters on the theory that it all evened out in the end. But this accounting method made it appear that the government got a very bad deal on cheap items, which suggested that taxpayers were getting fleeced. As James Q. Wilson notes, "A member of Congress who did not understand (or not want to understand) government accounting rules created a public stir."[14] In response to the scandal, Congress passed intrusive procurement regulations, including the Competition in Contracting Act of 1984 and the Procurement Integrity Act of 1989. While the purpose of the new rules was to protect the taxpayer, they made it even harder for federal procurement officers to do a good job.

By the late 1980s, government procurement officials and industry contractors alike were increasingly complaining that the new procurement rules were hampering performance in mission-critical areas. An adversarial relationship had emerged in which contractors were fearful of making mistakes or even communicating with government, lest they face the risk of criminal prosecution. One industry trade journal in 1988 pessimistically concluded that progress was unlikely in part because of the public image of all government contractors as "cheats."[15]

Yet pressure for reform was slowly building. In 1990, Congress set up a blue-ribbon panel to recommend options for streamlining defense acquisition. The so-called Section 800 panel (named for the section of the legislation that established it) issued an 1800-page final report in January 1993.[16] The study called for massive simplification and commercialization of the federal acquisition system.[17] While key members of Congress praised the commission's work, the report came too late to influence the staff of outgoing president George H. W. Bush.[18]

REINVENTING PROCUREMENT

For the Administration of "New Democrat" Bill Clinton, however, improving bureaucratic performance was a top priority. Clinton believed in activist government, but he recognized that public confidence and trust in the federal government had eroded. Clinton evidently felt that if he was to win public support for his activist policy agenda—which included the creation of new "health purchasing alliances" as part of his major health reform initiative— confidence in government's ability to manage complex operations would first have to be rebuilt. The bureaucracy would have to work better and cost less. In short, the relationship between citizens and their government would need to be "reinvented."[19]

Thus was born the Administration's National Performance Review (NPR or "reinventing government") initiative.[20] The core assumption of reinventing government was that good people were trapped in bad administrative systems—the procurement system chief among them.[21] In 1993, the Clinton Administration released a report ("From Red Tape to Results") that presented recommendations for procurement reform, including steps to make it easier for government agencies to buy off-the-shelf items.[22] Unlike most bureaucratic reform initiatives, the reinventing government effort could count on the personal support of a top Administration official—Al Gore.[23] The Vice President was eager to make the issue his own. When the initial NPR report was published, Gore went on the David Letterman late-night television show to poke fun at government procurement regulations. Gore put on safety glasses and aggressively smashed a government-issue ashtray with a hammer. This was a publicity stunt, of course, but a stunt with a message. Gore wanted to demonstrate to Americans that the contracting system was rigid and inflexible yet would crumble under force—like an overpriced, poorly made ashtray.[24]

Gore was the head cheerleader for procurement reform, but someone was needed to lead the initiative within the bureaucracy. The Administration turned to Steven Kelman, a Harvard public management professor who had written a book that argued for debureaucratization of the procurement system.[25] Clinton appointed Kelman administrator of the Office of Federal Procurement Policy at the Office and Management and Budget Administration— the government's top procurement position. Like Alfred Kahn before him, Kelman moved from being an Ivy League critic of an area of public policy to being a government executive cum entrepreneurial reformer responsible for fixing it.[26]

Kelman claimed that federal agencies were more focused on avoiding blame for procedural mistakes than on making good decisions. The procurement system was "like a police department that never mistreated suspects but also never solved crimes," he wrote.[27] Kelman acknowledged the need for anti-corruption measures but insisted that any set of buying rules primarily designed to make it impossible for actors to do something wrong could have the perverse consequence of making it impossible for them to do something *right*.[28] Kelman thus departed from the conventional view of law professors and public administration theorists that bureaucratic discretion constitutes a fundamental threat to democratic accountability and good government.[29] In Kelman's view, the government could not effectively serve the citizenry, its constituency, unless front-line contract officers were encouraged to use their good judgment to deliver public value.[30] Private sector firms develop informal performance-oriented relationships with long-term suppliers, Kelman pointed out, and public agencies should do the same.[31]

Kelman's appointment, together with Gore's enthusiastic support, the positive reaction to the Section 800 commission study, and growing frustration with the traditional purchasing system among contractors, bureaucrats, and some members of Congress, prepared the ground for the passage of three major procurement reform laws: the Federal Acquisition Streamlining Act of 1994 (P.L 103-355), the Federal Acquisition Reform Act of 1996, and the Information Technology Reform Act of 1996 (the "Clinger-Cohen" Act). The latter two laws were passed as part of the fiscal 1996 defense authorization act (P.L. 104-106). In addition, many important reforms were implemented through executive orders.

Key Changes in the Procurement System

Taken together, the 1990s reforms significantly deregulated the federal purchasing system. The 1994 Act waved paperwork and record keeping requirements for "small" purchases (less than $100,000) and authorized agencies to use purchase cards for "micro" transactions (less than $2,500). When offices ran out of supplies, agency managers would be allowed to send someone to a commercial store like Staples. Agencies were freed to let contracts to the best (not just the lowest) bidder, to take into account vendors' past performance, and the use of fixed-price performance-based contracts was encouraged to reduce the audit burden and cost overruns often experienced with cost-reimbursement contracts.[32]

The reforms included in the 1996 defense authorization changed the procurement process in four major ways. First, they made it even easier for agencies to purchase commercial items. Second, agencies were given more leeway to remove bidders who did not have a realistic chance of winning contracts at an earlier stage in the process. As noted later in this chapter, this change was a matter of some controversy. Third, agencies were given far more discretion to make information technology (IT) procurements. Under an existing 1965 law (the Brooks Act), the General Services Administration (GSA) managed

IT purchases for the entire federal government. As government agencies became increasingly dependent upon computers and rapidly evolving information systems in the 1970s and 1980s, the centralized IT acquisition process bogged down. When government tried to tackle IT problems, it was "like getting stuck in a swamp sometimes," said one government consultant in 1994.[33] To streamline the process, the 1996 reform revoked the Brooks Act. Under a new blanket purchase agreement, individual agencies were given the freedom to negotiate their own IT contracts.[34]

Finally, the 1996 law recalibrated the balance in the bid protest process between a contractor's right to fair treatment and the government's need to keep the costs of oversight within reason. While some argued that the ability of losing bidders to challenge contract award decisions kept the procurement system honest, many believed that the existing appeals process was expensive, inefficient, and vulnerable to contractor exploitation. The bid process for IT procurements was especially contentious. The 1984 Competition in Contracting Act made the GSA's Board of Contract Appeals the main forum for IT contract protests. The Board's formal litigation-intensive method for resolving contract award disputes illustrated the pathologies that Berkeley political scientist Robert Kagan calls "adversarial legalism."[35] During the months and even years it took to resolve disputes, agencies had to deal without needed products. Like doctors who order unnecessary tests to avoid malpractice suits, procurement officers spent time and energy on defense preparation.[36] Some vendors were believed to file bid protests not because they had been treated unfairly in the award process, but simply as a way to learn more about what procurement officers were looking for. While the Washington attorneys who handled these cases made out well, this was a socially inefficient way to encourage better communication between contractors and the government. The 1996 Act therefore stripped the Board's authority over IT bid protests. Losing vendors were required to lodge their protests with the General Accounting Office, which had a more streamlined appeals procedure. To reduce the use of appeals as an expensive information-gathering tool, agencies were required to notify unsuccessful firms within three days of awarding contracts. Losing bidders had a right to receive a prompt debriefing. Agencies were required to communicate the overall rankings of all submissions, as well as the technical ratings procurement officers had given them. Unlike most of the other cases discussed in this book, procurement reform sought not so much to scale back government as to expand governmental capacity.

The Politics of Reform Adoption

The passage of procurement reform was eased through use of multiple coalition-building strategies: skillful framing of the debate, creative use of symbols, manipulation of the procedural context in which decisions are made, and the use of tactical concessions and side payments.[37] Procurement reform advocates like Kelman emphasized that the changes would cut bureaucracy and make the government more business-like. Defense Secretary William J. Perry framed the debate in national security terms, arguing that without a more efficient procurement system the Pentagon would not be able to acquire cutting-edge technologies.[38]

While these frames resonated with many lawmakers, support for special-interest purchasing rules had not evaporated. Reformers were therefore forced to make several tactical concessions to build a winning coalition.[39] One involved protections for organized labor. Gore's reinventing government commission and the blue-ribbon panel set up by Congress in 1990 both called for contracts worth less than $100,000 to be exempted from the Davis-Bacon Act of 1931, which required the government to pay contactors no less than locally prevailing wages. Republicans and some economists argued that Davis-Bacon drove up the costs of federal contracts and inflated wages, but labor unions considered it sacrosanct. The provision was retained. Similarly, a modified preference was kept for small business.[40] The bill also established nonbinding goals for all agencies of awarding at least 5 percent of the total value of all contracts and subcontracts to firms owned by women, and made no change in the existing requirement that most companies receiving large contracts prepare subcontracting plans stating what percentage of work would be done by small and minority-owned businesses. The reform also left untouched "buy America" provisions designed to give domestic firms a business advantage over foreign competitors.[41] With these changes, the Senate approved the reform by voice vote in June 1994.[42] The House adopted the measure by a vote of 425-0.

The Clinton Administration was the prime mover behind the 1994 reforms, but Congress drove the 1996 changes. Bob Murphy, the head procurement officer at the General Accounting Office—which reports directly to Congress—argued that red tape continued to make it hard for the government to obtain maximum value for taxpayers. Murphy recommended a second round of legislation to further reduce transaction costs and create a more efficient process for resolving disputes over bid selections.[43] William F. Clinger, Jr. (R-PA), who became chairman of the House Committee on Government Reform and Oversight when the Republicans took control of Congress in 1994, had a similar view. "Some may say we should rest on our laurels. . . but clearly the system still cries out for fundamental change," he said.[44]

Clinger introduced a far-reaching reform bill (H.R. 1670), most of whose provisions ultimately found their way into law. One proposal that had to be modified before passage was a change in the statutory requirement that most federal contracts be awarded on the basis of "full and open competition." While competition can lower prices, Clinger and other reform advocates argued that administration of the "full and open" standard failed to deliver net benefits. The government was often forced to spend scarce time and resources evaluating bids from firms that were not truly competitive and therefore had no realistic chance of winning, causing long delays in the contract award process. Clinger believed that government should operate more like private firms and called for a new standard based upon "maximum practical competition." This proposal generated opposition from small business groups, which feared that the government would use its discretion to favor large firms with political connections.[45] In a key test vote in June 1995, the House rejected an amendment, 213-217, to strike the language proposing the new bidding standard. Ultimately, the requirement of full and open competition was retained to guarantee any firm the right to bid. But the government was allowed to limit the number of bidders at later stages of review to three when it would promote efficiency. The National Taxpayers Union and Speaker Newt Gingrich endorsed the compromise, and the political opposition weakened. An amendment to strip this section from the bill failed on the House floor 182-239.[46]

The House subsequently passed the revised bill 423-0 on September 14, 1995.[47] Clinger's entrepreneurial staff then pushed for the Act's inclusion in the fiscal 1996 defense authorization bill, which was already in conference committee.[48] Congress quickly passed the measure, but President Clinton vetoed it in December 1995 because of his opposition to a proposed antimissile program.[49] Republicans dropped the controversial missile program, and Clinton signed the defense bill in January 1996 with the procurement reforms folded in.[50] Some critics argued that the 1996 procurement overhaul received insufficient scrutiny from Congress—the Senate held no hearings on the topic—and that the reform would not have passed as a stand-alone measure.[51] But the procurement reforms had the strong support of both the Administration and lawmakers like Clinger and Senator William Cohen (R-ME), who were well positioned to get the reform on a moving legislative vehicle.

The regulatory reforms needed to streamline the procurement system generated even more conflict than the formal legislative changes. A key battle involved changes to part 15 of the Federal Acquisition Regulations (FAR), which govern all negotiated contracts. The modifications specified the way a contractor's past performance could be evaluated, the conditions under which government and procurement officers could communicate, when procurement officers could drop proposals based on an initial evaluation, and other acquisition terms.[52] When the new rules were unveiled in September 1996, they generated strong opposition from some industry trade associations which expressed concern about the harm to small businesses.[53] Law firms and bid preparation companies were also unhappy with the proposed changes, fearing they would "eat into the business by reducing the complexity of bid preparation and submissions . . . "[54] But political support for the changes increased as private sector vendors, especially those in the IT industry, got more involved in the process.[55]

The Effects of Reform

By nearly all accounts, the procurement flexibilities introduced in the 1990s improved the acquisition process. Surveys of procurement trends highlight five major changes in federal contracting behavior.[56] First, agencies increased their reliance on blanket purchase agreements to quickly acquire goods and services, reduce lead times, and lower administrative costs. The use of the General Service Administration's federal supply schedule, for example, more than tripled from 1997 and 2001.[57] Second, the government increased its purchases of commercial items, reducing the need for agencies to pay companies to develop unique items for their use. Several agencies increased their purchases of commercial items by more than 400 percent between fiscal years 1997 and 2001.[58] Third, agencies increased their use of government credit cards for many low dollar procurements. Credit card use increased by 160 percent between fiscal 1997 and fiscal 2001.

A fourth key change was that the acquisition process became less contentious and adversarial. The number of bid protests fell steadily during the 1990s. GAO protests, for example, declined from 3,377 in fiscal 1993 to 1,485 in fiscal 2005.[59] This decline is all the more striking because the GSA's authority to hear procurement protests was eliminated in 1996. If the level of procurement litigation activity remained constant, the number of protests heard by the GAO would have been predicted to rise. Instead, it appears that "any forum substitution was swamped by the decline in other protests."[60] Finally, some agencies began looking at contractors' track records when reviewing bid applications.[61] Implementation of other performance-based contracting methods, however, has been spotty.[62]

The performance of vendors also seems to have improved following the reforms. Contract officers reported that vendors were doing a much better job meeting commitments and sticking with contract delivery schedules. A 2004 Harvard University survey of 100 IT services projects found that average customer satisfaction with the vendors' performances was 9.3 on a 10-point scale. This was a significant increase from the average satisfaction of 6.9 that Kelman found when he asked the same question in 1990.[63] It is of course difficult to know how government performance would have changed in a world in which procurement reform did not occur in the mid-1990s. Yet consider the government's ability to rebuild the Pentagon a little more than twelve months after the 9/11 attacks.[64] It seems very likely that this massive construction project would have taken much longer if the government did not have access to new, more streamlined acquisition vehicles.[65]

THE PENDULUM SWINGS

The administrative efficiencies from reform generated support among key constituencies, including federal procurement officers, program customers, and "many in the information-technology industry and other nontraditional vendors whose relationship with government has been improved."[66] Nonetheless, the future of a high-flexibility, results-oriented procurement system is not entirely clear. Two main threats endanger the reforms' sustainability. The first is that the federal acquisition workforce is overstretched. Not enough well-trained contract officers are available to handle the growing burden of the procurement system.[67] The government employed 27,294 contracting officers in fiscal 2002, a decline of 4,500 from a decade earlier, even though the government's contracting work increased in both scope and complexity over this period.[68] A 2003 GAO study of the Department of Defense estimated that the defense contracting workload, for example, had increased by about 12 percent in recent years, but that the staff available to perform that workload had declined by about 50 percent over this time.[69] Ironically, some of the post–Cold War downsizing occurred during the same period the Clinton Administration was trying to boost government's administrative capacity. Surveys of procurement executives further suggest that resources for professional training are "woefully lacking," particularly within the civilian agencies, and that training has not kept pace with the growing complexity of the contracting system.[70] The government has a hard time retaining contract experts, and new employees often lack institutional knowledge and experience. If the human capital to run a high-discretion procurement system is not in place, support for the reforms may eventually decline. "We trusted individual contract managers to do the right thing. But we didn't give them resources or guidance on how to use their flexibility. People without expertise have been left to founder," said one Democratic legislative staffer who has become skeptical of the 1990s reforms.[71]

This raises the second reform sustainability issue—whether contract officers can preserve their autonomy. As Daniel P. Carpenter persuasively argues, bureaucratic autonomy, or the ability to create or implement policies free from the constraints of overseers, does not flow automatically from administrative expertise; it must be "forged" politically.[72] While a number of Progressive era agencies were able to use their reputations among diverse coalitions to gain a measure of autonomy from top officials, key elements of contemporary American politics frustrate agencies' efforts to resist intrusive political control. The risk with respect to procurement reform is not only that bureaucratic autonomy will be challenged following a change in governing coalitions. It is also that policymakers, regardless of their original support for reform, may be unable to commit to a high-discretion acquisition regime, even if they recognize the costs of overregulation. The short-run payoff from decrying "waste, fraud, and abuse" and enacting new procedural constraints may be very high.[73]

This eventuality is considered so predictable that both the scholarly literature and trade press on contracting regularly invoke the image of a "swinging pendulum." First, rigid rules give rise to administrative inefficiencies and pathologies, then the government enacts reforms to make the system more results-oriented, then "scandals" inevitably occur, and finally government adopts new rules and sends negative oversight signals to discourage innovation and crack down on abuses.[74] In sum, reformers and reforms may come and go, but the procurement system never changes.[75]

By late 2004, the political winds had decisively shifted toward increased oversight and more intrusive regulations of the procurement system. "The pendulum has clearly swung back in a hard way," said one attorney for government contractors. "Everything contractors do is going to be subject to scrutiny. They need to understand that they're in a different environment."[76]

The political climate changed for three interrelated reasons. First, the Bush Administration had a procurement reform agenda very much at odds with the spirit of reinventing government. Its goal was not to make government contracting more "business-like," but rather to give more federal jobs to private firms. Second, a series of contracting abuses, real or perceived, occurred on the Bush's Administration watch. These included allegations of overcharging and favoritism (especially by the mega-contractor Halliburton); the infamous Abu Ghraib incident (in which private employees working on a government IT contract were among those accused of torturing Iraqi prisoners), and charges of waste, fraud, and abuse during the painful-to-watch Hurricane Katrina recovery effort. Finally, the Democrats regained control of Congress in the 2006 elections and key committee chairs were eager to put contract officers back on a short leash. While the procurement reforms of the 1990s did not collapse, those who wanted to see the practice of results-oriented contracting consolidated and deepened were forced to retreat a bit and "play defense."[77]

The Bush Administration's Procurement Agenda

George W. Bush came to office with very different ideas about how to manage the executive branch than his predecessor. While Bill Clinton and Al Gore had campaigned on the need to deregulate the bureaucracy, Bush had pledged to open up more federal work to private sector competition. The Administration announced a "competitive sourcing" initiative to make it easier for agencies to privatize tasks that were commercial in nature and that could be performed by nongovernmental workers.[78] This initiative predictably sparked the ire of government employee labor unions, which formerly had been largely unconcerned with procurement reform issues.[79] It also gave procurement reform a partisan tinge.

Bush selected a former contract litigation attorney, Angela Styles, to serve as first chief procurement officer at OMB. Styles was fairly hostile to the 1990s procurement reforms agenda. During her Senate confirmation hearings, Styles stated that she was concerned that the "efficient procurement model" may have compromised important goals such as equity, integrity, and competition.[80] Styles sent an even stronger signal of her ambivalence about the 1990s reforms when she arranged a speech by Stephen Daniels, the chairman of the General Services Board of Contract Appeals, the litigation-prone body which had been stripped of its jurisdiction to rule on bid protest cases.[81] Daniels's speech ridiculed the reinventing government changes, arguing that they had weakened competitive requirements, inflated costs to taxpayers, and made it easier for unethical actors to influence the process. "Openness, fairness, economy, and accountability have been replaced as guiding principles by speed and ease of contracting," he complained.[82] The speech generated strong protests from much of the government contractor community. The Bush Administration did sign a modified version of the Services Acquisition Reform Act as part of the 2003 defense authorization bill. Introduced by Rep. Davis, SARA expanded the procurement reform framework to include a broader array of services that could be purchased under expedited procedures.[83] By all accounts, however, Administrator Styles devoted the bulk of her time to competitive sourcing and was less focused on broader procurement issues.

Her successor, David Safavian, who was appointed in November 2004, pledged support for the 1990s procurement reform framework. "I believe solutions can be achieved for most problems that do not erode the efficiencies Congress authorized over the past decade," he stated in response to questions from the Governmental Affairs Committee.[84] But Safavian, the former chief of staff of the General Services Administration, did not have much of an opportunity to lead. In September 2005, Safavian resigned shortly after being arrested in a corruption probe. While his arrest did not stem from his official duties as chief procurement officer, it cast a terrible light on the procurement community.[85] "The arrest of Safavian is going to put us in the freezer," said one industry expert. "The trend that we have seen over the last year or so of the pendulum swinging back toward an era of greater oversight is only going to get worse. The cumulative effect of all of these events will have an unfair but clear impact on the credibility of the procurement workforce."[86]

Perceived Contracting Abuses: Iraq and Hurricane Katrina

Safavian's resignation under pressure came at a time when the federal procurement system was already receiving intense scrutiny because of controversy about the role of government contractors in both the Iraq war and the Hurricane Katrina cleanup effort. Much of the controversy, to be sure, did not pertain to the routine purchase of commercially available goods and services (staplers, pens, pencils, cars, cafeteria service, etc.) but rather to the *nonroutine* purchase of government-specific items, where the problems of an inadequate contract management workforce really begin to emerge.[87] The controversy also pertained to the growing reliance on *mega-contactors* as service integrators / general contractors (a la Halliburton in Iraq).[88] While these emerging practices were not the main targets of reform in the 1990s, they fed into the general perception that "things had gotten too loose."

Many accusations of wrongdoing and abuse swirled around the Halliburton Company, a major construction and oil services firm that won large federal contracts to provide logistical support and repair the Iraq oil industry.[89] Vice President Dick Cheney had served as chief executive of Halliburton from 1995 to 2000. The main allegations, pushed by Congressman Henry Waxman (D-CA), were that Halliburton and its subsidiary Kellogg, Brown & Root (KBR) had been awarded the contracts outside a competitive bidding process and had used their privileged position to illegally and grossly overcharge the government for the services they performed. Intensifying the controversy was the demotion of a senior army contract officer who had questioned KBR's contract before a congressional panel, calling it the "most blatant and improper contract abuse" she had witnessed in her career.[90]

In 2005, federal auditors were conducting more than two dozen investigations into apparent bribery and kickbacks or false expense reports in the Iraq reconstruction. Critics argued that the lack of competition faced by KBR implied special treatment, but the Pentagon asserted that the firm had been selected because it possessed unique capabilities. KBR had a longstanding contract with the Pentagon dating back to 2001. In the months leading up to the war, the Pentagon hired KBR to draw up a classified contingency plan for dealing with any oil well fires in Iraq. With the war looming, the Pentagon gave the firm a temporary bridge contract to implement the plan. KBR had the personnel and the experience, and the Pentagon believed it could not afford to open a long bidding process at the time.[91] Reform defenders, including Kelman and Congressman Davis, argued that the charges of favoritism in the selection process were overblown.[92] Stronger evidence was present of problems in contract structures and management. Most of the no-bid contracts were supposed to be limited in scope and temporary.[93] A GAO review of Iraq reconstruction-related contracts found that these contracts often grew to include out-of-scope tasks that either should have been awarded through a competitive process or, if wartime circumstances made that impossible, better justified.[94]

Critics also complained about alleged cost overruns. Many government audits of the Iraq reconstruction effort were conducted in 2004 and 2005. These investigations turned up significant cost-control problems, and a former Halliburton employee was charged in federal court with defrauding the U.S. of more than $3.5 million.[95] Many of the disputed contracts were implemented under the Logistics Civil Augmentation Program (LOGCAP), which allows contracts to be let on a cost-reimbursable basis. Waxman and other watchdogs complained that these massive umbrella contracts invited private firms to gouge taxpayers. Others claimed that the use of LOGCAP contract vehicles was appropriate given the exigencies and uncertainties of war. The military's procurement needs were hard to predict yet they were also urgent—Pentagon planners could not be sure what services they would need, only that the services would be needed in a great hurry. These conditions rendered the initial use of cost-fixed contracts infeasible.

While some critics blamed the Halliburton scandal on the 1990s reforms, the main contract vehicles used by Halliburton and KBR actually predated them. LOGCAP had been established in 1985 to manage the use of civilian contractors who perform services in support of Defense Department missions during times of war and other military mobilizations. The program was first officially used in Somalia in 1992, *before* Al Gore went on the David Letterman show to smash a government ashtray. Like any contracting approach, LOGCAP has strengths and weaknesses. While LOGCAP contracts offer key performance advantages when acquisition needs are urgent and rapidly changing, they provide weak incentives to control costs until task orders are adequately specified and cost estimates are finalized. This clearly happened more slowly in the Iraq reconstruction effort than it should have.[96] It may be that the 1990s reforms, by emphasizing service delivery over cost accounting, contributed to this problem, although even that is not certain. In July 2006, the Army announced it was discontinuing its exclusive deal with Halliburton to provide logistical support to U.S. troops worldwide, and that it would split the work among three companies, with a fourth firm hired to monitor the performance of the other three. Halliburton would be eligible to bid for this work.[97]

The most serious collapse of contracting management occurred at the Abu Ghraib prison, where the Department of Defense used an existing Department of Interior information technology contract to hire private sector interrogators employed by CACI International Inc, a technology firm based in Arlington, Virginia. A detailed investigation concluded that the use of contract interrogators instead of appropriate government personnel contributed to the environment in which prisoner abuse occurred.[98] While interagency contracting, in which one federal agency needing services or supplies obtains them from another, may promote administrative efficiencies, the contract with CACI International was troubled from the start. Inadequate monitoring during the administration of the contract permitted inexperienced and little-supervised private employees to perform sensitive wartime tasks normally reserved for highly trained government personnel. By all accounts, the result was a serious breakdown of contractor oversight and accountability.[99]

Contracting abuses also were alleged to have occurred in the aftermath of Hurricane Katrina. The recovery effort posed an extraordinarily difficult challenge for government procurement officers. There was an urgent and appropriate desire to get goods and services to victims as quickly as possible. Thousands of Gulf Coast residents were homeless and literally possessed only the shirts on their backs. This was no time for bureaucratic paper pushing. Yet the rapid infusion of billions of dollars to private contractors inevitably creates temptations for mischief. As one contracting expert said, "The line between profiteering and doing good deeds in emergency situations can be very thin."[100]

Immediately after the disaster struck, Congress approved $62 billion in relief and reconstruction funds. At the request of the Bush Administration, Congress also raised the amount federal employees could charge on government credit cards for Katrina-related expenses to $250,000 from $25,000. At the same time, lawmakers were eager to demonstrate they had learned lessons from the Iraq reconstruction, and authorized $15 million to the Department of Homeland Security's Inspector's General office to track waste and abuse. Many of the contracts initially signed by the Federal Emergency Management Agency (FEMA) during the initial frantic effort to assist storm victims were awarded with no or limited competition. Government watchdogs and auditors immediately raised questions about the potential for waste, fraud, and abuse."[101] House Democratic Leader Nancy Pelosi (CA) and Rep. Waxman introduced legislation to create an anti-fraud commission to police federal contracts related to the hurricane.[102] Media coverage of the fraud issue was extensive. This level of media attention was arguably out of proportion to the true scope of the abuse problem. A Department of Justice Fraud Task Force on Hurricane Katrina produced forty arrests in six weeks, but many of these involved individuals falsely claiming to be disaster victims, not procurement fraud per se.[103] Under intense political pressure, the acting head of FEMA announced that the Katrina-related contracts that were awarded with little or no competition would be rebid.[104] The government further announced that it was rescinding the increase in the credit-card limit.[105]

The harsh reactions of the media and watchdog groups to the government's management of private contactors in the Katrina recovery effort confirmed that the political environment of procurement had changed since Al Gore went on TV to smash an ashtray. Initially criticized for being too slow to react to the disaster, FEMA was then attacked for agreeing to no-bid contracts with large companies in an effort to deliver services rapidly. The signals from political overseers were intense, multiple, and conflicting. In this highly politicized environment, contract managers were vulnerable to second-guessing almost no matter what they did.[106] Either they were too sluggish, or they were fleecing the taxpayer. "The effect of this dynamic has been to create an environment in which, frankly, mission focus has been too often supplanted by fear; an environment in which one government contracting officer told us people are not only afraid of making a mistake, they are afraid of making a decision. This is not a healthy environment," said one industry executive.[107] The risk aversion and fear of innovation that characterized the procurement system before the 1990s reforms had returned.

The Return of Congressional Oversight and Bid Protests

A final reason why the political climate became more hostile is that Democrats regained control of Congress in 2006.[108] Although the major procurement reforms were enacted during the Clinton–Gore Administration, the truth is that the reinventing government project was always more the darling of the presidential wing of the Democratic party than the congressional one. It was, after all, mostly the *Democrats* who controlled Congress during the years when the red tape that procurement reform was meant to cut was created. And it was mostly *Democrats* who chaired the key oversight committees whose behavior produced the bureaucratic pathologies that the reforms were supposed to cure. So it was no great surprise that the signals emanating from the Hill changed when Congressman Waxman assumed chairmanship of the House Committee on Oversight and Government Reform in January 2007. "Billions of dollars are being squandered, and the taxpayer is being taken to the cleaners," the new chairman announced.[109]

Under Waxman, the full committee and its four subcommittees held 38 hearings between January and May 2007. Some looked at decisions for specific contracts, including why the General Services Administration renewed a contract with Sun Microsystems despite performance concerns. This was a degree of legislative probing into the merits of individual purchase decisions rarely seen since the 1980s.[110] Waxman also proposed new legislation to correct perceived contracting abuses. On March 15, 2007, the House passed his "Accountability in Contracting Act," by a vote of 347-73. The measure would impose restrictions on cost-reimbursement type contracts and mandate tighter auditing of contract overcharges. The bill sparked strong opposition from industry groups, which argued that the reporting requirements would be burdensome and unproductive, but the measure's language was subsequently tucked in the defense authorization bill to increase its chances of enactment.[111] While Waxman's bill would not dismantle the 1990s reforms, it was a move in the opposite direction.

Waxman pinned the blame for the system's problems squarely on the ideology of the Bush Administration and the inadequacies of the federal contracting workforce. However, outside critics linked the perceived abuses to the Clinton era reforms themselves. "What went wrong is when we started reinventing government and using the streamlined model," said Danielle Brian, executive director of the Project on Government Oversight (POGO), a prominent watchdog group. At a forum sponsored by the Center for American Progress, Brian stated that the closest thing to a "silver bullet" to repair the procurement system would be if Congress "considered rolling back" the Federal Acquisition Streamlining Act and the Federal Acquisition Reform Act.[112]

Another indication of reversion toward a more adversarial, less flexible procurement process is that the number of protests filed by contractors also climbed. Firms that were not awarded contracts for which they submitted bids filed 1,327 protests with the GAO in 2006. This was not a huge number, and far lower than the number of protests in the 1980s, but it was 10 percent higher than in 2002. In addition, the number of firms taking their bid protests to court increased by 50 percent over this period.[113] Many reasons accounted for the increase in protests, including the possibility that overburdened procurement officers were making more mistakes. Even when they were ultimately rejected, however, protests can double or triple the time it takes for the government to award contacts.

CONCLUSIONS

Even the fiercest critics of the reforms concede there is no going back to the pre-1990s buying rules. MIL-SPECs, off-the-shelf purchases of commercial items, routine use of government credit cards—all these specific changes are now woven into daily governing routines. They have gained support among both procurement officers and contractors and others. As Kelman accurately observes, "[D]espite many real or alleged 'scandals,' reform has become rooted enough that it had not, as a result of the scandals, simply been swept away like a house of straw . . . "[114] These are no mean achievements, and they should not be denigrated.

Still, qualitative erosion of the reforms, especially the governing vision underlying those reforms, cannot be ruled out. While Congress has not restored the pre-1990s procurement rules and regulations, concerns are growing about the match between the new rules and the changing nature of the government's acquisition task, especially regarding the purchasing of government-specific items and the use of mega-contractors as general service providers. It is unclear whether Congress will tolerate a high-flexibility system for these evolving practices. As one reform advocate puts it, the risk is not that the "old red tape will be put back, but that new red tape will be created."[115] It also seems clear that the attempt of reformers to encourage more risk-taking and innovation among the procurement workforce is in serious jeopardy. The focus today is again on procedural compliance and avoiding trouble. Concerns about best value, public-private partnerships, and experimentation are being lost. Contract managers feel beleaguered and vulnerable.

While procurement reform has generated positive feedback within the bureaucracy, the broader political impact of the changes has been modest at best. Group identities and interests have not really changed. Most private-sector contractors supported the acquisition reforms when they were passed, and still do so today. Many Washington attorneys who handle government contract work still would prefer a more litigious and formal process. Unlike many high-cost legacy carriers that struggled to survive after airline deregulation, most high-priced federal procurement lawyers managed to escape bankruptcy. The most important institutional shift has been the stripping of the GSA's authority to adjudicate bid protests. This change appears durable, but affects only one piece of the acquisition process. There have not been lasting self-reinforcing changes in federal human capital investments or in the dynamics of congressional oversight. Political principals have retained the ability and the incentive to send contract managers conflicting signals (Buy cheaper! Deliver quality goods faster!). Agencies invite harsh rebuke even when their buying mistakes are relatively minor or made in good faith—*exactly* the situation that procurement reform was intended to change.

Procurement reforms were adopted in the mid-1990s because policy entrepreneurs were able to link a counter-intuitive diagnosis of the pathologies in the procurement system to much broader public concerns about government under-performance. But this fusion of expert analysis with public symbolism has not lasted. "Reinventing government" served Bill Clinton's electoral interests well, but it has not served as the launching pad for subsequent administrative reform efforts or remade electoral coalitions. Reinventing government was never about the elimination of administrative inefficiencies *per se*. It was about redefining the accountability relationships between bureaucrats and elected officials. It was about reshaping citizen expectations of government. Those were—and are—highly ambitious reform goals.

Some victories have been won, but transformational change in American public administration has not been easy to sustain.

CHAPTER 7

Unshackling an Unstable Industry: Airline Deregulation

THE AIRLINE DEREGULATION ACT of 1978 is a leading case of general-interest reform.[1] Between 1938 and 1978, the Civil Aeronautics Board (CAB) regulated the airlines as a quasi-public utility. The agency's mission statement was self-contradictory. It was to foster the development of the commercial airline industry and protect the public from monopoly and unreasonable prices and to shield the industry from destructive competition. The CAB controlled entry into the industry, determined travel routes, and in its last years regulated fares on the basis of a simple industrywide average cost-formula. Previous to that, it regulated prices by approving some tariff filings, disapproving others, then allowing the carriers proposing the disapproved prices to match the approved tariff. The CAB's policies boosted industry profit margins, but they also coddled inefficient carriers, stifled many innovations, including low-cost low-amenity service, and imposed large costs on consumers. In 1978, Congress passed a sweeping deregulation law despite strong opposition from labor unions and most of the incumbent carriers. Within a year of the reform's enactment, airlines were free to serve any route. By 1984, the airlines were competing virtually free from industry-specific economic regulation.

Airline deregulation has proved highly sustainable. This is a genuine puzzle for three reasons. First, certain issues and social pressures that promoted deregulation's enactment in 1978—such as severe inflation—have faded over time. The political climate is much changed, and the reform's original enacting coalition no longer governs. If airline deregulation had not already occurred, it is unclear it would be passed today. Second, the transition to a competitive market has been slower and far more turbulent than most economists predicted.[2] More than a quarter-century after deregulation, airports are congested, planes are crowded, and much of the airline industry is in financial turmoil.[3] Many of the larger carriers are struggling to control labor costs and match capacity with demand. Finally, there is a sense among some observers that the big carriers have tried to drive out smaller competitors through unfair practices. As NYU law professor and former CAB executive Michael E. Levine observes, the airline industry since 1978 has faced "the sorts of cyclical crises and accusations of monopoly and predatory-appearing behavior that often give rise to regulation."[4] Why have the big carriers failed to capture new rents through government restrictions on competition? Why didn't the September 11th terrorist attacks—which forced the grounding of flights across the nation and accelerated the industry's financial meltdown—lead to a fundamental reexamination of the government's supervisory role?

The central claim of this chapter is that airline deregulation has endured because policymaking has gradually but unmistakably been *reconfigured*, making it increasingly costly and unattractive to go back. Because the CAB was phased out of existence though a sunset provision contained in the 1978 Act, the federal government no longer possesses an independent commission with the political autonomy and capacity to supervise routes and prices on a continuous basis. Reregulation is still possible, but it would have to be carried out by a cabinet department subject to broad political pressures. Finally, the creative destructiveness of market forces has altered the industrial structure of the airline industry. The heterogeneity and instability of sector interests has ensured that almost any major new regulation the government proposes will encounter resistance from some quarter. At the same time, airlines, airport operators, service providers, and other economic actors have responded to the removal of regulatory barriers by making large-scale commitments in human and physical capital. It would be impossible to reinstate the old system without massive disruption. By changing the context in which the airline industry is governed and creating positive feedback effects, deregulation has promoted its own sustainability.

THE AIRLINE INDUSTRY BEFORE REFORM

The Airline Deregulation Act of 1978 removed many of the price and entry controls that had been imposed on the airline industry in the Civil Aeronautics Act of 1938. The New Deal measure created an independent regulatory agency, the CAB, to promote and supervise the industry.[5] The CAB was given broad authority to determine which commercial airlines (referred to as "trunk carriers") would be certified to provide long haul service, what interstate routes they would be permitted to fly, and what ticket prices they could charge."[6] The airline industry had "lobbied hard" for the 1938 Act,[7] and had suffered major losses during the Great Depression. The president of the Air Transport Association argued that without government regulation, "there is nothing to prevent the entire air system from crashing to earth under the impact of cut-throat and destructive practices."[8] The CAB allowed the industry to grow, but its decisions artificially protected the interests of incumbent carriers. From 1938 to 1978, the CAB did not allow the entry of a *single* new trunk airline.[9] The CAB also limited competition on existing routes. Only 10 percent of applications of existing airlines to enter an existing route were approved between 1965 and 1974.[10]

The CAB also tightly regulated fares. When a carrier wished to change its ticket prices, the CAB set it for hearing. Filings in response by rival airlines typically used this opportunity to argue that the proposed change would make it more difficult for the industry to maintain profitability. The CAB approved no tariff or indicated what kind of tariff it would approve. Subsequent filings conformed.[11] As a result, the CAB generally adjusted fares in unison and independently from costs. This disparity between fares and costs increased as new aircraft technologies were introduced.[12] The CAB typically set short-haul fares artificially low, with the costs passed along to long-distance travelers who paid expensive fares. By controlling ticket prices, the CAB encouraged nonprice competition, and carriers battled with one another to see who could offer the most luxurious flying experience. As business historian Richard H. K. Vietor writes in an insightful study of the evolution of the airline industry between 1925 and 1998, "On wide-bodied aircraft, lounges were introduced in first class, then in coach. When American installed piano bars, TWA countered with electronic draw-poker machines. Live entertainment proliferated, with musicians, magicians, wine-tasters, and Playboy bunnies."[13] These amenities were unavailable to ordinary Americans, who couldn't afford to fly given the high fares. As early as the 1940s, professional economists had criticized airline regulation. The overwhelming consensus among economists was that government regulation of the airlines' routes and prices was unnecessary and that greater reliance on the forces of market competition would deliver a better mix of fares and services for the public. Economists argued that regulated prices were too high on average, that many consumers would be willing to accept more crowded planes in exchange for lower fares, and that unregulated competition would yield a more efficient airline system. Strong consensus existed among academics that the airline industry was not a natural monopoly. While only a few airlines might compete on any given route, experts argued, "the threat of entry would hold fares down and constrain monopoly pricing."[14]

The CAB lacked authority to regulate carriers that operated only within one state. States like California and Texas had cities that were far enough apart to warrant air service. Economists seized on this "natural experiment" to show that fares on intrastate routes were often much lower than fares on interstate routes, even when the routes were the same distance.[15] An influential 1965 study, for example, found that the fares charged by Pacific Southwest Airlines between San Francisco and Los Angeles were more than 50 percent lower than the fares charged by CAB-regulated carriers between Boston and Washington, D.C.[16]

The Politics of Deregulation

Ultimately, the reform ideas of policy experts triumphed. Airline deregulation simply would not have occurred if professional economists had not made such a powerful analytic case for it. Yet, as Martha Derthick and Paul J. Quirk argue in their superb study of the politics of deregulation, the academic critique of the CAB's policies were not sufficient. Expert ideas had to enter into the stream of policy discussion in Washington. Political entrepreneurship was needed to make this happen.[17]

One of the most important reform advocates was Senator Edward Kennedy (D-MA). With the assistance of his staff aide, Harvard Law professor (and future Supreme Court justice) Stephen Breyer, Kennedy in 1974–75 organized congressional hearings on airline regulation that exposed the costs of the industry's anticompetitive behavior.[18] With growing public concern about severe inflation and the economic privileges of large corporations, Kennedy strategically linked airline deregulation to the consumer movement. To be sure, airline regulation was not a major contributor to the national inflation problem, but Kennedy and his staff realized that a political "hook" was needed to make the issue graspable for ordinary citizens. President Gerald Ford also took up the banner of reform. While Kennedy framed deregulation almost exclusively in proconsumer terms, Ford stressed that it would promote the free-enterprise system and curb "big government."[19]

Meanwhile, momentum for reform was building in the CAB itself. While the CAB had long protected the interests of incumbent carriers, its decision to impose a moratorium on new route cases and its application of a rigid fare formula sparked a great deal of criticism from the press and politicians. In 1975, under Chairman John Robson, the agency gradually relaxed the route moratorium and began to give carriers the flexibility to reduce fares. The pace of reform quickened under chairman Alfred Kahn, a Cornell University economist, who was appointed by President Jimmy Carter in 1977. Kahn had a rare combination of political skill and technical expertise. He was the "quintessential policy entrepreneur," who emerged at precisely the right moment.[20] Under Kahn's leadership, the CAB opened entry and allowed carriers to begin new routes without the agency's pre-approval.

Most of the trunk carriers adamantly opposed deregulation.[21] The airlines argued that the removal of government controls would lead to destructive competition. The fiercest opponents included financially strapped airlines such as TWA and Eastern, which feared entry into their most profitable routes,[22] but also included industry powerhouses like American and Delta. Eventually, a very few carriers, including only United among the trunklines, modified their position on deregulation. The industry's political retreat reflected less a sudden realization that deregulation would be economically advantageous for existing carriers than the momentum of reform, the inability of the big airlines to agree upon a common lobbying strategy, and the fear of ending up with the worst of both worlds—government regulation without governmental protection.[23] Once the governmental supports for the airline industry were removed, the cartel collapsed. Organized labor also fought to preserve government regulation of the industry. Unions representing pilots, flight attendants, transport workers, and other airline employees argued that deregulation would reduce wages and job security.[24] The CAB had not permitted any carriers to go bankrupt, its merger policies were highly favorable to labor interests, and an absence of the discipline of the possibility of competitive displacement meant wages and working conditions more favorable than market levels. Unions feared that the industry might consolidate, employees would lose jobs, and wages would fall.

While Congress faced intense pressure from organized interests to slow the movement toward deregulation, it acted to promote the general interest of consumers. The Airline Deregulation Act of 1978 provided for the gradual removal over six years of virtually all entry restrictions into the airline industry,[25] all restrictions on the selection of routes, and all constraints on pricing. The Act also contained a sunset provision that led to the CAB's demise at the end of 1984. A sunset provision for the CAB—a radical institutional change originally suggested by Ralph Nader—survived the legislative process in part because of its ambiguity. According to Derthick and Quirk, some reform advocates viewed it as a diversionary tactic that would provide an excuse for postponing genuine reform. Late in the game, however, some carriers decided they wanted a sunset provision in order to reduce political uncertainty. If the CAB were kept around, they reasoned, it might create regulatory mischief in the future.[26]

The final bill included two key compensation mechanisms to mollify opponents. Labor union concern that deregulation would hurt airline workers led Congress to include an employee protection program to provide temporary financial assistance to airline employees who lost their jobs or suffered pay cuts because of the bankruptcy or major contraction of a carrier caused by the Act.[27] Congress also sought to guarantee air service to small communities. While carriers were permitted to earn extraordinary profits on popular routes between large cities, they were forced to subsidize the air travel of sparse markets. Opponents argued that deregulation would end this cross-subsidization by freeing airlines to compete on the most profitable routes. Members of Congress from small cities and rural areas were especially worried about the impact on their districts. Congress therefore included subsidies in the bill to guarantee "essential" air services to eligible localities for ten years.[28] Once these modifications were made, the opposition to deregulation collapsed. The Senate passed the deregulation bill by a vote of 83 to 9. The House vote on final passage was 363 to 8.[29]

After deregulation, airlines had the right to carve out new routes for the first time in forty years. Beginning in 1982, airlines had full freedom to set fares.[30] By 1984, economic regulation of the industry had ceased, and the CAB no longer existed.

THE AFTERMATH OF DEREGULATION

The airline industry underwent profound changes after deregulation. A slew of new discount carriers began operations. Many of the start-ups quickly failed, but their entry into the industry forced the big carriers to dramatically lower their prices. Some of the leading carriers—such as Braniff, Eastern, and TWA—were unable to compete and disappeared. Formerly regulated carriers that survived the initial wave of market entrants had to reinvent themselves. They invested heavily in the development of frequent-flyer programs and computerized reservation systems to breed customer loyalty. They constructed hub-and-spoke networks with huge fixed costs to serve decentralizing cities and suburban areas. And they swallowed up smaller airlines under Washington's more accommodative antitrust policies.

A second wave of new no-frills airlines entered the market in the 1990s, intensifying the pressure on legacy carriers to reorganize their businesses to reduce their labor costs. In sum, deregulation has massively changed the identities, resources, and strategies of key sector actors. Those carriers who were unable to carve out a stable market niche have disappeared. Airline deregulation thus offers a powerful contrast to the standard functionalist argument that powerful group actors dictate policy reform outcomes.[31] *Rather than the big carriers obtaining the market rules and governmental frameworks they wanted, the deregulated airline market has structured the character and identities of the actors who could survive.*

The First Wave of New Entrants

Almost overnight, deregulation transformed the structure of the airline industry. Many new low-cost airlines entered the market (Table 7-1). Between 1978 and the end of 1983, the number of scheduled interstate carriers in the United States increased from 36 to 123.[32] While some of the startups existed only on paper, carriers like People Express, Air Florida, and New York Air were attracting customers in large numbers.[33] By the end of 1983, the start-ups were carrying about 10 percent of all domestic passengers.[34] Deregulation also permitted carriers formerly limited to intrastate operations to expand across state boundaries. For example, Southwest and PSA began to serve markets beyond Texas. Several of the new entrants had significant cost advantages over many of the legacy carriers, enabling them to charge very low fares. Their ability to offer cut-rate prices was due mainly to their lower wage costs and the simplicity of their operations, but also because they offered "no frills" service. People Express, Southwest, Midway, Air California, New York Air, and other new entrant airlines broke tradition by providing snacks but no meal service. Some of them did not even maintain ticket offices.

Table 7-1
First Generation New Entrant Interstate Carriers, 1978–1982

Entrant	Entry	Exit
Midway Airlines	1979	1991
New York Air	1989	1986
People Express	1981	1986
Jet America	1981	1986
Muse Air	1981	1985
Pacific Express	1982	1984
Northeastern Intentional	1982	1984
Hawaii Express	1982	1984
Air Atlanta	1984	1987
Florida Express	1984	1987

Source: Steven A. Morrison and Clifford Winston, *The Evolution of the Airline Industry*, (Washington: Brookings Institution), 1995.

New airlines have been likened to "newborn sea turtles trying to make their way to the sea: some will make it and some will not."[35] Most of the first generation of new carriers to crawl into the post-deregulation sea quickly drowned or were swallowed up by larger entities. Many had poor management and pricing strategies or were unable to generate enough confidence among consumers when legacy carriers matched their low fares. Of the fifty-eight carriers that started operations between 1978 and 1990, only one (America West) is still operating.[36]

Investments in Hub-and-Spoke Networks

The creative destructiveness of market competition came as a rude awakening to the long-coddled legacy carriers, which suddenly had to please price-conscious consumers. Deregulation could hardly have come at a less economically auspicious moment. During the late 1970s and early 1980s, the U.S. economy experienced high inflation, oil shocks, and slow growth. Previously, the airlines had been largely sheltered from external economic conditions. After reform, they had to bear the costs. The irony is that while the big carriers had fought to maintain the old regulatory regime, deregulation opened enticing new business opportunities for them. Freed from government controls, the legacy carriers almost immediately began abandoning less profitable routes and entering ones they had previously desired but had been unable to claim.

One of the most important responses of the legacy carriers was to reorganize their networks into "hub-and-spoke" systems. American established hubs at Dallas–Fort Worth and Chicago, United at Denver and Chicago, and Delta at Atlanta and Dallas–Forth Worth. Consumers benefited from more frequent flights, including frequent connecting service between smaller and medium-sized cities and from being able to avoid changing airlines when they made connections. While some hub-and-spoke networks existed prior to deregulation, the CAB generally assigned carriers linear routes. Carriers were prevented from realizing "the economies of scale or scope that would have been possible with a more integrated centralized structure."[37] The CAB's piecemeal route allocation process often resulted in nonstop service to locations that could not support it. In 1977, the average flight had only 55 percent of its seats filled.[38] Hubbing allowed the carriers to use larger planes and realize marginal cost savings though more efficient use of labor, fuel, and other inputs.[39]

The shift to hubbing had far-reaching unforeseen effects on carriers' investment decisions. As Vietor notes, "Four decades of CAB control had penetrated to the operational core of the regulated firms. Fleet competition and route structure, the essential plant and operating method of the airline business, had become artifacts of public policy. Moreover, most other aspects of the business—work rules and crew assignments, terminal and gate investments, organization of maintenance, and all critical marketing activities—were shaped to fit the routes and fleet."[40]

Historically, the major carriers had assembled fleets consisting of many large, wide-body planes. This decision was based on the reasonable assumption that most valuable service would occur on point-to-point routes and that wide-body planes had lower unit costs and permitted more onboard amenities, provided that airlines did not face competitors charging lower fares while offering more frequent service in smaller planes. The CAB didn't permit most carriers to create large hub operations. Wide-body planes allowed carriers to compete on new nonprice dimensions, such as piano bars. With the move to price competition and a hub-and-spoke system, smaller aircraft became far more attractive—even though the cost of retiring existing planes prematurely was high. Carriers wanted the fleet with low operating costs per aircraft-mile to permit high-schedule frequency into hubs. Moreover, the simple *uncertainty* about the nature of future competition also contributed to the increased desire for smaller planes, since "such planes provide greater flexibility to absorb added competition."[41] Carriers intent on constructing hub-and-spoke systems had to "substitute away from the wide-bodied planes favored during the regulatory years of nonprice competition, in order to increase load factors and reduce fuel expense."[42] Between 1978 and 1983, only one 747 (with 400 seats) was procured by U.S. carriers, even though passenger loads were climbing rapidly. The majority of new aircraft ordered were for planes with less than 150 seats.[43]

In addition to building "fortress hubs," the big carriers invested heavily in the development of centralized computer reservation systems to provide comprehensive information on all airlines to travel agents while promoting their own flights. These systems were made to be easy for use by travel agents. The number of travel agents increased from 14,804 in 1978 to 23,059 in 1983, and travel agent commissions on airline travel sales increased from $732 million in 1977 to $2.4 billion in 1983.[44] In sum, airline deregulation fostered the growth of a complementary industry. The travel agency industry would provide support for the reform path until its power was curtailed by the advent of Internet airline ticket purchasing in the late 1990s.

The carriers also developed "yield management systems"—sophisticated techniques and models to extract the maximum revenue per seat by charging different rates to different kinds of passengers. The fares were constantly being updated in response to changes in supply and demand. Competition in price became so fierce that some carriers were making 80,000 airline fare changes each day.[45] Implementing these complex yield management systems required firm-specific investments in both human and physical capital. Finally, the carriers spent heavily on marketing. They developed or expanded frequent flyer programs to build customer loyalty. The first major carrier to create a frequent flyer program was American Airlines in 1981. Within five years, virtually every other carrier offered one.[46]

The initial responses of carriers to deregulation shaped the dynamics of the industry going forward. The carriers that were quickest to establish computerized reservation systems, for example, had a huge advantage over slower movers because the incremental cost of adding another travel agency to an existing system was small. By the late 1980s, the computer systems of American (SABRE) and United Airlines (APOLLO) controlled 70 percent of the travel agency market. TWA and Eastern were effectively locked out.[47] Similarly, once frequent flyer programs were established, the travel choices consumers made affected their choice of airlines in the future.

Changes in Industry Structure: Mergers and Bankruptcies

One of the most striking developments in the airline industry since deregulation has been an almost constant evolution in the identity of sector actors as a result of mergers, bankruptcies, and the formation of marketing alliances. During the era of regulation, the CAB denied most merger requests except when carriers were on the brink of bankruptcy. No major trunk or regional carrier was acquired between 1968 and 1978. After deregulation, antitrust authorities stopped concerning themselves with the profitability of individual carriers. As long as the threat of entry is believed to exist, mergers have generally been permitted. A major wave of airline mergers took place in the mid-1980s as airlines scrambled to realize economies of scale and scope, resulting in an industry with a fewer number of big players (Table 7-2). The government permitted mergers between trunk carriers and local service airlines at their hubs (TWA and Ozark, Northwest and Republic) as well as mergers between

TABLE 7-2
Airline Mergers, 1978–2005

Year	Mergers
1979	North Central / Southern, Pan Am / National
1980	Republic / Hughes Airwest
1981	Continental / Texas International
1985	People Express / Frontier, Southwest / Muse
1986	Continental / Eastern, Continental / People Express
	Northwest / Republic, TWA / Ozark, Delta / Western
1987	American / Air Cal, US Air / Pacific Southwest, US Air / Piedmont
1992	US Air / Trump Shuttle, United / Air Wisconsin
2001	American / TWA

Source: Steven A. Morrison and Clifford Winston, "The Remaining Role for Government Policy in the Deregulated Airline Industry," in Sam Peltzman and Clifford Winston, eds., *Deregulation of Network Industries: What's Next?* (Washington, D.C.: Brookings Institution Press, 2000), 11.

trunk or local carriers to achieve national service goals (US Airways and Piedmont). The government also allowed carriers to establish marketing alliances, in which two or more carriers market the same flight even though only one provides it. Government officials have generally allowed these alliances as long as there is no sharing of revenue or profits in order to provide consumers with the opportunity to purchase itineraries they desire. Since deregulation, policymakers have assumed that markets are open and contestable. On occasion, antitrust authorities have concluded that a proposed merger would harm consumer welfare. In 2001, for example, the government blocked an attempted merger between United and US Airways. But merger opponents have had to overcome a strong evidentiary burden.

This shift in antitrust policy was not a necessary part of deregulation. Indeed, many experts, including Alfred Kahn, believe that antitrust enforcement since 1978 has been far too lenient, and that airline deregulation would have had even larger social benefits if the government had policed merger requests more aggressively. Yet even these critics acknowledge that the level of economic competition remains higher than it was prior to deregulation.[48] Despite the industry's increasing concentration, studies show that during the 1980s and 1990s airlines were more competitive at the crucial route level— where airlines compete head-to-head—than they were in the early to mid-1970s.[49]

The identity of industry actors has also changed through bankruptcies. Before deregulation, bankruptcy was extremely rare in the industry. The CAB "typically arranged marriages between failing carriers (i.e., Northeast) and survivors (i.e., Delta), transferring route and assets to the surviving carriers.

Since 1978, however, there have been more than 100 bankruptcy filings, although not all resulted in liquidation."[50] (See Figure 7-1.)

The 1980s were a particularly tumultuous period for the industry. After an initial period of success, virtually all of the first wave of new entrants failed financially. Once the legacy carriers developed competitive fare structures and hub operations, most customers preferred to stick with the airlines they knew.[51] Deregulation freed business tycoons like Eastern Airline's Frank Lorenzo to try and remake the industry, but the economic recession and overcapacity problems strained many carriers' ability to compete. In 1986, Lorenzo engineered a takeover of Eastern Airlines. Within five years, the carrier had collapsed under a mountain of debt. Another industry leader that ran into trouble in the 1980s was Pan Am, which tried without success to stay afloat by selling off its routes to United and TWA in a desperate cost-cutting measure. More bankruptcies piled up following the recession in 1991 and the terrorist attacks in 2001.[52]

As a result of bankruptcies, mergers, and route sharing, the identities and affiliations of the major actors in the airline industry has evolved almost continuously since deregulation (Figure 7-2). While some of the airlines that predated deregulation still exist, the remaining "legacy carriers" are the product of so many corporate restructurings that many are the same carriers in name only. Of the major carriers that predated deregulation, only United Airlines has had its identity remain basically unchanged, and that is only because the Department of Justice blocked its attempted merger with US Air in 2001 out of concern that the same carrier would control too many hub airports along the east coast.[53]

The Second Wave of Low-Cost Carriers

In the 1990s, a second wave of smaller entrants emerged, including Frontier, JetBlue, and ValueJet.[54] These new entrants were much better capitalized than their predecessors. They took advantage of the growing level of congestion at major hub airports. They sought out underserved cities (Oakland, Baltimore, Providence) or secondary airports (Dallas's Love Field, Chicago Midway) and provided no-frills point-to-point service. It turned out many Americans were willing to drive fairly long distances to non-hub airports in order to take advantage of the very low prices offered by the no-frills airlines. By 2004, low fare carriers accounted for about 25 percent of the domestic air market and the share is increasingly rapidly.[55]

What makes the success of these new entrants all the more remarkable is that the legacy carriers have enjoyed built-in institutional advantages. For example, at many hubs, airlines hold exclusive-use gate leases for as long as twenty years, locking out new entrants. The big carriers also dominate airport investments at their hubs. While the legacy carriers have benefited from these

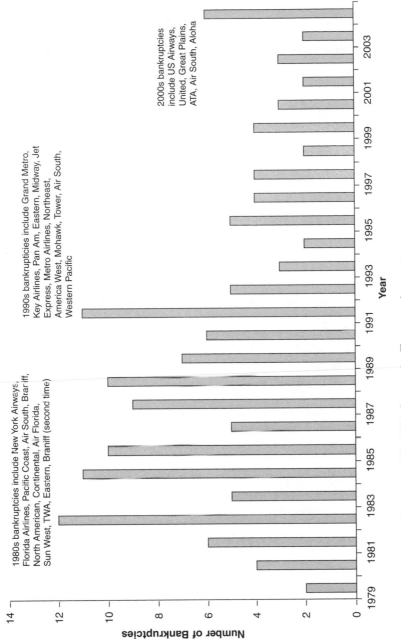

Figure 7-1. Airline Bankruptcies, 1979–2004. *Source: Air Transport Association*

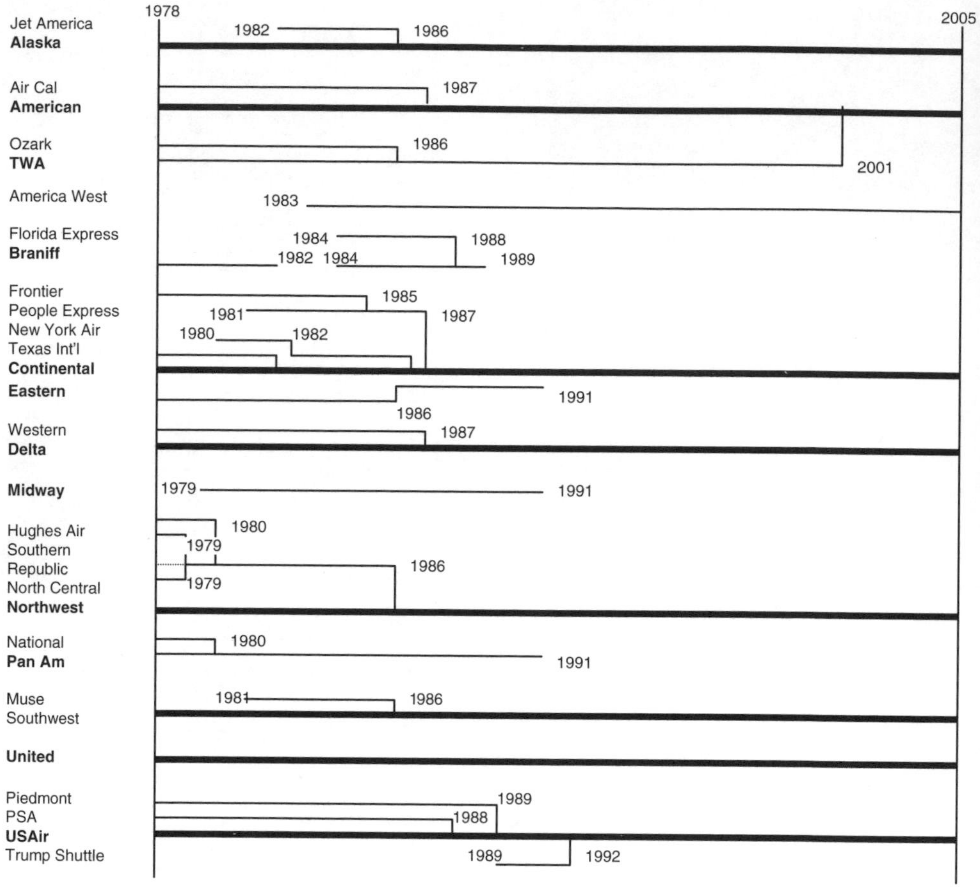

Figure 7-2. Chronology of Large U.S. Airlines Since Deregulation, 1978–2005. *Sources:* Richard H.K. Vietor, "Contrived Competition: Airline Regulation and Deregulation, 1925–1988," *The Business History Review* (Spring 1990): 99 and data compiled by the author.

privileges, their cost structures have been so high, and the desire of Americans for low airfares so strong, that the progress of the JetBlues and Southwests could not be stopped. It may be that the hub-and-spoke system—an innovation that the big carriers adopted as soon as they could following deregulation—is no longer the most efficient way to deliver air service. In a competitive market, the "right" business model is constantly being tested.[56]

Benefits for Consumers

By any reasonable standard, airline deregulation has been a dramatic policy success, vastly improving the welfare of American consumers (Table 7-3).

TABLE 7-3
Annual Gains to Travelers from Airline Deregulation (billions of 1993 dollars)

Category	Gain in Consumer Welfare
Fares	12.4
Travel Restrictions	−1.1
Frequency	10.3
Load Factor	−0.6
Number of Connections	−0.7
Mix of Connections (online or interline)	0.9
Travel Time	−2.8
Total	18.4

Source: Morrison and Winston (1995).

Fares are lower in general, most travelers have better choices, and flying remains safe. The best available social science evidence indicates that air travelers' fares were, on average, 27 percent lower in 1998 than they would have been had regulation continued. To be sure, not every passenger has enjoyed low fares. During the 1990s, for example, business travelers who wished to purchase last-minute tickets and were unwilling to accept Saturday-night stayovers were routinely forced to pay expensive fares. But most passengers who were able to book flights in advance enjoyed favorable prices. In 1998, 80 percent of passengers (accounting for 85 percent of passenger miles) paid lower fares than what they would have paid in the same economic environment if the old CAB regime had remained in place.[57] Travelers also have had more flights to choose from. In the decade following deregulation, demand for air travel more than doubled from 254 million domestic passengers in 1978 to 582 million in 1999.[58] Flying on a commercial airline is not dirt cheap, but it has become more like what riding Greyhound buses used to be—a relatively affordable but not especially glamorous way to travel for middle class people. While some have worried that deregulation would compromise safety, the number of fatal accidents on U.S. aircraft has continued to fall. Accident rates during the twelve years after deregulation were 20 to 45 percent (depending on the specific measures used) below their average levels in twelve years before the 1978 Act. Moreover, by giving intercity travelers an incentive to fly instead of drive, the low airfares made possible by deregulation reduced the number of auto fatalities.[59]

REREGULATING THE AIRLINE INDUSTRY?

Airline deregulation delivered a host of benefits: supersaver fares, frequent flyer programs, and more convenient flight schedules. But as passenger loads increased, so did complaints about poor service and concerns about anti-competitive behavior by the major airlines.[60] Beginning in the 1980s, some policy-makers argued that the federal government needed to play a more active supervisory role. The most serious attempt to reestablish federal control over aspects of the airline industry occurred in the late 1990s. The Clinton Administration endorsed the basic goal of deregulation, but insisted that "competitive guidelines" were needed to prevent the hub-and-spoke carriers from using predatory practices to drive out smaller airlines. The Administration ultimately dropped its efforts to adopt the guidelines after the major carriers and some outside experts criticized them as a misguided attempt to reregulate the industry. Similar legislative efforts to mandate improvements in passenger service also failed. Only with the terrorist attacks of September 11, 2001 did the federal government reemerge as a major determinant of the economic fate of individual carriers, and even then the approach chosen to assist troubled airlines (financial subsidies rather than new anticompetitive regulations) confirmed the legitimacy and embeddedness of the existing line of policymaking.

The relatively limited nature of the government's post-1978 interventions is puzzling in light of the widespread frustration with aspects of the airline industry's performance. Back in the 1970s, pro-reform advocates like Ted Kennedy linked deregulation to the consumer movement and to the public's desire for low prices. While ticket prices have fallen dramatically, the major consumer groups have become disenchanted with certain outcomes of the competitive market, arguing that it has resulted in a deterioration in air service quality and a loss of consumer "rights."[61] In an era in which the airlines have become fodder for late-night comics, it is no surprise that entrepreneurial politicians like Senators John McCain (R-AZ) and Harry Reid (D-NV) have pushed for the creation of "passenger rights" and tighter federal controls over the industry. Nor is it a shock that airline managers struggling to deliver profits to their shareholders would seek the security of government regulation. Certainly the carriers have not been shy about exploiting remaining vestiges of the pre-1978 regulated system to capture rents. As mentioned earlier, the big carriers often benefit from exclusive long-term gate-leasing arrangements and are able to dominate airport investments at their hubs. Finally, if bureaucrats seek more power and larger budgets, then reregulating the airlines would seem to have a natural constituency in the executive as well.

Rent-seeking behavior has not been eliminated from the airline industry—witness the industry's lobbying effort following the 9/11 attacks—but the old iron triangle relationship between the industry, lawmakers, and regulators has not reconstituted itself. Why not? Analysis of the reasons for the durability of airline deregulation, and the relatively modest scope of the government's post-1978 interventions, must turn to the reconfiguration of institutions, interests, and ideas.

The key institutional shift was the phasing out of the CAB. The importance of this change is twofold. First, since 1978 the government has lacked an agency whose central mission is to regulate airline routes and fares. When problems have emerged in the airline industry, the government has been forced to work through the Departments of Justice (DOJ) and Transportation (DOT), both of which have many other issues on their agendas. Executive policymaking with respect to the airline industry has consequently been episodic and *ad hoc*.[62] Second, the termination of the CAB meant that there was no longer an *independent commission* with the political autonomy to control the industry. The concentrated power of the CAB allowed the agency for decades to promote policies that were inimical to general-interests, but once the agency embraced economists' reform prescriptions, it was able to change course very quickly. Once the CAB was terminated, airline policymaking became susceptible to much broader political influences, including pressure from ideological conservatives opposed to new regulations and from economic actors vested in the new system. As former CAB executive Michael Levine observes:

> The change in institutions was subtle compared to the change in legislation. About 450 of the CAB's 800 employees went over to the DOT and became the core of the DOT's airline group. Only now [2005] are they beginning to retire out. The policy preferences of that group didn't change much. . . [They] liked deregulation as long as there was a proliferation of entrants and prices were declining and became worried about it when the opposite was the case (often because the market had been previously oversupplied for a period). What was different was that the Department was officially and overtly part of the Administration and thus explicitly subject to political and broad policy considerations. . . . As an example, when in 1998, the DOT staff [developed competitive guidelines to prevent large carriers from lowering their fares to drive out new entrants] . . . opposition came from many directions and the matter was unceremoniously dropped when the Republicans took the presidency.[63]

The ideational context of policymaking also changed. At the broadest ideological level, policymaking became more market-friendly. First, legal doctrines shifted in a way that discouraged new governmental interventions. For example, the Supreme Court established a high barrier to proving predatory pricing cases. "Cutting prices in order to increase business often is the very essence of competition," the high court ruled in a key 1986 decision. Actions against predatory pricing can be dangerous, the court warned, "because they chill the very conduct the antitrust laws are designed to protect."[64] The Republican takeover of Congress in 1994 further weakened political support for measures to reregulate aspects of the airline industry.

Most importantly, airline deregulation has created positive policy feedbacks that have profoundly altered the economic context of policymaking. Deregulation vastly increased the heterogeneity of sector interests as new carriers entered and legacy carriers adapted in different ways to the pressures of competition. Carriers still seek to capture new rents through anticompetitive regulations, but there is almost always an opposing airline to exert counter pressure. The political cohesion of the industry has declined. As Levine observes, when the CAB was established in 1938, and again in 1975–1977, "the large airlines were unanimous in their preferred policy—regulation by the CAB." By contrast, "Today there is no longer an 'industry position' on most matters of regulation and perhaps no 'industry' at all in its historical sense . . . Airlines have championed their own relief needs while opposing those of others."[65] The Air Transportation Association, the industry's most powerful trade association, has had difficulty reaching a consensus on regulatory issues since deregulation. The ATA requires unanimity among its members before it can endorse legislation, and any proposal to reregulate pricing, entry, or capacity would inevitably split its membership.[66] The interests of municipalities, airline industry employees, and even consumers have also fragmented since deregulation. The various "special" interests that comprise the airline sector have divergent and often conflicting objectives and incentives, increasing the organization costs "for any proponent of reregulatory policy change." [67]

Deregulation has created constituencies with a vested interest in reform by encouraging long-term, often asset-specific, investments in new aircraft, terminals, scheduling tools, and revenue-management software. "Fortress" hub operations were constructed at airports around the nation. Supporting industries and supplies (e.g., aircraft equipment suppliers, hotels, rental cars, restaurants, corporate office parks) grew up around them, creating strong but conflicting local constituencies. Any attempt to undo these changes would be massively disruptive not only for the airlines but for their host business communities. "The enormous growth and expansion in scope of the route system under deregulation," Levine argues, "has created many opportunities for complementary investments in hard assets and human capital, including the location of plants and offices by actors with no other connection to the industry.... They have become a very important force for policy conservatism, almost like a spontaneous and uncoordinated version of those in many congressional districts that have won contracts for key defense systems."[68] "You can't unscramble the egg," said Senator Jack C. Danforth in 1987. "We've set in motion forces that aren't going to be reversed."[69]

Predatory Pricing

After deregulation, the government must maintain a competitive environment and provide the physical and legal infrastructure necessary for market activity. But if government is essential after deregulation, and in any event *inevitable*, its residual presence in a policy sector with a long history of rent-seeking behavior and overregulation constitutes a serious threat to reform durability. There is fundamental political tension here. A government strong enough to make beneficial midcourse policy adjustments may also be strong enough to prevent the creative destruction and chaotic experimentation essential to a dynamic industry. As it has turned out, policymakers have largely erred on the side of non-intervention. They have accepted the outcomes from market competition—which were clearly beneficial in the aggregate—even when competition has been nasty, brutal and not completely fair.

A case in point is the failure of the Clinton Administration's "competitive guidelines" in the late 1990s. As noted earlier, the airline industry underwent considerable consolidation over the 1980s and 1990s as government antitrust authorities permitted mergers between former competitors. At some hubs, the big carriers controlled 80 percent or more of all flights. Critics argued that the big airlines were driving out their competitors through unfair practices. As soon as a new carrier enters their hub, the big carriers flood the routes of the upstart rival with rock-bottom fares. After the intruder is killed, the big airlines allegedly jacked up their prices again.[70]

In the late 1990s, the Clinton Administration took the position that the government needed to stop such "predatory pricing" practices. The Administration in 1998 drafted competitive guidelines to give the Department of Transportation the authority to begin enforcement proceedings against a major carrier if an established airline responded to a new entry into one of its local hub markets by selling seats at abnormally low fares. The Administration's proposal guidelines received strong support from some struggling new entrants. "The low fare industry has no prospects for success unless the line between vigorous competition and predatory conduct is drawn in an enforcement manner," testified the president of Spirit airlines, which was struggling to make inroads at Northwest's Detroit hub.[71] But big carriers vehemently opposed the guidelines, which they claimed represented a misguided attempt to "reregulate the industry." The airlines mounted a multimillion dollar lobbying campaign and ran ads in leading newspapers that characterized the proposals as an unwarranted government takeover over the airline business. One featured a photograph of a Department of Transportation bureaucrat with the words, "Flying this summer? Meet your new travel agent."[72] Economists were divided about the seriousness of the problems and whether they could be resolved. After heated negotiations with the Air Transport Association, House Speaker Newt Gingrich (R-GA) and other congressional leaders decided to delay implementation of the DOT's recommendations until after it heard from an expert panel of the National Academy of Sciences that was studying the issue. The panel was chaired by Harvard economist John R. Meyer and included Alfred E. Kahn, Roden Brandt, president of the failed start-up carrier Air South, and Randall Malin, a former executive vice president of marketing for USAir. The panel ultimately failed to reach consensus on the merits of

DOT's plan to protect start-ups, and the Administration abandoned its efforts.[73]

Unable to win the strong support of either Congress or outside experts for its competitive guidelines, the Clinton Administration took its case to the courts. In 1999, the Justice Department brought a predatory pricing suit against American Airlines, accusing the carrier of seeking to drive three new entrants—Vanguard Airlines, Western Pacific Airlines, and Sun Jet—out of its hubs by flooding its routes with below-cost seats. According to the Justice Department suit, once the new entrants reduced their services, American reestablished high fares. This was the first predatory pricing action brought by the government against an airline since deregulation. American Airlines claimed it had done nothing illegal. The trial court dismissed the case, arguing that American had merely responded to market forces. "There is no doubt that American may be a difficult, vigorous, even brutal competitor. But here, it engaged only in bare, not brass-knuckle competition," ruled the Court.[74] The decision was upheld on appeal.

Passenger Service

Policymakers have also considered imposing new rules to mandate quality improvements in airline customer service. As U.S. airports and planes became increasingly crowded during the late 1980s, and flight delays and late arrivals occurred more often, many people complained about poor service. Affluent business travelers in particular looked on the preregulation era with fond memories, perhaps recalling the long-ago joys of actually having an empty seat next to them and being served by a smiling attendant who was not harried. After a New Year's snowstorm in 1999 left thousands of Northwest Airlines passengers trapped inside aircraft on the Detroit tarmac for 11 hours, Congress began considering legislation to enshrine in law passenger "rights," such as being quoted the lowest available fare, receiving accurate information about flight delays, and getting larger awards for lost baggage. The effort was supported by the American Society of Travel Agents, the Consumers' Union, and the National Airline Passengers Coalitions. The major air carriers vigorously protested the need for the legislation. An airline industry spokesperson warned that "all the economic and social benefits of deregulation we take for granted will be at risk."[75] The congressional measure was forestalled after the airlines promised to institute a voluntary program to reduce flight delays and improve customer service.[76] While some members like John McCain continued to insist that an enforceable passenger bill of rights was needed, most lawyers argued that voluntary agreements were preferable.

After the September 11 attacks, security matters overwhelmed concerns about lost luggage, but this is the kind of populist issue that captivates Congress and it could easily come back. If the issue does return, however, it likely will be because a political entrepreneur sees an opportunity to gain attention, not because the public is clamoring for action. While people like to complain about their harrowing airline experiences, 75 percent of the flying public is satisfied with the job the nation's airlines are doing, according to a 2005 Gallup poll. Frequent flyers seem to understand that there is a tradeoff between fares and service quality: 61 percent say their flying experiences are "about as good as can be expected given the circumstances," and only 29 percent say providers can make air travel "much better for passengers without raising ticket prices significantly."[77]

Small Community Service

Another issue policymakers have periodically expressed concern about is the level of service in small and medium-sized communities around the nation. "Deregulation has been an unmitigated disaster for most rural areas and smaller communities," claimed Senator Bryon L. Dorgan (D-ND) in 1999.[78] "I voted for airline deregulation, and I apologize publicly," Senator Ernest F. Hollings (D-SC) said in early 2001.[79] When Congress deregulated the airlines, it established the Essential Air Service Program to provide subsidies to air carriers servicing small communities not located near major airports. The program was supposed to be transitional, giving small communities and airliners a decade to adjust to the competitive market. While the subsidies were supposed to end in 1988, Congress has kept the program going.

Spending has fluctuated over time. Budget shortfalls in the 1980s and early 1990s caused DOT to eliminate service guarantees and support for communities that are within 70 driving miles of a large or medium hub airport. Spending increased during the latter half of the 1990s. While the subsidies are large on a per-passenger basis, they are still too small to guarantee the quality of service that passengers desire. As a result, relatively few people who live in these communities use the federally subsidized air service, and the number of passengers served by the program has declined over time. The costs of the program rose from $37 million in 1995 to $113 million in 2002, but total passenger enplanements per subsidized community declined from 592,000 to 477,000 over the same period.[80] Many people preferred to drive or fly out of nearby airports with cheaper fares or more flights. In 2000, the median number of passengers of each EAS-subsidized flight was just three.[81]

The continued existence of federal subsidies for small community service more than a quarter-century after deregulation is not altogether surprising. Politicians from rural areas like the program and most taxpayers are indifferent to it—the costs are too diffused for them to notice. While federal subsidies are arguably inefficient—if states derive economic benefits from air service to small communities, they could provide the subsidies themselves—they do not jeopardize the sustainability of the reform itself. On the contrary, the provision of the subsidies is premised on a basic acceptance that route and pricing decisions should be made by the marketplace. The transition payments were always intended for marginal communities, and the eligibility criteria have been tightened over time.

The program has not expanded for two main reasons. First, commuter airlines are increasingly reluctant partners in the small community program. The program is dependent on small 15-to-19-seat propeller planes, but the commuter lines are more and more using 50-seat regional jets. In addition, high labor turnover has resulted in periods of heavy flight cancellations, which in turn have harmed the program's reliability. As one analyst notes, the natural incentives of the commuter lines are to "find ways to escape the program" rather than to put energy into developing small community markets.[82]

Second, deregulation has not in fact been an unmitigated disaster for small communities. While some small communities have been losers, many others have been winners. Some cities that initially attracted low-fair carriers later lost them. Others that were losers later gained when discount carriers began operations at relatively proximate airports. With carriers largely indifferent to the program, and a constantly changing set of affected communities, the subsidy program has generated enough support to maintain itself but not enough to undermine the basic commitment to the market process.

Government Aid After September 11

A key test of the sustainability of any policy reform is what happens when there is an unanticipated exogenous shock that suddenly transforms the political environment. Do policymakers abandon the reform, pushing a new line of policy development? Or is the continued maintenance of the reform taken for granted even as other policy arrangements are fundamentally revised? For airline deregulation, the key test came on September 11, 2001. The terrorist attacks forced the government to temporarily shut down the nation's airports for several days. After the airports were reopened, many Americans were reluctant to fly, and the airlines suffered heavy financial losses.

Within weeks of the terrorist attacks, Congress passed a $15 billion assistance plan to help the airlines recover. Airlines would have to document their direct losses from the attacks to qualify for a share of a $5 billion federal grant. The federal government also agreed to provide up to $10 billion in loan guarantees to help airlines gain emergency access to capital. The Department of Transportation directed the grant program. The loan guarantees would be managed by a four-member Air Stabilization Board consisting of officials from the Departments of Treasury and Transportation, the Federal Reserve, and the General Accounting office. The House passed the airline aid bill 356-54, and the Senate cleared it by voice vote.[83] The speed with which Congress approved this package was a tribute not only to the ability of American government to move quickly in times of crisis, but also to the political clout of the airline lobby, which extracted more money from taxpayers than their industry lost during the brief shutdown. While the airline industry is often internally divided, the bailout package demonstrated that it remains a formidable actor when it is united. The airlines drew on the resources of 27 in-house lobbyists, supplemented by lobbyists from 42 Washington firms, and included former White House aides and former Republican National Committee chairman, Haley Barbour. The airline lobby focused its efforts on leading members of Congress. The industry did have some strong arguments to make: The government had grounded their planes for security reasons, costing the airlines millions of dollars in lost revenues. In addition, industries related to air travel, such as tourism, had connections to virtually every congressional district in the nation. House Speaker Dennis Hastert's Illinois district, for example, had strong ties to Chicago's O'Hare International Airport and United Airlines. "It was masterful," said Senator Peter G. Fitzgerald, an Illinois Republican who opposed the airline rescue package. "The airline industry made a full-court press to convince Congress that giving them billions in taxpayer cash was the only way to save the Republic."[84] The White House originally proposed giving $5 billion to the airlines but without loan guarantees. The Administration ultimately offered a compromise proposal that created a special board to oversee the loan guarantees and to ensure that loans did not go to airlines that were insolvent.

A critical dilemma for the Air Transportation Board was helping the airline industry recover without artificially interfering with the marketplace. U.S. airlines, particularly the legacy carriers, were in deep trouble even before September 11. During the late 1990s economic boom, business travelers willingly paid high fares to avoid Saturday night stay-overs, and labor unions won rich new contracts. But in the months leading to September 11, the economy slowed, and business passengers started to balk at high ticket prices. The legacy carriers faced intense competition from low-cost airlines, and the growth of the Internet empowered consumers to search for the lowest possible fares. The combination of greater competition and price transparency placed unprecedented pressure on the legacy carriers to reduce their costs and cut capacity. While airline deregulation occurred more than 25 years earlier, some of the most significant competitive changes were occurring only now, brought about by these very recent technological and economic changes.[85] Key lawmakers were emphatic that they did not want the Board to postpone the steps the legacy carriers needed to take to operate profitably in the new era of cut-throat competition. "We ought to respond to events from [September 11] forward, not the underlying problems that the airline industry may have created for itself prior to that," agreed Senator Christopher J. Dodd (D-CT).[86] Leading newspapers took similar editorial positions, warning that a bailout package would only push back restructuring in an industry with excess capacity.[87] Yet the struggling carriers pushed hard for government assistance.[88]

The Air Transportation Stabilization Board was given an almost impossible mission. Before it could issue a loan guarantee to a carrier, it had to determine that the applicant was an important part of the national air network, that the loan would be prudently incurred, and that the applicant could not easily raise the money privately. In sum, the Board could only assist strong carriers with sound business plans, but if a carrier's business was strong and sound, it would have little trouble raising capital privately, rendering it ineligible for government assistance. The Board could not eliminate this tension. All it could do was try to manage it.[89]

The Board wound up not using most of the $10 billion available under the loan guarantee program, approving only 7 of 16 applications for a total of $1.6 billion (Table 7-4). Many airline interests were disappointed the Board did so little. "The White House opposed the Board from the beginning, and the Board has made applications too difficult ever since," complained Duane E. Worth, president of the Airline Pilots Association.[90] Despite the intervention of Speaker Hastert on its behalf, United Airlines was rejected three times for loan guarantees.[91] The Board rejected United's first application for a $1.8 billion guarantee in late 2002, saying its costs were too high and its business plan inadequate.[92] It rejected a second application from United for a $1.6 billion loan, arguing that the airline has not shown that it was a necessary part of the nation's commercial aviation system or that it could not get the capital it needed on its own.[93] United then reduced its request by $500 million, but the Board voted against its application by a 3-0 vote and told the airline it would not be given a fourth chance.[94]

While some experts complained that the existence of the Board had reinforced the industry's dependence on Washington, the government's assistance ultimately offered no reprieve from competition for the struggling big carriers. While they suffered heavy losses after the terrorist attacks, American, Continental, Delta, and Northwest all decided not to apply for loan guarantees because they wanted to avoid the Board's scrutiny and having to give the government a stake in their businesses. US Airways received $900 million in loan guarantees, more than any other carrier, yet was unable to escape bankruptcy. The main airlines that were helped by the loan guarantees were America West and Frontier, which already had low costs and good business models.[95] Frontier repaid its $63 million loan early in 2003. In addition to the original $15 billion bailout package, Congress also offered carriers some money after September 11 to help with insurance coverage and security costs. But John Mica, chair of the House Transportation Aviation Subcommittee, told airline executives in mid-2004 that they should not expect any additional federal aid, and that they had to be prepared to "fend for themselves" in the current marketplace.[96] In the end, the program guaranteed only

TABLE 7-4
Federal Loans to Carriers After September 11

	APPLICATIONS FOR THE AIR CARRIER LOAN GUARANTEE PROGRAM			
APPLICANT	Applied	Request ($Millions)	Status	ATSB Decision
United Airlines	6/24/02	$1,100.0[1]	Denied	6/28/04[1]
US Airways	6/7/02	900.0[2]	Approved	3/31/03[2]
America West Airlines	11/13/01	379.6	Approved	12/28/01
ATA Airlines	6/13/02	148.5	Approved	11/20/02
Evergreen Int'l Airlines	2/25/02	90.0[3]	Withdrawn[3]	12/20/02[3]
Frontier Airlines	6/28/02	63.0	Approved	2/14/03[4]
Spirit Airlines	3/28/02	54.0	Denied	8/14/02
National Airlines	5/3/02	50.5	Denied	8/14/02
Aloha Airlines	6/28/02	40.5	Approved	12/23/02
Gemini Air Cargo	6/28/02	29.7	Denied	6/2/03
World Airways	6/28/02	27.0	Approved	12/30/03[5]
Great Plains Airlines	6/28/02	17.0	Denied	12/20/02
MEDjet International	6/28/02	7.7	Denied	11/26/02
Vanguard Airlines	12/6/01	7.5	Denied	7/29/02
Frontier Flying Service	1/29/02	7.2	Denied	5/31/02
Corporate Airlines	6/28/02	7.0	Denied	11/26/02

[1]Previously rejected 12/4/02 @ $1,800M and 6/17/04 @ $1,600M.
[2]Conditionally approved 7/10/02 and 2/11/03; restructured 3/12/04 with repayment of $250M.
[3]Conditional approval of $90M followed initial request of $148.5M; application withdrawn in June 2003.
[4]Conditionally approved 11/5/02.
[5]Conditionally approved 4/23/03.
Source: Air Transport Association

$1.6 billion in loans and actually earned a profit for the U.S. Treasury of more than $300 million.[97]

CONCLUSIONS

The airline deregulation case demonstrates that policy reform is a dynamic process in which outcomes are never completely settled. The collapse of many larger carriers, the rise and possible fall of the hub-and-spoke system, the re-configuration of the industry—these and many other developments were not predicted, or predictable, at the time of reform enactment. Deregulation has stuck in the face of these surprising events not because market competition has delivered only benefits—although most citizens *are* better-off—but because key private actors were forced to accommodate themselves to the new regime. Rather than these powerful actors generating the reform (deregulation), the reform has played a substantial role in generating the properties of the surviving actors.

Economic policymaking with respect to the airline industry has been successfully reconfigured through changes in both institutions and group affiliations. Airline deregulation fundamentally destroyed the structural underpinnings of the old policy subsystem. The CAB was abolished, eliminating the government's major institution for regulating entry and determining ticket prices. Had the CAB continued to exist, it is probable that more extensive interventions would have taken place, especially given media attention to the airline industry's problems and the presence of key politicians in both the executive and legislative branches who were supportive of significant regulatory interventions. The reform has also created positive policy feedback effects. While the major carriers fought deregulation's adoption vehemently, once it occurred they were forced to adapt their business strategies and long-term capital investments to market competition. Airlines that couldn't compete in the harsh new environment either went bust or were taken over. Like all businesses, air carriers have tried to use their available political resources to gain economic advantage. By dramatically reducing government involvement in ticket pricing and route schedules, however, deregulation lowered the economic return from such rent-seeking efforts. Airlines still look to Washington for assistance to a degree that vigorously free-market economists find displeasing, but they can no longer count on being protected from competition. The most striking thing about the government's response to the September 11 attacks is not that it provided financial assistance to the industry but that it didn't fundamentally challenge the legitimacy of current policy arrangements. If the industry had been subject to government regulation when the planes brought down the World Trade Center, it seems inconceivable that deregulation would be on the policy agenda today.

The relative timing of the reform's enactment has had long-lasting effects on its durability. Deregulation occurred just before Ronald Reagan was elected president, allowing the initial transition to market competition to occur under the protection of an ideologically sympathetic Administration. By the 1990s, the political climate had shifted, some of the weaknesses of the new system were becoming visible, and the public concerns that had originally sparked deregulation's adoption (e.g., price inflation) had largely faded. By then, however, deregulation had already been in place for more than a decade, and the economic organization of the airline industry had already shifted. A final reason airline deregulation has stuck is because the identity of the "losers" from reform has not been constant. Some small cities that complained about sacrificing low-fare services later gained them. In other cases, smaller cities have attracted low-fare carriers but then lost them because residents were not supporting them. By generating a constant ebb and flow in the fortunes of various interests and groups, the deregulated market has inhibited the development of a concentrated and aggrieved political constituency with a stake in deregulation's repeal.

In sum, the very fluidity and complexity of the deregulated market has inhibited significant government reregulation. Deregulation has generated new problems (e.g., crowded planes, flight delays, and so on) while foreclosing a policy alternative (extensive government regulation of prices and entry) that had once been feasible. The reform has endured not because it has eliminated economic frictions and political distress, but because it has changed the menu of policy solutions.[98]

CHAPTER 8

Making Pollution Control Pay: Emissions Trading for Acid Rain

ECONOMISTS HAVE LONG ARGUED that "command-and-control" regulation is a poor way to control pollution. The cost of curbing pollution typically varies widely across firms yet government regulations impose one-size-fits-all solutions. Some firms may be unable to meet pollution control requirements without shedding jobs. Others may have the capacity to reduce emissions below mandated levels, but government rules give them no incentive to do so. A cap-and-trade system—in which the government sets a cap on the total level of pollution, and individual firms obtain emissions allowances to use or trade as they wish—is generally a far more efficient solution.[1] Because the allowances constitute a form of wealth, firms face powerful incentives to employ whatever pollution abatement methods will minimize their costs, allowing aggregate pollution reduction targets to be met in the most socially cost-effective manner possible. In sum, "cap and-trade" programs harness the pursuit of private interests to the achievement of public goals—the *sine qua non* of reform sustainability.[2]

For two decades, economists tried and mostly failed to convince policymakers that a better way to reduce pollution is to establish a market for emissions allowances and let the private sector figure out the most efficient control methods.[3] Some environmental advocates viewed the concept of emissions trading as morally offensive since it seems to give businesses a "license to pollute."[4] Others believed emissions trading was an idea that could work in theory, but not in practice. Yet Congress in 1990 followed experts' advice and established an innovative cap-and-trade program to curb sulfur dioxide emissions.[5] In so doing, Congress withdrew substantial economic rents from well-organized constituencies, such as miners' unions, that profited from inefficient regulatory protections on the use of high-sulfur coal.

By any measure, this environmental policy reform has been a stunning success. The sulfur dioxide emissions trading market today is robust, and environmental outcomes have vastly improved. Sulfur dioxide emissions in the United States, which were predicted to climb without the program, have declined by 41 percent since 1980.[6] Signs of recovery are evident in some acid rain sensitive regions. Although initially viewed with skepticism, the acid rain program now enjoys the broad support of industry and environmental groups.

The emissions trading program constitutes a case of successful policy reconfig-uration—the strongest form of reform sustainability. It has changed the terms of the debate and become a platform for the launching of other environmen-tal policy initiatives. An array of private-sector actors—including utilities, pollution abatement technology firms, and brokers—have made extensive economic commitments based on the expectation that the emission trading market will remain active in the future. This self-reinforcing process has not only made the acid rain emissions trading market hard to dismantle, it has all but eliminated any reason for doing so.

THE PRE-REFORM SITUATION

Environmental policymaking is riddled with tensions and contradictions.[7] On the one hand, Americans overwhelmingly favor stricter laws to protect and improve the environment. Support for the environment is bipartisan and not confined to narrow ideological factions. On the other hand, Americans are pragmatic about their environmentalism. They do not favor pollution control at all costs. Industrial workers have a palpable fear that tough environmental mandates will cost them their jobs. And managers worry that installing expen-sive pollution abatement equipment will harm firm profits.[8] When pollution control measures are perceived to impose concentrated costs on identifiable groups, they may generate intense opposition, resulting in policy stalemate.

No environmental issue reflected these tensions more strikingly than acid rain during the 1970s and 1980s.[9] Technically known as "acid deposition," acid rain occurs when sulfur dioxide and nitrogen oxides react in the atmo-sphere to form sulfuric acid and nitric acid. When the acids fall to earth (as rain, snow, or dry particles), often hundreds of miles from their release points, they pollute lakes and streams, damage forests, and threaten human and ani-mal health. Most of the harm in North America was concentrated in the east-ern United States and parts of Canada. Beginning in the late 1970s, Congress attempted to address the acid rain problem, but a politically acceptable solu-tion was elusive.

Regional divisions and patterns of labor organization sharpened the conflict over the acid rain issue. The main source of acid rain was the burning of high-sulfur coal in electric utilities. Most of the high-sulfur coal came from mines located in West Virginia and other states east of the Mississippi. Western mines, in contrast, generally produced coal with much lower sulfur content. Western utilities burning locally mined low-sulfur coal therefore had much lower sulfur emission levels than Midwestern utilities. Coal miners in the Midwest and Appalachia, unlike those out West, were heavily unionized. The United Mine Workers claimed that any effort to impose tighter controls on sulfur dioxide emissions would force big power plants in states like Ohio to abandon high-sulfur coal and switch to the cleaner Western variety, threatening tens of thousands of good union jobs.[10] The UMW's arguments carried great weight with Democratic lawmakers.

Bowing to labor union pressure, Congress in 1977 amended the Clean Air Act of 1970 to require new power plants to impose scrubbers regardless of whether they burned clean or dirty coal. This change incensed owners of low sulfur–burning utilities and other Western interests. Congress also permitted large Midwestern power plants built before 1971 to continue using high-sulfur coal, thus leaving essentially untouched the "Big Dirties" most responsible for the acid rain problem. While environmental groups preferred stronger measures, they entered into a "strange bedfellow" coalition with high-sulfur interests and embraced the 1977 Clean Air Act Amendments, both to avoid antagonizing organized labor and because they thought the acid rain problem would quickly resolve itself as power plants with clean technology came on line.[11] But these expectations proved unrealistic. Because new pollution sources faced much tougher federal emissions controls than old ones, there was an economic incentive to keep existing plants in operation almost indefinitely.[12]

During the 1980s, acid rain became a salient issue on the Congressional agenda. Many hearings were held to gather testimony from environmentalists and others concerned about the degradation of forests and lakes in the U.S. and Canada (Figure 8-1). More than 70 bills to combat the acid rain problem were introduced in Congress over the next decade, most calling for reductions of between six and twelve million tons of sulfur dioxide per year.[13] While the bills were aggressively pushed by policy entrepreneurs such as Congressman Henry Waxman (D-CA), they were prevented from reaching the House floor by Energy and Commerce chairman John Dingell (D-MI).[14] In 1988, Environment and Public Works Committee member Senator George Mitchell (D-ME) spent months working with miners' unions trying to craft a compromise between high-sulfur interests and the environmental lobby.[15] Mitchell managed to win the tentative support of Senator Robert Byrd (D-WV) for an acid rain plan that would have eventually reduced sulfur dioxide emissions from power plants by ten million tons. The measure required older dirty plants to install scrubbers but would have let them pass on the costs to electricity ratepayers across the nation. The deal collapsed, however, at the eleventh hour after the National Clean Air Coalition, the key environmental group in the debate, signaled its opposition.[16] "A few who say they support the Clean Air Act joined with the many who oppose it," lamented Senator Mitchell. "They remained rigid and unyielding, wholly unwilling to compromise . . . in the meantime, the health of many more American children will suffer, more lakes will die, more forests will wither."[17] President Ronald Reagan's indifference to the acid rain problem further weakened the incentives for Congress to strike a compromise, despite mounting evidence that the existing regulatory approach was grossly inefficient. In 1984, for example, the Office of Technol-

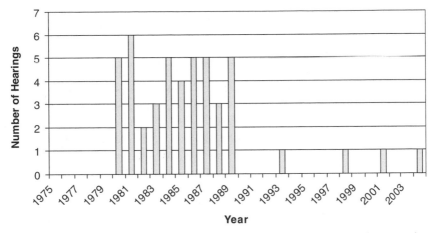

Figure 8-1. Congressional Hearings on Acid Rain, 1975–2004. *Source:* Policy Agendas Project, University of Washington.

ogy Assessment released a study concluding that if utilities were permitted to choose their own method for controlling sulfur dioxide, they could save about $1 billon a year over mandated controls.[18]

THE POLITICS OF REFORM ADOPTION

Ultimately, fresh thinking and new leadership were required to break the impasse.[19] Aiming to capture moderate voters concerned about pollution, George H. W. Bush in the 1988 campaign promised to be the "environmental president" if elected to the White House. After his victory over Michael Dukakis, Bush moved quickly to make good on his campaign promise.[20] While Reagan's environmental appointees had maintained tense relationships with environmental groups, Bush named former World Wildlife Fund and Conservation Foundation executive William Reilly to head the EPA.[21] Bush's chief of staff, John Sununu, had been a fervent supporter of strong acid rain measures during his previous tenure as governor of New Hampshire. In his first major address to the new Congress, President Bush pledged that he would shortly propose legislation to reduce acid rain emissions, stating the "time for study has passed and the time for action is now."[22] The political equation on the Hill also changed in ways that promoted reform prospects. As noted earlier, Senator Mitchell, whose state was among those most soaked by acid rain, had been an ardent supporter of tighter standards, but he was never able to win the outright support of Senate Majority Leader Byrd, who remained concerned that Mitchell's bills might cost his West Virginia constituents their jobs. In the

101st Congress, however, Democrats selected Mitchell to replace Byrd as Senate Majority Leader.[23]

Bush's Acid Rain Proposal

In June 1989, Bush submitted a major revision of the Clean Air Act calling for sulfur dioxide emission levels to be reduced 10 million tons below 1980 levels through the use of an innovative cap-and-trade system.[24] The reductions would be phased in over a decade. During Phase I (scheduled for 1996–2000), the owners of 107 of the nation's dirtiest utility plants would be required to bring their emission levels of sulfur dioxide down to 2.5 pounds per million BTU of electricity generated. Utility executives (subject to a veto of the governors in their states) were free to decide how to comply. They could, for example, decide to install scrubbers, switch to low-sulfur coal, or use less high-sulfur coal by establishing incentives for their customers to conserve energy. Utilities also could purchase allowances from other units that had surplus allowances to sell, but trading was restricted to plants within an individual state or utilities system. In Phase II, scheduled to begin in 2000, the standard would tighten to 1.2 pounds per MBTU. An additional 200–300 more plants would be brought into the market, and most of the restrictions on trading would be lifted.

Bush's acid rain proposal—quite similar to the plan ultimately enacted by Congress—drew heavily on the market-oriented ideas of the Environmental Defense Fund. While the concept of pollution markets dates to the 1960s, EDF economist Daniel J. Dudek first presented a detailed emission trading program for acid rain at a late 1987 Columbia University conference on new directions in environmental policy. The Bush Administration became aware of the proposal about six months later, after it gained the support of Project 88, a bipartisan group established to recommend environmental initiatives for the next president.[25]

The EPA had mixed reactions to the tradable emissions proposal. The agency had experimented quite successfully with a number of small market-oriented programs during the 1970s and 1980s.[26] For example, "netting," which was introduced in 1974, allowed a firm that created a new source of emission in a plant to remain in compliance with emission limits by reducing emissions from another source in the same plant. A second program—the so-called "bubbles" initiative—allowed firms to trade emission credits with outside firms on a limited basis. These experiments produced billions of dollars in cost savings without harming the environment, suggesting that market approaches to pollution control might have genuine promise. But the experiments were very narrow in scope and did not displace the preexisting command-and-control system. Trades could not occur under the bubble and netting programs without the preapproval of government officials, and firms were prohibited from buying or selling credits unless they were already in full regulatory compliance. These limitations prevented the full benefits of emissions trading from being realized.[27]

Bush's emission trading proposal was far more ambitious than anything the EPA had attempted before. Some EPA analysts viewed command-and-control regulations as a more certain method of pollution abatement. The agency was a frequent target of litigation in the 1970s and 1980s, and court rulings often construed clean air policy in terms of rights and duties, rather than an opportunity to devise more efficient ways to balance environmental benefits and economic costs.[28] "The EPA staff was not especially sympathetic" to the Bush proposal, Dudek recalled. "They saw our trading approach as untried, risky, and a burden for EPA to enforce."[29] The agency would have an important role to play under the new program. It would need to monitor pollution levels, ensure that plants had sufficient allowances for their emissions, and guarantee the integrity of the trading process.[30] Some lawmakers weren't certain the agency was up to the task. Rep Dingell, for example, questioned the agency's ability to do "an adequate and fair job in implementing this legislation."[31]

Organized interests also had mixed reactions to the initial release of the Bush proposal. Executives of Western utilities embraced the emissions trading plan, praising its flexibility. But Eastern utilities expressed concerns about compliance costs and the rate increases they would have to pass on to their consumers.[32] Environmental groups, with the exception of the EDF, were mostly reserved. David Hawkins of the National Clean Air Coalition stated, "The environmental community is starting out skeptical."[33] Unsurprisingly, the most hostile reactions were from mining unions. "All [the Bush proposal is] is a disincentive to burn coal, period," said Bill Banig, lobbyist for the United Mineworkers of America.[34] But Administrator Reilly signaled his strong support for the cap-and-trade approach, provided the administrative kinks could be worked out. After extensive study within both the White House and the EPA, the Bush Administration's cap-and-trade plan was approved for formal submission to Congress. A reworked version of the plan was ultimately enacted as Title IV of the Clean Air Act Amendments of 1990 (P.L. 101-549). The conference bill passed in the House by 401-25 and in the Senate by 89-10 and was signed into law on November 15, 1989.[35]

Building a Winning Coalition

A striking feature of the legislative debate over Bush's acid rain proposal was the extent to which the logic of emissions trading was accepted. As political scientist Kevin Esterling points out in his study of the role of information in legislative deliberation, even prospective reform losers conceded that a market-based approach to the acid rain problem was more flexible and effective than traditional command-and-control regulation.[36] That left opponents to focus their criticisms on the plan's workability and distributive fairness.[37] Three major issues generated conflict: first, whether compensation should be given to Eastern miners who might lose their jobs as Midwestern power plants switched to low-sulfur coal; second, whether the distribution of allowances was equitable; and finally, whether the dirtiest plants should receive subsidies to help them transition to the new system. Coalition leaders responded strategically to these three concerns by making design modifications and offering side payments. The amount of compensation provided to reform losers, however, was constrained by President Bush's credible threat to veto any clean air bill that raised taxes.

The most emotional and closely fought issue during Congressional debate involved whether to compensate the estimated 3,000–5,000 Eastern miners who were projected to lose their jobs under the acid rain program. The chief advocate for the miners was again Senator Byrd, who argued that Bush's proposal "would decimate high-sulfur coal and cause economic disruption in the Midwest."[38] As the new chairman of the Senate Appropriations Committee— with the power over the allocation of congressional earmarks—Byrd was seemingly well-positioned to protect his constituents. Byrd initially called for the government to spend up to $1.4 billion to give miners from 50 to 100 percent of their average salary and benefits over a six-year period, but lawmakers balked at the price tag. Byrd modified the proposal to reduce its maximum cost to $700 million. He then modified the proposal a second time to reduce it to $500 million. Byrd's scaled-down proposal lost by just one vote in the Senate, 49-50. The major reason the measure failed is that the White House convinced wavering lawmakers like Joseph Biden (D-DE) that it would veto any law that contained the Byrd Amendment.[39] The final bill included some aid for displaced workers, but it was mainly a symbolic gesture.[40] However, high-sulfur coal interests did win one concession. The conference committee agreed to give bonus allowances to Phase I units that complied with the law through installation of scrubbers instead of shifting to low-sulfur coal.[41]

The initial distribution of emissions allowances among polluting entities also sparked conflict. The Bush plan called for Phase I allowances to be distributed to incumbent generators at no charge, based on each plant's historic energy usage over the prior three years.[42] Auctioning off these valuable pollution rights was never on the table.[43] "Grandfathering" existing units was crucial to building political support for the stringent cap on emissions. Yet some market actors argued it would harm their interests. In particular, independent power producers that would be covered under Phase II were anxious that big Midwestern utilities would hoard their allowances, out of fear of being caught short in the future.[44] To ensure liquidity in the market and guarantee new or rapidly growing plants equitable access to allowances, the final bill required the EPA to hold back 150,000 or 2.8 percent of the 5.3 million allowances available for Phase I, and 250,000 allowances or 2.8 percent of the 8.9 million allowances for each year of Phase II. These allowances would be placed in a special reserve and auctioned off each year to the highest bidder.[45] The money raised at the auctions would then be returned on a pro rata basis to the firms from which the EPA withheld them to create the reserve pool, underscoring that the allowances were valuable economic assets.[46]

The final controversial issue concerned whether and how to ease the transition costs for Midwestern utilities that burned high-sulfur coal. Philip R. Sharp (D-IN), chairman of the Subcommittee on Energy and Power and a former political science professor, pushed a plan to levy fees on sulfur dioxide emissions from plants across the nation.[47] The revenue would be funneled to Midwestern utilities to compensate them for the cost of installing scrubbers. But Sharp's proposal violated President Bush's no-new-taxes pledge and was unacceptable to key lawmakers such as Henry Waxman who believed industry should bear the costs themselves.

Once they recognized they could not win direct compensation payments, Sharp and other Midwesterners on the conference committee shifted tactics and worked to obtain extra pollution allowances for utilities in their districts. The final bill—over the protests of EPA Administrator Reilly—contained an additional 200,000 Phase I credits for units in Illinois, Indiana, or Ohio.[48] Environmental groups went along with these additional credits in order to get the law passed. "Our basic position was the Midwest did not need the extra tons," said Marchant Wentworth, an environmental lobbyist. "The data supports that. But it was a political problem . . . [Representative] Sharp needed something big to take back."[49]

A Limited Compensation Scheme

The nature of the compensation or side payments provided to ease the initial adoption of a general-interest reform can signal a reform's future sustainability. The very fact that so much political lubrication was required to pass the Freedom to Farm Act, for example, was a bad omen for the reform's long-term durability, especially since there was nothing to prevent farm interests from demanding additional payments in the future. Seen in this light, the side payments provided in the acid rain program are notable for their immediacy, relative efficiency and self-limiting nature.[50] Dirty states actually did worse in winning additional allowances in Phase II than would have been predicted based on their representation on key congressional committees. This may have reflected the declining power of high-sulfur miners relative to pro-environmental interests.[51] Not only were the side payments contained in the acid rain bill relatively small, they were provided in a form (legal rights to emit pollutants rather than discretionary appropriations or tax breaks) that made it hard for high-sulfur coal interests to ask for more. Any future effort to increase the supply of allowances for Midwestern utilities in a particularistic way not only would seem unfair, it would *directly reduce* the market value of allowances held by plants in other states, ensuring a political backlash. *In sum, the main compensation payments for reform losers were not only front-ended (creating some immediate buy-in from economic interests), but they were relatively insulated from the political interventions of future Congresses.*

WHY THE ACID RAIN EMISSIONS TRADING PROGRAM HAS STUCK

Several factors have rendered the acid rain program politically sustainable over time. The first and most obvious reason is that the program has worked. Acid rain emissions have dropped significantly, compliance costs have been remarkably low. It is hard to argue with success. Second, the EPA has overseen the evolution of the emissions trading market with an appropriate mix of firmness and restraint. The agency has treated emissions allowance as property rights, promoting confidence in the market. At the same time, the agency has implemented a very stringent emissions monitoring system to prevent sources from exceeding their allowances.

Shifts in coalitional dynamics have also contributed to the reform's sustainability. Actors previously uninvolved in the environmental policy debate—including brokers who earn commissions on allowance trades—have become key players in the arena. Finally, the rules of the acid rain program have encouraged private actors to make asset-specific long-term investments. If a firm has more allowances than it needs to cover its emissions in any given year, it may save the surplus for future use or sale. This unique intertemporal design feature ("banking") has generated a process of self-reinforcement, in which regulated firms develop major stakes in the program's future maintenance.

Environmental Policy Achievements

One excellent reason the emissions trading program has endured is because it has been good for the environment. While a full evaluation of the 1990 Clean Air Amendments is beyond the scope of this chapter, a recent analysis of Title IV estimates annual benefits in 2010 at $122 billion and costs for that year at $3 billion—*a 40 to 1 benefit-cost ratio.*[52] Total annual emissions of sulfur dioxide in the U.S. fell from by five million tons between 1990 and 2004—a decline of about 34 percent—despite a tripling in fuel usage over this period (Figure 8-2). The decline in emissions has resulted in tangible improvements in environmental conditions, such as fewer acidic lakes.[53] There is little doubt that Title IV was responsible for these improvements. While emission levels fell steadily during the 1980s, the reduction in the first year of the program's implementation was much greater than during any prior year.[54] The positive impact of the

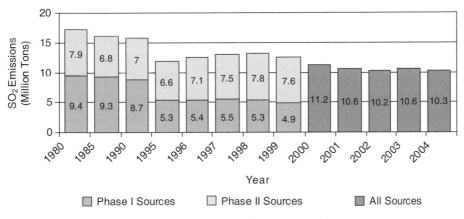

Figure 8-2. Trends in SO$_2$ Emissions, 1980–2004. *Source:* EPA

Acid Rain program has been broadly acknowledged. The major environmental policy worry about the establishment of a nationwide acid rain trading market is that it would create hotspots, meaning spikes in pollution in concentrated areas or during specific time periods. The fear was that dirty Midwestern plants would buy up all the allowances in order to maintain their existing emissions levels. Acid rain reductions might be achieved not by decreasing acid deposition in the eastern part of the country where reductions were most critically needed, but rather by making the West even more pristine.[55] But these fears have not come to pass. The largest SO$_2$ emissions reductions have been achieved in the highest SO$_2$-emitting states, including Pennsylvania, West Virginia, and Ohio.[56] According to the EPA, "trading did not cause geographic shifting of emissions or increases in localized pollution" and the human health and environmental benefits have been "delivered broadly."[57] The wide distribution of benefits has been helpful to the program's appeal because clean air has been framed in terms of legal rights, available to all.

A Robust Market Emerges

In 1992, the Tennessee Valley Administration publicly inaugurated the emissions trading market by announcing it had purchased the right to emit 10,000 tons of sulfur dioxide from Wisconsin Power and Light.[58] It took a long time for the new market to grow. Trading volume was initially quite low. Indeed, a 1995 news article in *The New York Times* raised the distributing possibility that the emissions trading "market is simply not working."[59,60]

The market was slow to consolidate itself for several reasons. First, because mandated emissions reductions were phased in over several years, there was no sense of urgency to buy and sell allowances immediately. Second, many utilities simply lacked experience with the new market. Their expertise was in scrubbers, not pollution credits. "You have a lot of really bright engineers who have a preference for technology over financial tools," said one New York broker for emissions trades.[61] Finally, the market was subject to high transaction costs. Early trades "required considerable legal advice, cost as much as $5 per ton in brokerage fees, and took months to complete."[62] By 2004, however, transaction fees had fallen to 50 cents per ton, and trades could be completed in a matter of weeks.[63] Unlike the market-trading experiments of the 1980s, the Acid Rain Program eliminated the cumbersome preapproval of individual trades. Private parties handled the deals themselves, with the assistance of professional brokers. The number of allowances traded increased about 400 percent, from 881,852 to 4,407,302, between 1994 and 1996.[64] The market was conservatively valued at $2.5 billion in 2003.[65]

Early trades were mostly between economically related organizations—such as multiple plants of a single firm. Residual political uncertainty existed about how state public utility regulators would treat allowance transactions in setting rates, dampening power plants' willingness to make deals with other entities. But the market became more efficient over time as public and private actors gained knowledge of how the market worked.[66] By 2004, about half of all transactions took place across firm boundaries (Figure 8-3). Active futures emerged at the New York Mercantile Exchange, providing speculators with the opportunity to buy and sell sulfur dioxide emissions options.[67] The SO_2 market today is both mature and liquid. It features an active spot market as well as multiple hedging instruments including forwards, options, future vintage trading, and swaps.[68] The EPA web site identifies some 14 brokers that buy and sell allowances, as well as four environmental organizations that retire allowances, meaning they purchase them in order to prevent the allowances from being used to offset emissions.[69]

While most emission allowances have been traded privately, annual allowance reserve auctions have also been successful. The first reserve auction, held in 1993, reaped about $21 million.[70] The 1999 auction generated $53.5 million. The Chicago Board of Trade initially won the right to administer the auctions in a three-way bidding war with the New York Mercantile Exchange and the New York–based financial broker Cantor Fitzgerald.[71] The bidding war took place despite the fact that the winning bidder was not compensated by the EPA for conducting the auction, and (unlike brokers for the regular allowance trading system) was not permitted to charge fees. All three bidding firms sought to position themselves to sell other market-oriented environmental products in the future.[72]

The Durability of Property Rights

A precondition for the emergence of a successful pollution trading market are secure property rights. A market will not develop if potential traders fear *ex*

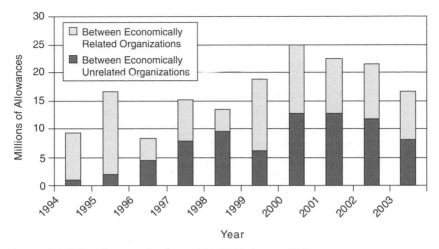

Figure 8-3. SO$_2$ Allowance Trading, 1994–2003. *Source:* EPA

post governmental confiscation of their allowances. To be sure, political un-certainty cannot be eliminated entirely. Future Administrations and Con-gresses always retain the legal authority to revise the rules of the allowance trading game—just as tomorrow's political actors are free to alter taxes or regulations that affect the value of *any* economic asset. The key issue is therefore not whether the property rights in emissions allowances have been absolute, but whether they have been "secure enough" to promote investor confidence.

The historical experience suggests they have been. The 1990 Act itself expressly states that an allowance "does not constitute a property right."[73] This provision—which was included in the law to protect the government from having to defend itself against alleged "takings" violations if it subse-quently lowered the SO$_2$ emissions cap—initially led some skeptics to say that the market-building effort was bound to fail.[74] Yet, in practice, the al-lowances have been treated by the EPA as de facto property rights.[75] The al-lowances are freely tradable, and when the program began, the EPA "con-sciously allocated allowances to eligible parties for years beyond 2010 to provide confidence that they would be treated essentially as durable prop-erty rights."[76] As one legal scholar notes, the fact that the right to emit sul-fur dioxide is not absolute *lowers* the economic value of the allowances, but does not destroy it.[77]

Like any well-functioning competitive market, the sulfur dioxide allowance market continually takes into account new information, and changes in al-lowance prices frequently reshuffle the identities of market winners and losers. The initial price for emission allowances was close to $150 per ton. Average prices then fell to about $70 by 1996, after which they rose to about $200.[78] One reason early prices were relatively low is because an exogenous policy shock—railroad deregulation—reduced the cost of transporting low-sulfur coal from Wyoming to the Midwest. This made it easier than anticipated for utilities to comply with their emissions caps, reducing the market demand for allowances.[79] Allowance prices remained fairly steady over the remainder of the 1990s, except for a temporary jump in 1999 due to planning for Phase II. By late 2004, however, allowance prices had climbed significantly to $700, closer to the price level expected when the program was first designed. A major reason for the increase in prices in 2004 is because the EPA was then weighing a new clean air rule (discussed in the following) that would require additional reductions in sulfur dioxide emissions from Eastern utilities. The allowance trading market is efficient enough to take into account fresh information like this almost immediately. "Usually companies don't get a clear signal until after [an environmental] rule is finalized," said Brian McLean, director of the EPA's Office of Atmospheric Programs. "But it's clear the [allowance] prices were rising as we started to discuss the new program. They anticipated the change."[80]

When allowance prices climbed, many utilities found themselves priced out of the market. It became cheaper for them to install advanced scrubbing equipment and use *high-sulfur* coal than to purchase credits from other sources. The effect has been to provide a massive economic windfall to the high-sulfur mining industry. "Over the next five years, Consol [a high-sulfur coal firm] will nearly double its coal cash flow due to the phenomenon of high-sulfur coal being priced upward due to the number of scrubbers being added, and if coal prices rise it will do even better," said one industry expert.[81] *In sum, a number of the economic interests that initially opposed the enactment of the Acid Rain Program have developed a stake in the reform's maintenance.*

Credible Enforcement

The sustainability of a cap-and-trade program requires not only low transaction costs so that actors can deal, but also transparency to demonstrate that promised emission reductions are being achieved. Here again, the EPA has governed the emissions trading market effectively. When the market was first opened, court challenges to EPA acid rain rules and the lack of an official allowance tracking system increased nervousness among potential traders. The EPA hoped it could get away with maintaining a compliance tracking system, rather than a more elaborate system that would record individual trades. But no private entity stepped forward to assume the burden of recording allowance trades. EPA staff recognized the agency would have to fill this gap to enable the market to function.[82] The EPA publicly recognizes any trade in which an allowance is used for compliance.

Sulfur dioxide emissions are subject to a continuous emission monitoring system (CEMS). Affected sources must report hourly emissions data each quarter. These reports are then posted on the EPA web site. The EPA uses computer programs to audit the submitted reports for integrity and to prevent and detect errors.[83] If a utility exceeds its SO_2 emissions, the EPA imposes a stiff penalty of $2,000 per ton, indexed to inflation. In 1997, the penalty was about twenty-five times the value of current allowance prices. Utilities that break the rules also have their allowance holdings reduced the following year.[84] Compliance has been extraordinarily high, approaching 100 percent. In 2004, for example, only four units out of 3,391 were out of compliance, meaning they did not possess enough allowances to cover their annual emissions. The owners of the four units were fined approximately $1.4 million.[85]

The EPA itself has thus been a major contributor to the reform's sustainability. The agency has provided the institutional supports and enforcement mechanisms without which the market could not function while simultaneously allowing market forces to determine the price, ownership, and utilization of allowances. As a study by leading environmental economists concludes, "The EPA deserves significant credit for resisting opportunities to review and approve compliance and trading decisions by private parties and for focusing instead on the integrity of emissions monitoring and on a strict, no excuse, banker-type accountability for emissions and allowances."[86]

Private Sector Reactions

With the exception of the initial displeasure of high-sulfur coal miners' unions, the reactions among private actors to the creation of the emissions trading market have been overwhelmingly positive. One piece of evidence is the absence of intense conflict over the program's implementation. When the EPA tried to enforce Clean Air Act regulations in the 1970s and 1980s, it was constantly forced to defend its actions in court. The EPA became a leading governmental poster child for Americans' penchant to resolve political conflicts through protracted and highly adversarial litigation.[87] In sharp contrast, there have been few legal challenges to emissions trading, "and none of the challenges [have] delayed implementation of the program."[88]

The private sector has embraced emissions trading for two main reasons. First, and most directly, emissions trading—in contrast to the rigidity of command-and-control regulation—gives power plants the flexibility to identify the least costly ways to reduce emissions. Plants may decide to switch to low-sulfur coal, or they may opt to install scrubbers or purchase allowances from other sources—whatever makes most economic sense given their own production functions. Utilities not only can make their own choices, they can *revise* their pollution abatement strategies over time if doing so makes sense, given changes in market conditions. All this promotes huge efficiency gains. In sum, the *emissions trading market* has been institutionalized—but the strategies of individual market actors are not "locked in," except as a result of their *own* prior irreversible investment decisions. According to the Government Accounting Office, compliance costs fell from $1.3 billion under traditional regulation to $725 million in 1997.[89]

The emissions trading market not only has been embraced by regulated sources, it has generated support from an array of private sector actors, including brokers, traders, and pollution-abatement firms. The creation of the Acid Rain Program has transformed investment patterns in at least three industries. First, the increased demand for low-sulfur coal by some eastern utilities encouraged new investments in rail technology to transport coal.[90] This market demand, coupled with deregulation of the railroad industry, led to improvements in coal hoppers and track upgrades. Second, emissions trading transformed the technology of scrubbing. Before 1990, scrubber systems generally included a spare module to maintain compliance with emission rules when any one module was inoperative. Once firms could use emissions allowances to cover any temporary outages, they no longer needed spares, reducing their capital costs by as much as a third. Furthermore, because sources could bank their excess allowances, there was a growing demand for improvements in scrubber design.

Finally, the creation of the sulfur dioxide emissions trading market essentially created a new industry of brokers and traders who handle most purchases and sales of emissions allowances and futures contracts. There is real money to be made in handling these deals. One hedge fund, TEP Trading Two, posted returns of 10 to 20 percent in 2005–06 as allowance prices rose. "If you can channel greed, for lack of a better term, you are going to clean up the environment a whole lot faster than a government saying thou shalt reduce pollution," said the firm's manager.[91] In the late 1990s, brokers who served the Acid Rain Program formed a trade organization, the Emissions Marketing Association, to promote market-based emissions trading.[92]

Emissions Banking as a Self-Reinforcing Process

One of the most important reasons for the success of the Acid Rain Program is that a major element of its policy design—emissions banking—generates a self-sustaining process. Sources that reduce their emissions below required levels may "bank" the surplus allowances for future use, or sell them to other utilities. Banking promotes the program's political maintenance in two ways. First, banking lowers compliance costs by giving firms flexibility in the *timing* of their investments in pollution abatement technology. Many investments in abatement technology are asset-specific and irreversible. Without allowance banking, sources would face strong incentives to make "just in time" investments to satisfy immediate emissions compliance requirements. Banking al-

TABLE 8-1
Origins of 2004 SO$_2$ Emissions Allowances

Type of Allowance Allocation	Number of Allowances	Explanation
Initial Allocation	9,191,897	Initial allocation in 1990 Act, based on units' historic usage
Allowance Auction	250,000	Special reserve for allowances allocated at market
Opt In	99,198	Allowances for units entering the program voluntarily
Total 2004 Allocation	9,541,085	
Total Banked Allowances	7,574,959	
Total 2004 Allowable Emissions	17,116,044	

Source: EPA, *2004 Acid Rain Progress Report*, 5.

lows firms to choose whatever investment schedule is most economical given their particular situations.[93] Because regulated firms retain more discretion over their own financial operations, they are far more accepting of emissions trading than traditional command-and-control regulation. Second, banking encourages firms to make early emissions reductions and hold some pollution credits either as assets that could be sold for cash or to cover their own emissions in the future. Any repeal of the emissions trading program would cause those long-term investments to be lost. "Once firms had built up a bank of unused allowances," a study by the environmental research organization Resources for the Future observes, "they had a vested interest in maintaining the value of those banked credits, and thus in furthering the program itself."[94]

During the program's early years, utilities "overcomplied" with emissions limits, banking nearly 11.6 million allowances by the end of Phase I. When Phase II began in 2000, firms began to withdraw allowances from the bank. Emissions have exceeded annual allowance allotments, but emissions are still far lower than they would have been in the absence of the program. In 2004, there were 17.1 million emissions allowances, of which 7.6 million had been carried over from prior years. Sources emitted only 10.3 million tons in 2004 (Table 8-1).

Policy Launching Pads

The U.S. acid rain program has attracted "worldwide attention and emulation," serving as a platform for new political actions.[95] The program's success has spurred the development of other cap-and-trade programs from the regional to the international level.[96] The EPA has expanded emissions trading to pollutants like nitrous oxide and ozone. In the mid 1990s, the Los Angeles air basin created the first tradable permit program developed by a local jurisdiction. Called RECLAIM (Regional Clean Air Incentives Market), the program is designed to reduce emissions of both nitrogen oxides and sulfur dioxide emissions.[97] The Northeast NO_X Budget trading program began operations a few years later to reduce smog in selected states.[98] In addition, the Clinton Administration aggressively promoted emissions trading during the negotiations that led to the Kyoto Protocol, the international agreement to curb greenhouse gases. While the Bush Administration withdrew the United States from Kyoto, the treaty took effect in 2005. The European Union began trading in carbon emissions in January 2005.[99]

In 2002, the Bush Administration sought to build on the success of the Acid Rain Program though its Clean Skies initiative.[100] The goal of the program was to curb SO_2, NO_X, and mercury emissions by an average of 70 percent below current levels by the year 2020. The more ambitious pollution reduction goal reflected a growing recognition of the health and environmental risks from ambient air pollution. Clear Skies would have established a new cap-and-trade system of these three pollutants while eliminating a number of remaining heavy-handed regulations, including a provision that requires companies to install new emissions controls in old power plants when they are upgraded. While many policy experts argued that this "new source" requirement created disincentives for the dirtiest plants to modernize and bred litigation, environmentalists argued that its repeal would increase the risk of hot spots.[101] Environmentalists also objected to the failure of Clean Skies to include a cap on carbon dioxide emissions. The Clear Skies Proposal died in the Senate Environment and Public Works Committee after Republicans James M. Jeffords (I-VT) and Lincoln D. Chafee (R-RI) joined all seven Democrats on the committee in opposition.[102]

Following the legislative failure of Clear Skies, the EPA took a step in the same direction through administrative action, adopting the Clean Air Interstate Rule (CAIR) in March 2005. CAIR sets new limits for the release of sulfur dioxide and nitrogen oxides from power plants in 28 mostly Eastern states and the District of Columbia.[103] Sulfur dioxide pollution is expected to decline by approximately 50 percent over the next decade under the rule, relative to allocations in Phase 2. To produce these pollution reductions, CAIR layers a new cap-and-trade program *atop* the existing Acid Rain Program.[104] While a number of business groups preferred Bush's Clear Skies initiative because of the greater political stability of policymaking by statue, most environmental groups applauded the rule's adoption.

The EPA gave careful consideration to interactions between the existing Acid Rain Program and the new cap-and-trade initiative. The core policy question was how to require additional reductions in sulfur dioxide and other pollutants while maintaining "the integrity of the title IV market for SO_2 allowances."[105] The agency explicitly recognized "the large investment in pollution controls that firms had made under Title IV that enable companies to sell excess emission reductions."[106] Title IV sources in the northeast would be required to comply by using more than one allowance for every ton emitted. This would, in essence, change the terms of trade. To avoid disrupting the market, the EPA provided for a *gradual phase-in* of the new exchange ratios. Allowances banked before the 2010 implementation date could be used at the existing one-to-one ratio. Allowances of vintage 2010 through 2014 would be worth 0.5 tons of SO_2 and those of vintage 2015 and later would be worth 0.35 tons of SO_2.[107] In a similar vein, the EPA opted to allocate SO_2 allowances under the CAIR program in proportion to *the original allocations under the Acid Rain program*. Several utilities complained that this allocation was inequitable, arguing that the distribution of CAIR allowances should reflect actual emissions levels from recent years.[108] The EPA's explanation for its chosen allocation approach is instructive.

> If the EPA adopts an approach that does not preserve the structure of the title IV allowance market and the value of those allowances, the confidence in the cap-and-trade policy instrument . . . would likely decline. Such an outcome could result in a reduced willingness of the owners of sources . . . to invest in control technologies . . . or to purchase allowances for compliance, for fear that the rules might change. . . . The preservation of title IV allowances for use in CAIR, then, is integral to the viability and effectiveness of both title IV and the CAIR trading.[109]

In sum, the market-based line of policymaking initiated in the Acid Rain program has been deliberately extended. Furthermore, the investments stimulated by the existence of the allowance trading market have been respected to the extent feasible given the political desire to impose a tighter cap on emissions levels.

CONCLUSIONS

The acid rain program is a prime example of a general-interest reform that neither public opinion nor business preferences would have simulated on their own. While Americans (and Canadians) clearly wanted the acid rain problem addressed, the notion that sulfur dioxide emissions could be curbed more cheaply and effectively through an emissions-trading market than through government regulations was not intuitively obvious. The general public *got* a novel emissions trading system; it did not demand one. The creation of the sulfur dioxide emissions trading market in 1990 must be seen not as the inevitable result of exogenous political forces, but as a remarkable victory for policy expertise and political leadership.

The reform's sustainability has been as impressive as its original enact-ment.[110] The emissions trading market has lasted not because it has "frozen in place" environmental outcomes, or even pollution control technologies, but rather because it has given firms the flexibility to find the cheapest emissions control methods in exchange for the achievement of overall pollution reduc-tion goals. That political bargain has stuck long after its enacting coalition left the political stage because the Acid Rain Program has worked well on the ground, because it has been embedded in well-designed governance structures, and because it has generated a new constellation of interests that have devel-oped stakes in the program. Emissions trading programs clearly are not envi-ronmental panaceas; they cannot be implemented unless technical conditions are favorable.[111] When those favorable conditions are obtained, however, these market-oriented reforms can reconfigure political dynamics in powerful and self-reinforcing ways.

CHAPTER 9

Conclusions: The Patterns and Paradoxes of Policy Reform

> Every abuse ought to be reformed, unless the reform is more dangerous than the abuse itself.
>
> —Voltaire

> Every reform was once a private opinion, and when it shall be a private opinion again, it will solve the problem of the age.
>
> —Ralph Waldo Emerson

IT IS NO SMALL THING to win the adoption of general-interest reforms in the United States. Reformers must convince a majority that existing policy arrangements are defective and that the role of government should change. Often, they must carry out difficult political tasks, including imposing losses on powerful clienteles and withdrawing concentrated benefits. Expert ideas, political entrepreneurship, side payments, and parliamentary tactics are often essential to reform adoption. But what is required to *initiate* policy reform should not be confused with what is required to *sustain* it. While the passage of a reform may offer immediate political dividends, sustaining the reform may be a losing proposition, even when doing so would generate net social benefits. It takes time for reforms to embed themselves in governing routines, but time is a luxury reform advocates may not have. Reform coalitions may hold power only momentarily, giving opponents an opportunity to wait for the political winds to shift. In sum, political uncertainty and contestation do not end when reforms are enacted. When reforms *do* stick, it is because they realign public authority, generate positive feedback effects, and, in many cases, unleash the creative destructiveness of market forces. When reforms fail to do these things, they are vulnerable to reversal or erosion. This is the basic lesson of sustainable reform in the United States. *Reforms endure not because they are "frozen in place" or because their background conditions do not change. Rather, they endure because they reconfigure the political dynamic.*

By way of summary and conclusion, this chapter draws out the central lessons from the analysis presented in this book. First, I discuss the broad implications for current debates in political science. Next, I review the main patterns and paradoxes that emerge from the case studies. I conclude with some practical lessons for governance.

THE LIMITS OF GENERAL-INTEREST LAWMAKING

My argument builds on an important political science literature regarding the passage of general-interest legislation.[1] R. Douglas Arnold in his insightful book *The Logic of Congressional Action* shows how coalition leaders can manipulate the procedural and information context of decisions to ensure that election-maximizing lawmakers are willing to cast votes for reform bills that impose costs on their constituencies and on organized interests.[2] The key to the Arnold model is that lawmakers are responsive not only to the fixed preferences of well-informed voters, but also to the *potential* preferences of constituents who could become active and attentive if provoked. Lawmakers want to avoid taking public stands that might come back to haunt them in a future election campaign. The task of coalition leaders is therefore to persuade lawmakers that it is a politically safer (or at least equally safe) to support a reform proposal than to oppose it. Coalition leaders do so through manipulation of the procedural context of votes and through the strategic framing of the policy debate.

Arnold's model is elegant and ingenuous, but it skirts the key question of what happens *after* the general-interest prevails in Congress. The existence of inattentive voters makes reform *possible*, but the preferences of such voters must somehow get institutionalized in governing routines or market processes if reforms are to become durable. Coalition leaders are the indispensable actors in the Arnold model. They would include leaders such as President Ronald Reagan, Congressman Dan Rostenkowski and Senator Bill Bradley in the tax reform case, and Senator Jacob Javits for ERISA. Without their initiative and creative contributions, general-interest reforms would not get on the legislative agenda or get passed.

Severe limits exist, however, as to what coalition leaders can achieve at the moment of reform enactment. First, reforms are seldom self-implementing. There is inevitably hard follow-up work to be done: administrative rules to write and enforce, political bargains to explain and defend, and long-term policy outcomes to monitor. Coalition leaders might perform this critical second-stage work, but they often lack the incentive or ability to do so.[3] Many issues and causes compete for their attention, and tackling new challenges often seems more rewarding than retackling old ones. Even if coalition leaders *do* remain interested in shepherding a reform through to its successful consolidation, they may not be in a position to do so. Coalition leaders can lose their ability to shape the agenda. Just a decade after tax reform, for example, almost the entire cast of key players was gone from power. (Ronald Reagan became an ex-president in January 1989, Dan Rostenkowski was forced to resign his leadership post under a cloud of corruption a few years later, and in 1996 Senator Bill Bradley announced he would not stand for reelection.) The politicians who succeeded each of these three men had very different tax policy agendas. In the strong civil service systems of some European parliamentary democracies, well-placed senior officials can promote a reform's sustainability. The U.S. federal bureaucracy, however, is heavily politicized and dominated by short-lived appointees who often lack the institutional memory or incentives to serve as agents of reform continuity.[4]

THE LIMITS OF STRUCTURAL POLITICS

If coalition leaders may not be around to safeguard their reform creations, and bureaucrats cannot be relied upon, perhaps reforms can be protected through structural design. Terry Moe argues that farsighted reformers recognize that their political enemies may one day be in power and therefore design cumbersome rules and procedures to insulate their reform achievements from future political contestation—even when doing so frustrates their own future political control. According to Moe, the desire to reduce political uncertainty results in the creation of durable yet irrational structures that are "flawed by design."[5]

While Moe's structural model offers powerful insights into long-term processes of policy development, it has three key limitations for an understanding of reform sustainability. First, Moe's framework largely focuses on battles over administrative structures at the initial moment of choice. It says relatively little about downstream structural developments. Yet post enactment institutional changes may be of critical importance in the trajectory of reforms. For example, the lapsing of budget deficit–control rules had massive implications for Congress's ability to sustain its 1986 commitment to tax neutrality and base broadening. *The institutional development story must be followed all the way through.*[6] Second, Moe rightly emphasizes the manipulation of political transaction costs, but his model gives scant attention to the role of interest-group investments and other policy feedback effects in the reform process. As the airline deregulation case study shows, the generation of asset-specific investments may be a far more influential source of reform sustainability than the creation of procedural veto points over the long run. Finally, Moe pays less attention to the key influence of *non-institutional* factors. General-interest policies are more than a bundle of structures and rules; they also embody "theories" about the proper interactions among people with specific capacities, ideas, and professional norms. The failure to adequately recruit, motivate, and train the federal purchasing workforce, for example, has threatened the long-term sustainability and effectiveness of a high-flexibility procurement system.

The fate of reforms also depends on their interaction with other unfolding developments, such as changes in the market price of crops in the farm subsidy case. The capacity of reforms to *absorb* changes in their environment is an important source of policy resilience.[7]

BEYOND THE DICHOTOMY OF PUNCTUATED EQUILIBRIUM

My argument also suggests the limitations of punctuated equilibrium models of policymaking, which hold that long periods of stability are followed by short bursts of rapid change.[8] As Kathleen Thelen has persuasively argued, strong versions of punctuated equilibrium models are often based upon a sharp juxtaposition between periods of stasis and innovation, but the real world often does not admit to such neat divisions.[9] Consider the mixed fate of agricultural reform. The subsidy regime has remained largely intact (at least though 2007), even as farmers' planting decisions have been largely deregulated. Similarly, the corporate side of the federal tax code has been relatively stable since 1986, amidst the rapid growth in tax expenditures for social purposes. *Parts of a policy system may be undergoing rapid transformation while other components remain stable.*

Not only can change and stability occur simultaneously, but the *pace* of major policy change may occur more slowly than is implied in punctuated equilibrium models. While change can indeed result from short bursts of rapid reform (or from rapid anti-reform thrusts), it can also unfold gradually.[10] There was no single moment, for example, when ERISA ceased promoting the retirement security of workers. Rather, the regulatory safeguards imposed by ERISA interacted with unexpected shifts in both employer and employee preferences to slowly establish a new U.S. pension regime organized around defined contribution plans.[11] Similarly, the Tax Reform Act of 1986 was never repealed, but twenty-odd years after its passage it is harder and harder to see evidence that it was ever enacted.

A third limitation of punctuated equilibrium models is that they downplay variance *among* punctuations. Yet policy punctuations are clearly not all the same. There is a critical difference, to invoke a physical analogy, between letting the air out of a balloon and piercing it with a pin. The balloon shrinks in both instances. But the second balloon is a "goner," while the first balloon is just waiting for an actor to perform a simple act (blow in air) to revert it to its former state. In a similar vein, general-interest reforms that challenge the policy status quo are not all created equal. Some have greater potential to generate durable change than others. A reform that recalibrates public authority or injects market pressures into a previously regulated economic arena is more likely to reconfigure interests, investments, and incentives than one that "just" withdraws public subsidies from some constituency.

Fourth, punctuated equilibrium models say relatively little about what happens *after* policy monopolies are destroyed.[12] The implication would seem to be that a new policy subsystem soon emerges to fill the resulting power vacuum. But policy dynamics can, at times at least, be far more complicated than that. As the airline deregulation case shows, the termination of the CAB and its associated regulatory structures unleashed powerful market forces subject to *no* actor's control. It is a stretch to describe the post-deregulation airline industry as a new "equilibrium."

Finally, punctuated equilibrium models suggest that policy change occurs through shifts in decision-making venues.[13] This is often the case. Yet venue shifts may be ephemeral or incomplete. Newt Gingrich temporarily shifted power over farm spending to the House budget committee in 1995–1996, for example, but the agricultural committee was soon able to regain control. After ERISA, control over corporate pension policy was only partially shifted to the PBGC. Decision-making authority was divided amongst Congress, the IRS, the courts, and multiple other institutional actors. While strategic players clearly do shop for venues to promote their reform projects, "decommissioned" venues can pop back up or reconstitute themselves. Rather than permanent venue shifts, it is sometimes more accurate to think in terms of *ongoing venue clashes* among sites with disparate powers and interests.

IMPLICATIONS FOR THE STUDY OF AMERICAN POLITICAL DEVELOPMENT

My argument builds upon the literature on American Political Development (APD) in its effort to bring a historical dimension to bear in the empirical study of policymaking, but it also seeks to challenge and add to this literature in several ways. In particular, I believe APD scholars should study a much wider array of public policies, be more attentive to the interplay between markets and governance, and devote far greater attention to what happens after the moment of legislative enactment.

An impressive historical literature exists on the enactment of procedural reforms within Congress as well as rich APD literatures on the expansion of U.S. administrative capacities and on the policy feedback from welfare state programs, but scholars have given much less attention to the dynamics of general-interest reform measures.[14] Over the past quarter-century, broad coalitions have repeatedly emerged in the United States in support of efforts to recast the agricultural, transportation, tax, environmental, and many other policy arenas. As the national government has grown larger and more cumbersome, the sense that existing programs and policies need renewal and repair has grown. There is a strong pragmatic problem-solving streak in American democracy that can be readily if not always successfully tapped into by policy entrepreneurs. To be sure, reform projects may serve as vehicles to advance narrow political agendas. For example, the Freedom to Farm bill was part of Newt Gingrich's attempt to consolidate the power of the new Republican majority on Capitol Hill, and procurement reform was part of President Clinton's attempt to rebuild public trust in activist government. Yet policy reforms often emerge out of the efficiency-oriented ideas of think tanks or academic experts and frequently generate bipartisan support. The policy reform process involves a struggle not only over the size and scope of the American state, but over the content and manner of specific policy interventions. The empirical study of general-interest reforms thus provides a more balanced portrait of the character of American national policymaking.

A troubling separation is apparent in the political science discipline in which political economists and rational choice theorists study markets (often with little attention to their historical and institutional contexts) and with which APD scholars study the political power of business (often with little attention to the social impact of economic decisions). More attention is needed from APD scholars, I believe, as to how *markets* shape politics and policymaking over time.[15] Many of the cases examined in this book involved conscious efforts to free or harness market forces by removing market-distorting subsidies or regulations or creating new marketable goods. Markets are complex social coordination mechanisms. They produce outcomes that cannot simply be "read" off the preferences of any individual officeholder or even a single dominant faction. Markets also exist in both politics and time. An understanding of the logic of market-oriented policy requires some knowledge of economics, but an understanding of the political sustainability of market reforms requires attention to institutional configurations and policy feedback. In sum, the study of policy reform provides an opportunity to develop a wider and more solid base of evidence to test claims in the APD literature.

It also provides an opportunity to enrich our understanding of *policy development*. As Paul Pierson stresses, historically oriented scholars must study not only *what* happened in the past, but *how* policies have come to be what they are.[16] All too often, however, the focus of policy scholarship is on the initial passage of a big piece of legislation. The problem with this empirical focus is that a lot of the action occurs "after the curtain falls on the high drama of legislative enactments."[17] As we have seen, self-reinforcing reforms can reconfigure the political dynamic while reforms that fail to gain traction may gradually disappear from political view. As Martha Derthick observes, policymaking consists of "a compound of exciting, innovative events in which political actors mobilize and contest with one another, and not-so-exciting routines that are performed without widespread mobilization, intense conflict, or much awareness of what is going on except the involved few."[18] These crucial subterranean routines exist even in the highest-profile policy sectors—as Derthick showed in her landmark book on the evolution of the Social Security program—but they are particularly important in more obscure but still important sectors like taxation and procurement. This is another reason to expand the empirical scope of APD inquiry: to tease out key developmental patterns.

The analytic challenge is to identify *mechanisms* of policy consolidation and collapse.[19] I have explicated four basic post-enactment reform paths (entrenchment, erosion, reversal, and reconfiguration) and showed how these paths are stimulated by distinct combinations of policy feedback effects. The existence of these four reform paths underscores that the absence of partisan conflict does not mean the lack of policy accomplishment, and that the most sustainable policy reforms may generate the most dynamic social change. By casting a broader empirical net, taking into account the influence of market forces, and thinking systematically about how policies unfold over time, APD scholars thus can learn not only about the broad contours of the American state, but also about the micro-level forces that drive specific policy outcomes.

EXPLAINING PATTERNS OF REFORM SUSTAINABILITY

The enactment of a policy reform, then, signals not the end of the political story, only the start of a new chapter. Many of the stories told in this book have been tales of disappointment and dashed expectations, although even reforms that have been seriously unraveled (e.g., the Tax Reform Act of 1986) often leave behind a significant residue of accomplishment. Other stories contain elements of irony or even farce (e.g., *rising* farm subsidies after the passage of the Freedom to Farm Act, *declining* enrollment in defined benefit pension plans after ERISA). Still others, such as the creation of a sulfur dioxide emissions trading market, have produced far sunnier outcomes.

What accounts for these patterns? Why do general-interest reforms have different trajectories after passage? The conditions associated with reform paths are manifold and complex, and the influence of any given explanatory factor is often contingent on the presence of other factors. Nonetheless, it is possible to reach some conclusions about the overall patterns of reform sustainability.

One important conclusion is that reforms may persist for reasons other than those which prompted the reforms' original adoption. In recent years, political modelers have argued that the longevity of public creations such as laws and agencies depends in part upon the partisan configuration of enacting coalitions as well as upon the persistence of these coalitions over time. According to this line of scholarship, the durability of previously enacted political bargains will be threatened, for example, when control of government flips from one party to another, or even when there are losses in the partisan composition of seats falling short of switches in party control. This argument has an empirical basis.[20]

My analysis suggests, however, that a focus on macrolevel partisan coalitions offers only limited insight into the substantiality of any *specific* general-interest reform.[21] First, reforms not infrequently collapse even when the partisan composition of their enacting coalitions remains stable. Consider the immediate reversal of Medicare Catastrophic Coverage Insurance. Consider too the reversal of farm subsidy cuts after 1996. Second, electoral trends may fail to generate the predicted policy effects. Airline deregulation passed in 1978, when Democrats controlled both Congress and the White House. The shift to divided government in 1981 might have been expected to have threatened the reform, yet it had the opposite effect. Ronald Reagan's election permitted the newly deregulated market to take wing with the protection of a conservative Administration. In contrast, the sustainability of the Tax Reform Act of 1986 "should" have been enhanced when President Reagan was succeeded in 1989 by his own vice president, yet George H. W. Bush almost immediately set about trying to undo it.

Reforms clearly can and do persist for reasons other than those which prompted the reforms' original adoption. Airline deregulation was adopted in response to concerns about rapid inflation, for example, yet it has lasted even though consumer prices have since stabilized. ERISA was primarily a response to funding problems in defined-benefit pensions, but today it sticks mainly because business groups favor its preemption of state health reform efforts. The political conditions at the moment of reform adoption can provide *clues* to future reform trajectories, but only clues. Indeed, even when a plausible story can be told about the impact of electoral coalitions on a reform's longevity, the real action may be happening much closer to the ground.[22] In sum, election outcomes are important, but policy development needs to be studied as a distinct political process in its own right.[23]

A second conclusion is that whatever benefits for sustainability it may offer, the initial passage of a reform by a lopsided majority provides no guarantees that the reform will be protected from subsequent attack.[24] Major general-interest reforms are typically enacted by bipartisan coalitions that emerge when (1) Washington elites agree upon the existence of a problem and the urgent need for the government to do something and (2) strong blame avoidance dynamics that lead lower-ranking actors to want to avoid being seen publicly as blocking action (see column two in Table 9-1 for the final passage votes on the reforms). Once reforms have been put in place, however, the blame avoidance dynamics can weaken, allowing opportunities to erode the changes without suffering political pain. Members of both parties were perfectly happy to hold hands and vote for farm subsidy cuts in 1995 and then to vote to restore the subsidies in

2002.[25] A large majority can vote for reforms—only to have other, equally lopsided majorities undo them later.

Third, the relative timing of reforms matters greatly.[26] All reforms face sustainability threats from external developments like changes in economic or macro political conditions, but it makes a huge difference *when* those threats arise in the life of a given reform. Agricultural reform offers an instructive example. Before farmers had the opportunity to learn how to get along without reliance on federal subsidies, and also before the agriculture market really adapted to the new system, their market incomes declined due to an exogenous shift in demand conditions. The subsidy cuts might have endured if market conditions had been more favorable for the first several years of Freedom to Farm's implementation. In contrast, one reason why the welfare reforms enacted under President Clinton have lasted is arguably because the labor market was so robust during the 1990s, providing almost ideal circumstances for the target population to adapt to the new system. By the time the economy took a downturn in early 2000, most former welfare recipients were working and the reform had been perceived as "successful" long enough to make it difficult for politicians to challenge that narrative. While counterfactual analysis is always hazardous, if the timing of the recession had been different, and unemployment had spiked five or seven years earlier, it is a reasonable bet that political support for maintaining 1990s-style welfare reforms would have weakened.[27] This underscores the role of historical contingency in the reform consolation process, as well as the limits to reformers' influence and control.

Fourth, reforms that prove unsustainable in key respects can nonetheless shape the development of subsequent public policies through negative lesson-drawing. A clear desire not to repeat the embarrassing reversal of the Medicare Catastrophic Coverage Act, for example, is a major reason Congress chose to make participation in the new Medicare prescription drug program voluntary and to push most of the costs onto general taxpayers.

The fifth and most important conclusion is that there are systematic patterns in reform trajectories. While the path of any given reform can never be preordained, there is nonetheless systematic variance across reforms in their respective prospects for policy sustainability. My analysis has centered on the influence of two factors: shifts in institutional configurations and the generation of policy feedback effects (Table 9-1).

Shifts in Institutions

Changes in institutions shape reform trajectories, but not all institutional changes have the same impact. As Karen Orren and Stephen Skowronek suggest, there is a clear hierarchy of institutional shifts.[28] The most powerful changes involve the termination of an existing instructional structure or capacity (*dismantling*), or the construction of a new institution (*institutional as-*

Table 9-1
Institutional Shifts, Policy Feedback, and Reform Trajectories

Reform	Final Passage Vote in House and Senate	Institutional Shifts	Interest-Group Feedback	Investment Feedback	Post-Enactment Trajectory
Tax Reform Act of 1986	292-136; 74-23	No shifts in legislative or bureaucratic structures; reform layered atop existing tax legislative process.	Tax sector is cluttered with constituency demands; groups fail to counteract one another; no major constituency emerges with a clear stake in TRA's preservation.	Negative or nonexistent policy feedback; most of the impacts of the reform were transitory.	Commitment to tax neutrality and base broadening gradually but unmistakably eroded over time. While corporate tax shelters were closed down, new individual tax shelters have popped up.
Freedom to Farm	318-89; 74-26	Narrowing of USDA governing authority over acreage set-asides; no changes in congressional committees; farm lobby–Congress nexus essentially unchanged.	Only modest changes in the configuration of agricultural interests; farm organizations remained potent in electoral politics.	Some agricultural interests develop stakes in maintenance of planting flexibility; investments in previously disfavored crops like soybeans increased significantly.	Subsidy cuts quickly reversed (Congress essentially says "Never mind!;") but deregulatory provisions (e.g., removal of acreage controls) have been largely sustained.
Airline deregulation	363-8; 83-9	Dismantling of the CAB via sunset provision.	Rapid and repeated shifts in the identities of sector actors as airline industry witnesses hundreds of start-ups, mergers, and bankruptcies.	Deregulation stimulates massive, often asset-specific, investments in new travel routes by carriers, airports, and myriad complementary interests and service providers.	Sustained despite many problems in the airline industry; dramatic reconfiguration of entire sector.

Procurement reform	1994 reform: 425-0; voice vote in Senate; 1995 reforms: 287-129; 56-34 (passed as part of defense authorization bill).	Displacement of authority over IT bid protests from GSA to GAO.	Reforms gain major support inside the federal procurement bureaucracy and among government contractors, but the reforms are not consolidated on Capitol Hill.	By all accounts, federal government made inadequate investments in hiring and training of procurement experts following the reforms, raising concerns about the long-term durability of a high-discretion acquisition system.	Deregulation of controls on many commercial items seems likely to persist, but congressional oversight dynamics continue to focus on fraud, waste, and abuse. The attempt to create a new culture of risk tasking, innovation, and entrepreneurship among contract officers never really gains traction.
Acid Rain Emissions Trading	401-25; 89-10	New EPA emissions monitoring and allowance banking systems.	Environmental groups, initially skeptical of emissions trading, became supportive; new actors emerged to service the market, including environmental allowance brokers.	Sulfur dioxide emissions trading develops into a multibillion dollar market. Allowance banking gives participating sources direct stakes in system's durability, and a range of private actors make economic investments based on expectation of the market's continuation.	Successful reconfiguration of acid rain policymaking; trading market deeply rooted.

Table 9-1 (Continued)
Institutional Shifts, Policy Feedback, and Reform Trajectories

Reform	Final Passage Vote in House and Senate	Institutional Shifts	Interest-Group Feedback	Investment Feedback	Post-Enactment Trajectory
ERISA	407-2; 85-0.	Creation of Pension Benefit Guaranty Corporation.	Reconfigured interests of, and coalitional patterns among, labor, large corporations, and some insurers, creating a broad lobby (ERISA Industry Committee—ERIC) to defend the preemption clause and other provisions against major revision.	Reform stimulated firms to expand and formalize HR divisions to comply with pension and welfare plan regulations.	Reform has stuck, but some of its most important downstream effects (e.g., shift to defined contribution plans) were largely unforeseen.
Medicaid Catastrophic Coverage Act	328-72; 86-11	No shifts in legislative or bureaucratic routines.	AARP leadership withdraws support for reform after revolt from own membership.	None.	Stunning reversal—one of the shortest lived pieces of social policy in U.S. history.

sembly). The prime example of dismantling was the elimination of the CAB via a sunset provision in the airline deregulation law. The belief that government could improve social outcomes by regulating the airline industry did not die out in 1978. With the CAB out of existence, however, airline regulators no longer possessed a semi-autonomous bureaucratic niche from which to launch new policy initiatives. The elimination of the USDA's legal authority to order acreage set-asides, in a similar vein, helped sustain the planting flexibility provisions of the Freedom to Farm Act. Institutional assembly is also important. The creation of the intertemporal allowance banking system successfully promoted the credibility of the sulfur dioxide emissions trading program.[29]

Next in the institutional design hierarchy are *displacements*, meaning the transfer of governing authority from an existing structure to a new one. While the new institutional venue may be more supportive of the reform's purposes than the original one, the old institutions may remain in tact, giving reform opponents a base from which to mount future challenges. The shift of bid protest review authority from the GSA to the GAO to reduce the amount of adversarialism and the length of delays in the federal procurement process, for example, did nothing to alter the behavior of congressional oversight committees or inspectors general's offices. Least influential of all, yet perhaps most common, are *layerings*—the placement of new rules and structures atop old ones with conflicting principles. Examples include the levying of redistributive charges on Medicare beneficiaries atop a Medicare program historically funded through general revenues and payroll taxes, and the grafting of a farm subsidy market-transition schedule atop an agricultural-congressional political exchange system keyed to the electoral cycle.

Effective institutional design is crucial when reforms contain multiple unrelated parts that were stitched together at enactment. Tax reform, for example, was the result of logrolling between advocates of lower tax rates and advocates of fewer tax breaks. While there is an *economic* connection between these two tax reform components, there is no necessary *political* connection: tax rates can, and were, lowered in the 1990s even as tax breaks proliferated. In contrast, a market-oriented reform like airline deregulation cannot easily be pulled apart without destabilizing the entire system. The more a reform has multiple "separable" parts, the easier incremental de-reform becomes, and the more institutional safeguards are necessary to raise the transaction costs to particularistic demands or rent seeking and keep the package stuck together.

In sum, institutional shifts clearly affect reform sustainability, but the devil is in the details. The institutional structures established to protect reforms may conflict with the mandates from preexisting institutions, or they may lack the necessary incentives or capacities. This is a more complex story than is suggested by rational choice arguments about procedural "hand-tying."

Interest-Group Feedback

The interplay between reforms and clientele groups is also of crucial importance. The most sustainable reforms do not simply *outlast* changes in the interest-group environment. Rather, they transform group identities, incentives, and coalitional alignments. Reforms may lead to the formation of entirely new interests. For example, after ERISA, the business community organized the ERISA Industry Committee to fight state attempts to eliminate or water down ERISA preemption rules. Similarly, airline deregulation led to the emergence of new discount carriers which have been a key force in preserving the reform. Reforms may also build interest group support by concentrating some of their diffuse benefits on identifiable actors, such as a subgroup of reform beneficiaries or service providers (e.g., farmers who gained from the deregulation of planting and land use decisions, government contractors that internalized efficiencies after procurement reform). Sustainable reforms solve collective action problems.

But the interest group feedback from major general-interest reforms is often weak or nonexistent. Many of the reforms have failed to build clienteles, leaving them vulnerable to reversal and erosion. The base-broadening aspects of the Tax Reform Act of 1986, for example, have few defenders among the thousands of lobbying groups that press for special tax provisions on Capitol Hill. The reform simply never built a positive constituency.

Indeed, the Tax Reform Act of 1986 is a paradigmatic instance of what I call *winnerless reform*, meaning a reform whose benefits are scattered so widely across society that it generates no influential clientele-group defenders. There is a bitter irony here. The more "general" a general-interest reform is, the more widely dispersed its benefits across society, and the more badly it needs countervailing interests to defend it against future potential attacks, the less likely the reform is to generate such allies.

A second potential clientele feedback from reform is the weakening of organized enemies. As mentioned in chapter 2, it is possible for reforms to disable rent-seeking groups through a process of "stigmatization," in which the public reputation of groups is tarnished in the reform battle. This dynamic appeared in some of the cases, but it met with only limited success. For example, reformers were able to generate some political and media criticism of the affordability and fairness of agricultural subsidies, but more direct attacks on the public standing or moral deservingness of farmers were largely repelled.[30] The image of the family farmer is apparently too strong for stigmatization to work. In contrast, reformers made some headway in labeling business tax breaks as corporate welfare.

Perhaps the more common way that reforms weaken the power of clientele enemies is through a change in the cohesion of group actors. This can happen in either of two ways. First, groups whose incentives or strategies are incompatible with the reform may simply be weeded out. This scenario is most likely to occur in the wake of the establishment of competitive markets. Consider the demise of rent-seeking legacy carriers such as Pan Am. The creative de- structiveness of market forces can destroy the once powerful as well as the pre- viously weak. Second, reforms can greatly multiply the number and hetero- geneity of interests within a given policy sector, increasing the organizational costs of mobilizing groups around a rent-seeking agenda. Again, market forces may come into play. Even thirty years after deregulation, the rent seeking mentality of many legacy carriers has not entirely disappeared. But the post- reform emergence of scores of new carriers greatly lowered the economic and political cohesion of the airline industry, thus weakening the pressures for reregulation. While each individual airline would still like to receive govern- ment subsidies and protectionism, the airlines increasingly check and balance one another, since more rent for one would reduce the profits of the others. *The unleashing of market forces is an especially powerful mechanism for reconfigur- ing the interest group pressures that impinge on government over time.*

The Stimulation of Investments

Finally, reforms may cause actors to make extensive physical or financial in- vestments all connected to the maintenance of the reform.[31] Examples include the reorganization of airline fleets and routes over the past quarter-century; the growth of myriad service industries around airport hubs; the banking of sulfur dioxide pollution allowances under the acid rain program; the construc- tion of private employee pension and health insurance plans around the regu- latory framework of ERISA; and extensive shifts in farmers' land use and planting decisions. When reforms stimulate such extensive investments, the options available to subsequent policymakers narrow. Even if the federal gov- ernment had wished to reregulate the airline industry after the 9/11 terrorist attacks, for example, it could not have easily done so. Such investments do not rule out future policy choices—rather, they channel and constrain them.[32] When the EPA in 2005 wished to tighten pollution controls on power plant emissions, it was able to do so. However, the agency was forced to construct the rule atop the preexisting acid rain program to avoid disrupting the sulfur dioxide emissions market.

Temporal Forces and Reform "Cycles"

Reforms unfold in time in part because they interact with the larger economic and social context of governance, which is never static. The temporal dy- namic that has received the most attention in the American politics literature is the "reform cycle." In the 1950s, pluralist theorist David Truman described the "balance wheel" in American politics: clientele groups who triumph in one round lose out to other groups in the next.[33] Samuel Huntington has argued that American political history undergoes a sixty-year cycle of "creedal passions" in which reformers seek to narrow the gap between American political ideals and the actual performance of U.S. governing institutions.[34] In a provocative updating of the reform cycle model, Andrew McFarland claims that economic interests normally have a more stable incentive to participate in policymaking than reform groups who challenge them.[35] Within a few years, however, producer groups tend to abuse their unchecked power. The resulting "excesses" then give reformers an incentive to get into action. But after winning a few victories, most reformers lose interest in the issue, and the reform cycle begins again. Cyclical pressures emerge when the government faces a dilemma over how to balance the pursuit of two attractive, yet contradictory, goals.[36] Politicians cope with the tradeoff by favoring one phase of the cycle and then the other. Negative feedback from the pursuit of one goal eventually leads more attention to be given to the second.

My analysis provides some support for the claim that governance oscillates between reformist and anti-reformist impulses, but policy dynamics are ultimately too varied to be reduced to the single image of a single cycle.[37] A cycle has only two phases (reform and anti-reform), but the case-study chapters provide evidence of four dynamics (entrenchment, reversal, erosion, and reconfiguration). The probability of one of these dynamics coming into play at any given moment depends in part on how long a particular reform has been in existence. Reforms appear to be at highest risk for outright reversals (e.g., Medicare Catastrophic Coverage Act and farm subsidy reform) during the first few years post-enactment, before actors have become heavily invested in the new system and policies have had the chance to "take."[38] Erosion, in contrast, is a malady of middle and old age. Once a reform has been around for some period of time, repeal becomes increasingly costly, yet the reform has had years to become encrusted with the provisions of antithetical policies. Reconfiguration is the slowest-moving process. The sulfur dioxide emissions trading market did not establish itself overnight; it took time for actors to gain the confidence to trade. Airline deregulation, arguably the most successful instance of reconfiguration, is *still* a work in process. Three decades after the removal of governmental protections, the remaining legacy carriers have not yet fully adjusted their cost structures to the relentless competition of a dynamic market.

Reform cycle theory has several other limitations. First, the negative feedback from reforms often does not lead to the restoration of the policy status quo ante.[39] Congress backslid on the reform commitment to tax neutrality, for example, less through the re-creation of old corporate tax breaks than though the creation of new social tax provisions that did not predate the reform. As Frank Baumgartner and Bryan Jones argue, when policy subsystems break down, outcomes can go off in many directions.[40]

A second limitation of the model concerns its assertion that reform cycles in issue areas proceed in phase. In any given year, argues McFarland, "the political power of producer groups will be relatively high in many issue areas simultaneously, while in another year the political power of countervailing groups and autonomous government will be relatively high in many issue areas."[41] This is an intriguing hypothesis with some empirical support, but it cuts too deeply. Reform and anti-reform thrusts may occur at the same moment in different arenas. During the late 1990s, for example, particularism was creeping back into the federal tax code even as the consolidations of airline deregulation and emissions trading were taking place.

The reform cycle model also underestimates the role of positive feedback and momentum, as Eugene Bardach argues.[42] When one policy actor takes actions supportive of a reform, she may persuade others who were previously less committed. Such "bandwagon effects" emerged within the bureaucracy (less so on Capitol Hill) in the case of procurement reform. Moreover, as we have seen, reforms may build up constituencies, like the low-cost airlines and rental-car agencies located near airport hubs, which make long-term economic investments based on the expected continuation of the new system. These extensive commitments and adaptations stave off attempts to reverse course. In sum, there is not a single grand reform cycle, but rather particular dynamics connected to particular reform measures at certain moments in time.

PARADOXES OF REFORM

An understanding of these empirical patterns may be useful to reformers who wish to see their policy achievements endure. Unfortunately, the political dynamics of reform can be more difficult to manage than the preceding discussion might suggest. Attempts to ease the initial adoption of a reform can create sustainability problems later on, and attempts to solve these problems can sometimes backfire. Five paradoxes arise in the effort to sustain reforms over time.

> *Paradox 1: Side payments are often needed to grease the passage of general-interest laws, but the very act of compensating losers serves as a reminder of government's awesome power to deliver particularistic benefits.*

A major challenge at the enactment stage is to reduce the number and intensity of reform opponents. Reformers therefore often understandably find themselves agreeing to provide compensation schemes and side payments in one form or another. But these tactics are double-edged. On the one hand, the harnessing of self-interested motives may be the only feasible way to win passage of reforms serving general-interests. In a pluralistic democracy, there is no moral shame in giving actors a tangible reason to support general-interest policies.[43] On the other hand, distributing such pay-offs may only reinforce skepticism about whether the reform process will continue. The behavior of actors depends substantially on their highly unstable beliefs about the future.[44] If actors believe they've really been "beaten," they will adapt their ways. If, however, they believe they've only lost one round, they will look for ways to fight another day. All things being equal, the larger the side payments needed to cobble together a reform coalition, the lower the groups' belief that that they have lost and will continue to lose in the future. If payments are not credibly tied to the reform's long-term maintenance, they can undermine their own cause by discouraging interest-group actors from adapting to the new system. Moreover, the buy-outs may send negative signals about the government's larger commitment to efficient public policymaking. As Daniel Shaviro observes, while the provision of transition relief may facilitate the curbing of inefficient public policies in *particular* cases, its long-term effect may be to increase political demand for inefficient subsidies and regulations in the first place.[45]

There is no clear solution to this political incentives problem. An important challenge that policymakers must confront after reform is sticking to the transition payment schedule embedded in initial reform enactments. This obviously did not happen in the Freedom to Farm case. Congress extended the market transition payments and, when those additional payments were deemed inadequate, it grafted huge new farm subsidies atop them. It is hard to imagine a more powerful way for Congress to have signaled the weakness of its commitment to agricultural reform. In contrast, the in-kind transition schemes contained in the acid rain (e.g., extra pollution credits for some dirty regions) and airline deregulation (subsidies for air service to small communities) measures did not mushroom out-of-control. A major reason is because implementation of the transition schemes was mediated by the interests of third parties. After the acid rain program was adopted, Congress could not suddenly come back and grant more pollution credits to particular regions without reducing the value of emissions allowances held by other areas, which would inevitably trigger a political backlash. That helped give the new emissions trading market credibility. Similarly, growth in the small community air service program was checked by the relative (un)willingness of commuter carriers to serve small isolated cities. Commuter air carriers were simply not eager (even with generous public subsidies) to provide service to every community that lost flights after deregulation. Greater profits could be captured elsewhere. In sum, the transition schemes for both the acid rain program and airline deregulation were self-limiting. Transition schemes unmediated by the interests of market actors are far more difficult for policymakers to control.

Paradox 2: The very macro political changes that have made reforms easier to pass have arguably made them harder to sustain.

During the 1960s and 1970s, the American political system became more transparent, open, ideational, and participatory.[46] The media became more aggressive, and policy elites lost their monopoly on political authority. The number of think tanks, foundations, nonprofit groups, and "public-interest" groups mushroomed, and many iron triangles disintegrated. These changes reduced the autonomy of elected officials and made it easier for critics to challenge inefficient and inequitable public policies. Expert ideas came to matter more. As Derthick and Quirk argue, if microeconomists had not made the theoretical case for airline deregulation, the reform "would not have occurred."[47] It is an interesting empirical question whether the substantial influence of outside experts reflected the relatively weak party system of the 1970s and if it continues in the current era of more intense partisanship. It would take another study to resolve this question, but it is noteworthy that some of the 1990s reforms were also driven by expertise. The Freedom to Farm Act, for example, almost exactly followed "what standard welfare economics has promoted for decades: the replacement of market-distorting interventions by lump-sum payments."[48] And the deregulation of the federal procurement system came directly out of the ideas of Harvard public management expert Steven Kelman.

What seems clear is that the macro political developments of the 1960s and 1970s did not push uniformly in the direction of effective governance. After reform enactment, opponents can use modern political technology to reframe their causes in the most favorable possible light. Ordinary citizens, as the Medicare Catastrophic Coverage Act case highlights, can be highly vulnerable to elite distortion and misinformation about the true consequences of reforms. Individual candidates also have a greater ability and incentive to use polling to identify policies that resonate with large swaths of voters. While such opinion surveying can help elected officials craft acceptable solutions to important public problems, it can also facilitate pandering and symbolic policymaking, as in the creation of scores of questionable special tax breaks for various social purposes in the 1990s. In sum, macro political changes have arguably made it easier for politicians to embrace novel policy reforms, but not necessarily easier for them to stay the course.

Paradox 3: The prospects for sustainable reform increase when Congress has a long history of delegating its power, but Congress is unlikely to delegate control over the sectors most in need of reform.

A significant threat to the sustainability of many general-interest reform measures is the particularistic interventions of future Congresses. Those legislative interventions are far less likely to occur after reform if the enactment of the reform follows a long history of delegation to bureaucrats or other actors. If Congress was content even *before* the reform to play a less interventionist role in a given policy arena, the enactment of the reform should constitute less of a challenge to its institutional authority. In contrast, when the prior line of policymaking has served as a platform for members of Congress to engage in position-taking, credit-claiming, political advertising, and related activities, incumbents may find it difficult to abide by reforms that disrupt their regular supply of electoral benefits.

Striking differences exist in the structure of policy inheritances across the cases. Consider the contrasting fates of airline deregulation and tax reform. The difference is not only that the airline deregulation involved the removal of price and entry restrictions and that tax reform involved federal subsidy reductions. The key difference is that the two reforms did not demand the same level of behavioral change from Congress. To maintain a clean tax code, Congress had to reject its inherited patterns of tax favor provision. Taxation is such a valuable arena for particularistic credit claiming that Congress has long written meticulously detailed laws that give the executive almost no discretion. By contrast, even prior to airline deregulation, Congress had established an independent agency (the CAB) with far more power over the airline industry than the IRS has ever possessed over taxpayers.[49] In sum, airline deregulation and taxation inherited different political economies. These differences in policy legacies, in turn, shaped the prospects for durable reform in each sector. It is one thing for Congress to eliminate policy inefficiencies in an arena (airline regulation) where civil servants have been dominant policy actors, and quite another to do so in an arena (taxation) where Congress itself has a tradition of pulling the policy strings.[50] The use of the tax code for political purposes is deeply institutionalized in the United States. The 1986 Act did not remove tax policy as a key tool in the members' credit claiming toolbox. Any effort to really deny Congress's ability to use tax policy for political purposes—to make it more akin to monetary policy, for instance—would have added another level of political complexity, as well as engendered intense opposition, and probably would have killed the reform effort in its tracks.

Paradox 4: *Midcourse policy corrections are sometimes essential to achieve the general-interest purposes of reform measures, but the more interventionist the government remains after reform the greater the risk that the reform will be undermined through political manipulations.*

No matter how clever or farsighted reforms are, it is impossible for them to avoid every conceivable design mistake or to anticipate every possible contingency. When things go wrong after reform enactment, policymakers may have an opportunity to promote general-interests by making social welfare–enhancing midcourse adjustments. While the failure to intervene may not always result in a reform's collapse, it can lead to unplanned or even perverse outcomes if a reform is not updated to take account of changing social conditions. Something like this seems to have happened with respect to ERISA's regulations of defined-benefit plans. These regulations have stuck, but they cover a shrinking portion of the workforce.[51] If ERISA's rules had been changed to reflect vast changes in employer and employee preferences regarding the design of fringe benefits, the reform might have better achieved its original goals.

Yet, as Eugene S. Bardach observes, the more active and interventionist the government is in managing reforms (either to update the reform as conditions change or to provide funding, trained personnel, or other inputs needed to make a reform operational), the longer the reform "remains a target for rent seeking and other such distorting forces."[52] In the agricultural reform case, for example, Congress was eager for political advantage in 2002 when it tried to "rescue" farmers from the hardship of "unexpectedly" low farm prices. Policy inertia has a cost, but so does a political unwillingness to accept that even appropriate and relatively effective reforms will create some ugly surprises, as well as generate some losers.

No perfect solution exists to the post-reform tradeoff between harmful policy inertia and counterproductive micromanagement. In the acid rain case, for example, the government managed this tension about as well as possible. The EPA skillfully monitored emissions and penalized violations, as well as organized annual auctions, but outside this it allowed market actors to trade and use their allowances as they saw fit. Environmental policymakers were patient when the emissions trading market did not take off right away. They did not try to force trades to occur before actors were ready for them. A case also can be made that federal policymakers have behaved responsibly in permitting airline competition to continue unfettered after deregulation, even though rent-seeking by carriers did not come to an end and market competition for passengers was often brutal and even a bit underhanded.[53] In contrast, policymakers were too quick to jettison the market-transition payment schedule of the Freedom to Farm Act when commodity prices fell more rapidly than expected. Leadership (and human agency) matters so obviously in the reform enactment phase that it is easy to overlook the more subtle role it plays during the second phase.

Paradox 5: *Reforms are enacted to solve problems, but what they really do is create new ones.*

Sustainable reforms do not eliminate social difficulties.[54] The continuing painful adjustment to airline deregulation is a case in point. Many air carriers have been teetering on the edge of bankruptcy, meal service on even long flights increasingly consists of a tiny package of pretzels, travel delays are common, and many flights are oversold. Yet despite these difficulties and petty annoyances, the air travel system still delivers social value. Tickets are relatively cheap, flying is no longer a travel mode reserved for an economically privileged few but something that is affordable to middle-class American families, and the pressure on the commercial airline industry to shed inefficiencies and meet consumer demand is tremendous. As the late Aaron Wildavsky argued, progress in policymaking consists not of eliminating problems but rather of substituting lesser troubles for greater ones.[55] *Sustainable reforms redefine the problems that policymakers attend to and the menu of alternatives they choose from.*

SOME PRACTICAL IMPLICATIONS

Reform sustainability and good government are not identical. They can even be in tension with one another. Policymakers sometimes must abrogate an existing reform commitment in order to promote the social welfare. Sometimes a reform solution that was appropriate yesterday no longer makes sense today. Yet a government that lacks any capacity to sustain general-interest measures over time, whose actions reflect nothing more than the current play of interests or the policy fads of the day, will accomplish nothing worth supporting. No proposed reform would be worth fighting for if its advocates know in advance that it will be unraveled soon after enactment.

Favorable policy inheritances, good timing, and other "politically uncontrollable" factors shape reform trajectories, as we have seen. However, sustainable reform is also partly a matter of strategy and policy design.[56] Reformist politicians can take five steps to give general-interest policies at least a fighting chance of surviving the myriad threats to sustainability: cultivate clienteles, create sunk costs, harness the power of market forces, change the game, and integrate political sustainability considerations into policy design.[57]

Cultivate Clienteles

Reform initiatives last when their supporters are more influential politically than the groups opposing them. This sounds like a truism, yet experts often seem to think that general-interest policies will endure simply because of the vast social benefits they offer. They may not. It is essential for reformers to think about which *specific groups* will benefit from reforms and if these groups will mobilize to defend their gains. Reforms without interest-group friends have nothing to protect them beyond policy inertia and the support of academic experts. In the hyper-competitive world of American politics, that is rarely enough.

Of course, the producers and other groups who reap the gains from reforms can *themselves* become threats to the general good.[58] This risk arises even when reforms are highly successful and long-lasting. Low-cost air carriers would not exist but for airline deregulation. They are the products of a market paradigm. Yet they have been unwilling to pay the market price for landing slots at certain airports.[59] Instead, they have lobbied the government to make the slots available to them on a special basis. (The legacy carriers have naturally opposed these actions.) Reformers thus must worry not only about whether vested interests will emerge after reform, but about whether vested interests can be constrained if they do.[60]

Create Sunk Costs

One way to narrow the potential for post-reform interest-group mischief is to create sunk costs. If the enactment of a reform induces actors into making substantial, asset-specific investments, the actors will accommodate themselves to the reform since they have little to gain from its repeal. In contrast, support for a reform will not grow after enactment if actors can avoid up-front investments but face high marginal compliance costs over time.

Harness the Power of Market Forces

All things being equal, reforms are far more likely to endure when they seek to reinforce, rather than offset, market forces. Their creative destructiveness can destroy or weaken policy subsystems, and their profit incentives can generate interests with a stake in safeguarding the reform.

Of course, markets are not panaceas. Market-based reforms will be sustainable and effective only if the underlying market is competitive. Many areas of governmental activity do not satisfy this criterion. The free market is not going to mobilize the socially optimal level of tax revenue, and even "contracting out" initiatives requires government contract officers. Even when market-based reforms are appropriate solutions, the government must possess the capacity to prevent actors from self-dealing and manipulating prices. The disastrous experiment with electricity market liberalization in California is a reminder that efforts to facilitate new markets may produce poor outcomes for firms and consumers alike if market rules are technically flawed and lack credibility.[61]

Any time a reform shifts market risks to individuals or groups, there is a danger that short-term responsiveness to constituent demands will lead politicians to undo the gains that come from reliance on market forces, as occurred in the Freedom to Farm case. "Privatization" of the Social Security program would create similar dilemmas. As Hugh Heclo observes, various political risks will arise should a private Social Security system ever be established.[62] For example, some individual account holders will inevitably demand the right to withdraw or borrow sums before retirement for various good causes, such as a family emergency. They may also try to blame negative market outcomes on "bad advice" from financial brokers. If the government signals (even unintentionally) that it will rescue people if they have bad stock market experiences, it will create a moral hazard, encouraging workers to invest in even riskier assets.[63]

One way to potentially limit these risks is through institutional structures and rules (like those governing monetary policy) that insulate the policies from subsequent political intervention. If it is not feasible or desirable for elected officials to extract themselves entirely from a given arena, reformers could seek to create a "relational contract" that specifies in advance the criteria to be used in deciding what the government should do when contingencies arise.[64] In the farm subsidy case, for example, the rule might have provided that market transition payments will be increased by 10 percent for every 10 percent decline in prices relative to an agreed-upon baseline, but then automatically return to the original payment schedule by some particular date. Farmers would likely have still lobbied for emergency assistance in the late 1990s, but they would have faced a higher burden.

Change the Game

A fourth way to improve the probability that a reform will be sustained over time is to "change the game." Game changing goes well beyond a temporary shift in a policy venue—it involves the redefinition of the actors, a modification of the "rules," and changes in the political stakes.[65] Many of the cases examined in this book featured reform victories within the context of an ongoing game whose rules are biased against general-interests. For example, in 1986, tax reformers scored an impressive victory, which has created a few enduring benefits, but the legislative game of cutting tax breaks and lowering tax rates in one round (and then doing the reverse in the next round) did not change. Similarly, agricultural reformers in 1996 cut crop subsidies, yet Congress continued to play the same electoral / credit-claiming / pork barrel farm politics game. A more far-reaching agricultural reform would create a new high-level "reputation" game by taking U.S. farm subsidy levels out of the domestic policy realm and making it largely a matter of international treaty obligations.[66] Congress's failure to implement promised farm subsidy cuts would then become extremely damaging to the president's international standing and weaken the nation's ability to achieve other foreign policy goals. Reformers sometimes may be better off trying to change the game than trying to steal a victory under unfavorable rules.

Integrate Sustainability Considerations into Policy Design

The most important thing reformers can do to manage these risks is to think about them from the start. *Political sustainability considerations should be an integral part of policy design.* All too often, however, they are ignored or treated as a mere afterthought. Reformers and policy analysts instinctively distinguish between what is desirable and what is feasible. This distinction has a logical basis. Just because something is possible does not mean it is the best of all worlds. Yet it seems somewhat perverse to describe a policy as "desirable" if it cannot be enacted or sustained. By the same token, a policy that generates supportive constituencies and is capable of sustaining its own legitimacy and warding off enemies has much to commend it, especially if it also represents a technical improvement over the status quo. As Steven M. Teles writes, "Policies are more than mechanisms for the solving of problems: They are also contexts in which future policy battles will be fought."[67]

In crafting policies, reformers must not simply identify the policy which works best "in theory." Nor must they stop at identifying the best policy that can be passed under current conditions, which, after all, may soon change. Reformers must also consider the downstream political reactions a policy will generate from affected interests and whether these reactions will likely increase or decrease the odds that the policy will endure and that government will be able to serve the general good in the future.[68] This is not to imply that political sustainability is a more important consideration than economic efficiency in policy design. The point is that a *dynamic* view of the potential gains from reform is required.[69] Reformers should select policies that are best not only in a static sense, but that seem likely to generate more, rather than less, social progress over time.

Consider the current debate over the best policies to reduce greenhouse gases. Most everyone now recognizes that imposing "command-and-control" regulations from a centralized bureaucracy would be a very inefficient way to tackle global warming. Two market-based policies currently vie for elite support: carbon taxes (which impose a fixed price on every ton of carbon emitted) and cap-and-trade (which limit the total quantity of carbon emissions and allow the market to set the price for each ton). Economists generally agree that carbon taxes are both easier to administer and are a more efficient response (than cap-and-trade) to the high degree of uncertainty over the potential costs to the economy of carbon emissions reductions in the future.[70] Nonetheless, lawmakers seem to favor cap-and-trade over carbon taxes. It appears that members of Congress are behaving precisely as Doug Arnold's model would suggest. They are thinking about the traceability of costs and benefits and how best to avoid electoral retribution for "doing the right thing." Lawmakers are attracted to a carbon cap because it promises a definite reduction in emissions while the environmental benefits of a carbon tax are elusive. Moreover, voters are unlikely to notice the connection between slower economic growth and the creation of a cap-and-trade scheme, whereas the costs of a carbon tax are easily grasped.

What has received far less attention is that a cap-and-trade might be more effective than taxes at creating a "dynamic that over time would accelerate innovation and shape the incentives on future Congresses to continue on a path to further drive down greenhouse gas emissions."[71] A cap-and-trade system may create a business constituency with an interest in reducing the national emissions cap over time. The emissions permits would create hundreds of billions of dollars in annual trades. As Rand senior scientist Robert Lempert points out, "Congressional hearings on lowering emissions caps will no longer pit only those segments of society who lose most from climate regulations against environmental groups and scientists representing a diffuse general good. Rather, specific commercial interests will be eager to testify that deeper reductions are possible and environmentally beneficial."[72] Whether or not cap-and-trade is in fact the best feasible solution to global warming would require another book (and another author), but political considerations such as these must figure prominently in the analysis.

THE REFORM SUSTAINABILITY PROBLEM IN PERSPECTIVE

Assessments of political sustainability must attend to empirical facts, but they also must reflect judgments about what is achievable and desirable in a democratic polity. Many experienced Washington hands view the failure of reforms to stick as "par for the course." Tax policy insiders were skeptical, for instance, that the political configurations that produced the miraculous Tax Reform Act of 1986 would survive, even as they hoped that a remnant of its spirit would live on. "Like a child's room," writes former Treasury official Eugene Steurele, "one has little expectation that when [the tax code] is cleaned up it will stay tidy forever. By the same token, however, permanent improvements can often be made along the way."[73] Just as parents learn to pick some battles with their children and avoid others, so idealistic yet savvy reformers must reflect on which potential reform targets are worth the effort.

Because battles over reforms sometimes get caught up in broader partisan and ideological conflicts, it is easy to lose sight of the fact that reform decisions also reflect normative tensions between the values of commitment and discretion, and between the payoff from the avoidance of foreseeable policy mistakes on the one hand, and the payoff from the preservation of the flexibility necessary for beneficial social learning and policy evolution on the other. The often circuitous paths that reforms take matter not only because they create winners and losers at certain moments in time, but because they shape the possibilities for governance in the future. Strategic leaders will want to think carefully about the reform legacies they leave to their successors.

Notes

1. *The New York Times*, "A Tax Law to Hail. Yes, a Tax Law," October 22, 1986, A30.

2. Michael J. Graetz, "Tax Reform Unraveling," *Journal of Economics Perspectives*, vol. 21, no. 1 (Winter 2007): 69–90.

3. Jeffrey H. Birnbaum, "Historic Tax Code Changes Eroded in Years Since 1986," *The Washington Post*, June 7, 2004, A1.

4. Quoted in Steven Pearlstein, "Tax Reform Falling Prey to Tax Cuts," *The Washington Post*, December 18, 1994, A1.

5. Quoted in David E. Rosenbaum, "Reform Taxes? Give us a Break!" *The New York Times*, December 25, 1994, Section 4, 1.

6. General-interest reforms face tremendous "political risk," to borrow a helpful concept from Hugh Heclo. They are highly vulnerable to "being destabilized as time passes, unexpectedly rendering the plan's original design unsustainable in its promised operations and purpose." Such riskiness, Heclo points out, "is not the same as uncertainties about the future in general. Uncertainties—for example, an unexpected change in the economy or demographic trends—can beset any policy. The forces of 'political' riskiness have to do with pressures that are fashioned and put in play by a particular policy approach." Hugh Heclo, "A Political Science Perspective on Social Security Reform," in R. Douglas Arnold, Michael J. Graetz, and Alicia H. Munnell, eds., *Framing the Social Security Debate* (Washington, D.C.: National Academy of Social Insurance, 1998), 71. Heclo nicely analogizes reforms to vessels that aim not only to stay afloat but to maintain their course amid unpredictable political storms. This brings to mind Paul Light's provocative work on the "tides of reform"—reform ideas and fads tend to come and go in the United States, and often a new reform may contradict the potential benefits of a prior one. Paul C. Light, *The Tides of Reform: Making Government Work, 1945–1995* (New Haven: Yale University Press, 1997). See also the helpful discussion in Jeanne Rose Century and Abigail Jurist Levy, "Sustaining Your Reform: Five Lessons from Research," in *Benchmarks: The Quarterly Newsletter of the National Clearinghouse for Comprehensive School Reform*, vol. 3, no. 3 (Summer 2002): 1–7.

7. See Alan S. Gerber and Eric M. Patashnik, *Promoting the General Welfare: New Perspectives on Government Performance* (Washington, D.C.: Brookings Institution, 2006).

8. Alfred E. Kahn, "Airline Deregulation," *The Concise Encyclopedia of Economics*. Liberty Fund, Inc. Ed. David R. Henderson. *Library of Economics and Liberty*. Retrieved June 16, 2004 from www.econlib.org/library/Enc/AirlineDeregulation.html.

9. Forrest Maltzman and Charles R. Shipan, "Continuity, Change, and the Evolution of the Law," *American Journal of Political Science*, forthcoming.

10. Andrea Campbell, *How Policies Make Citizens: Senior Political Activism and the American Welfare State* (Princeton: Princeton University Press, 2003); and Suzanne

Mettler, *Soldiers to Citizens: The GI Bill and the Making of the Greatest Generation* (New York: Oxford University Press, 2005).

11. Terry M. Moe, "The Politics of Structural Choice: Toward a Theory of Public Bureaucracy," in Oliver E. Williamson, ed., *Organization Theory: From Chester Barnard to the Present and Beyond* (New York: Oxford University Press, 1990); Karen Orren and Stephen Skowronek, *The Search for American Political Development* (New York: Cambridge University Press, 2004).

12. Christopher R. Berry, Barry C. Burden, and William G. Howell, "Matters of Life and Death: The Durability of Discretionary Programs 1970–2004," University of Chicago Harris School of Public Policy Working Paper, 2006

13. Jacob S. Hacker, "Privatizing Risk without Privatizing the Welfare State: The Hidden Politics of Social Policy Retrenchment in the United States," *American Political Science Review* 98:2 (May 2004): 243–60.

14. Frank R. Baumgartner and Bryan D. Jones, *Agendas and Instability in American Politics* (Chicago: University of Chicago Press, 1993). In more recent work, Baumgartner and Jones have become quite attentive to some of these complexities. See Frank R. Baumgartner and Bryan D. Jones, eds., *Policy Dynamics* (Chicago: University of Chicago Press, 2002).

15. Jeffrey Pressman and Aaron Wildavsky, *Implementation*, 3rd Edition (Berkeley: University of California Press, 1984), 162.

16. Eugene Bardach, *The Implementation Game: What Happens After a Bill Becomes a Law* (Cambridge, MA: MIT Press, 1977).

17. *Ibid.*

18. I thank an anonymous reviewer for helping me clarify this section.

19. "[P]olicy entrepreneurs are strategic actors that do not want to waste their time on challenges that will be ignored," Michael C. MacLeod, "The Logic of Positive Feedback," in Frank R. Baumgartner and Bryan D. Jones, *Policy Dynamics* (Chicago: University of Chicago Press, 2002), at 58; on this point, see also John Kingdon, *Agendas, Alternatives, and Public Policies*, 2nd Edition (New York: HarperCollins, 1995).

20. On the importance of commitment problems in policymaking, see Murray J. Horn, *The Political Economy of Public Administration* (New York: Cambridge University Press, 1995); for an application to the design of budgeting institutions, see Eric M. Patashnik, *Putting Trust in the U.S. Budget: Federal Trust Funds and the Politics of Commitment* (Cambridge: Cambridge University Press, 2000).

21. On the limited attention spans and constrained information-processing capacities of political elites, see Bryan D. Jones and Frank R. Baumgartner, *The Politics of Attention: How Government Priorities Problems* (Chicago: University of Chicago Press, 2005).

22. "Tax Legislation Should Be for Long-Term as well as Fair," *Engineering News-Record*, March 9, 1992, 70.

23. James Wetzler, quoted in Jeffrey H. Birnbaum, "Fundamental Tax Reform: Public Perception and Political Rhetoric," *National Tax Journal*, vol. 51, no. 3 (September 1998), 566.

24. It is sometimes argued that a reform and its sustainability are not distinguishable—if a general-interest policy doesn't endure, it must mean that genuine reform never occurred in the first place. In sum, a reform is not "real" until it has influenced its sustainability. But this confuses matters—if a reform presumes its own sustainabil-

ity, then it is not possible to study the conditions under which reforms stick. For an exactly analogous argument about the need to distinguish between a policy and its implementation, see Pressman and Wildavsky, *Implementation*, xxii–xxiv, fn. 4. The tautological view that reforms determine their own sustainability not only is confusing from a definitional standpoint, it downplays the courage politicians may display when they adopt general-interest reforms. Reforms may not always live up to their hype, but their adoptions should not be dismissed as meaningless or trivial events even if they are later eroded or reversed. For a parallel discussion, see Christopher Hood, *Explaining Economic Policy Reversals* (Buckingham: Open University Press, 1994), 144.

25. Theodore J. Lowi, *The End of Liberalism: The Second Republic of the United States*, *2nd Edition* (New York: Norton, 1979); Grant McConnell, *Private Power and American Democracy* (New York: Knopf, 1966); and Mayhew, *Congress: The Electoral Connection*.

26. David R. Mayhew, "Congress as Problem Solver," in Alan S. Gerber and Eric M. Patashnik, *Promoting the General Welfare*, 228. Mayhew pointed out in his 1974 book that a key "reform recourse" to which Americans have turned to improve congressional performance has been to strengthen the political parties. For a sober analysis of why the emergence of cohesive unified parties in the U.S. since the 1980s has not brought about better government, see Morris P. Fiorina, "Parties as Problem Solvers," in Gerber and Patashnik, *Promoting the General Welfare*, 237–55.

27. Mayhew, *Congress: The Electoral Connection*, 138–40.

28. *Ibid.*, 135.

29. Mancur Olson, *The Logic of Collective Action* (Cambridge: Harvard University Press, 1965). See also Jonathan Rauch, *Government's End: Why Washington Stopped Working* (New York: Public Affairs, 1994).

30. Martha Derthick and Paul J. Quirk, *The Politics of Deregulation* (Washington, D.C.: The Brookings Institution, 1985).

31. R. Douglas Arnold, *The Logic of Congressional Action* (New Haven: Yale University Press, 1990).

32. Gary Mucciaroni, *Reversals of Fortune: Public Policy and Private Interests* (Washington, D.C.: The Brookings Institution, 1995).

33. Adam Sheingate, *The Rise of the Agricultural Welfare State: Institutions and Interest Group Power in the United States, France, and Japan* (Princeton: Princeton University Press, 2001).

34. Mark K. Landy and Martin A. Levin. *The New Politics of Public Policy* (Baltimore: Johns Hopkins University Press, 1995).

35. James Q. Wilson, "New Elites, New Politics, Old Publics," in Landy and Levin, eds., *The New Politics of Public Policy* (Baltimore: Johns Hopkins University Press, 1995), 249–67.

36. Paul Pierson, "The Study of Policy Development," *Journal of Policy History*, 17.1 (2005), 34–51.

37. *Ibid.*

38. On the need to study U.S. budget policymaking from a developmental perspective, see Patashnik, *Putting Trust in the U.S. Budget*.

39. See, for example, Robert H. Bates and Anne O. Krueger, *Political and Economic Interactions in Economic Policy Reform: Evidence from Eight Countries* (Cambridge: Blackwell Publishes, 1993); and Kurt Weyland, *The Politics of Market Reform in Fragile*

Democracies: Argentina, Brazil, Peru, and Venezuela (Princeton: Princeton University Press, 2002).

40. A good deal of ink has been spilled among social scientists who study economic policy reforms in developing nations over the perceived failures of the so-called "Washington consensus." The economist John Williamson coined this term to describe a least-common denominator set of policy prescription being recommended by Washington-based institutions for Latin American nations in the late 1980s. The policies included tax reform, privatization, deregulation, trade liberalization, fiscal discipline, and a competitive exchange rate. Caution must be exercised in drawing any simple comparisons between the reform experiences of developing nations and those of the United States. First, there are vast differences in the economic, political, and cultural settings of governance in these nations. Moreover, the meanings of key reform concepts often do not travel across national boundaries. In most of the world, for example, the term "privatization" refers to the selling of government-owned assets. The United States, however, has few government-owned enterprises to shed. The general-interest reforms I discuss are in general far less daring and draconian than the ones attempted in nations like Argentina, Brazil, and Peru. These important caveats aside, it is noteworthy that scholars of economic reforms in developing nations have recently acknowledged the need to pay far greater attention to the political requisites of reform sustainability. See, for example, Joseph Stiglitz's essay, "Reflections on the Theory and Practice of Reform," in Anne O. Krueger, eds., *Economic Policy Reform: The Second Stage* (Chicago: University of Chicago Press, 2000), 551–84; Pedro-Pablo Kuczynski and John Williamson, eds., *After the Washington Consensus: Restarting Growth and Reform in Latin America* (Washington, D.C.: Institute for International Economics, 2003); and Dani Rodrik, "Goodbye Washington Consensus, Hello Washington Confusion?"*Journal of Economic Literature*, vol. 44, no. 4 (December 2006), 973–87,

41. For an important exception, see Maltzman and Shipan, "Continuity, Change, and the Evolution of the Law."

42. For an argument that legislative action cannot be reduced to roll call voting, see David R. Mayhew, *America's Congress: Actions in the Public Sphere from James Madison to Newt Gingrich* (New Haven: Yale University Press, 2000).

43. See, for example, Theda Skocpol, "The Origins of Social Policy in the United States," in *The Dynamics of American Politics.* Lawrence C. Dodd and Calvin Jillson, eds. (Boulder, Colorado: Westview Press, 1994); Paul Pierson, *Dismantling the Welfare State: Reagan, Thatcher, and the Politics of Retrenchment* (New York: Cambridge University Press, 1994); and Jacob S. Hacker, *The Divided Welfare State* (New York: Cambridge University Press, 2003).

44. Many intriguing public policy ideas that would seem to merit serious debate (e.g., school vouchers, dramatically higher salaries for public school teachers, universal health insurance, Social Security privatization, a federal value added tax, gay marriage, European-style gun control, legalization of marijuana, reinstatement of the draft, to name just a few ideas) lack this degree of expert consensus.

45. Hebert McClosky and John Zaller, *The American Ethos: Public Attitudes Toward Capitalism* (Cambridge: Harvard University Press, 1984).

46. Henry E. Brady, David Collier, and Jason Seawright, "Refocusing the Discussion on Methodology," in Henry E. Brady and David Collier, eds., *Rethinking Social Inquiry* (Lanham, MD: Rowman & Littlefield, 2004), 12.

47. For a similar intellectual approach to the study of policy reform in foreign nations, see Bates and Krueger, *Political and Economic Interactions in Economic Policy Reform: Evidence from Eight Countries.*

48. See the discussion of durability in Karen Orren and Stephen Skowronek, *The Search for American Political Development* (New York: Cambridge University Press, 2004).

49. See, for example, Lester M. Salamon, ed., *Beyond Privatization: the Tools of Government Action* (Washington: Urban Institute Press, 1989).

50. The main alternative to Wilson's framework is Theodore Lowi's threefold classification of the world into distributive, regulatory, and redistributive policies. For purposes of my study, however, Wilson's framework is the more useful. In the Wilson construct, costs and benefits are variables, and one can examine how various quantities of these variables affect government action. In finding the Wilson framework more helpful to a study of reform sustainability, I am employing a similar analysis to R. Douglas Arnold's *The Logic of Congressional Action* (New Haven: Yale University Press, 1990), which offers a brilliant analysis of how general-interest reforms are adopted in the first place.

CHAPTER 2
POLICY REFORM AS A POLITICAL PROJECT

1. On the organizational and moral difficulties of eliminating ineffective or outdated policies, see Eugene Bardach, "Policy Termination as a Political Process," *Policy Sciences*, 7 (1976): 123–31.

2. Robert J. Samuelson, "Seduced by 'Reform,'" *The Washington Post*, June 2, 2004, A25.

3. On the related concept of policy drift, see Jacob S. Hacker, "Privatizing Risk Without Privatizing the Welfare State: The Hidden Politics of Welfare State Retrenchment in the United States," *American Political Science Review*, 98, no. 2 (2004): 243–60.

4. In a provocative essay, Lawrence Brown distinguishes between "breakthrough" and "rationalizing" policies. My empirical focus is on the latter. Brown argues that rationalizing policies has grown more prominent as the scope of government has expanded. See Lawrence D. Brown, *New Policies, New Politics: Government's Response to Government's Growth: A Staff Paper* (Washington, D.C.: The Brookings Institution, 1983).

5. Hugh Heclo, "Clinton's Health Reform in Historical Perspective," in Henry J. Aaron, ed., *The Problem that Won't Go Away: Reforming U.S. Health Care Financing* (Washington, D.C.: The Brookings Institution, 1996), 18.

6. Aaron Wildavsky, *Speaking Truth to Power* (New York: Transaction Press, 1979).

7. Brown, *New Policies, New Politics: Government's Response to Government's Growth.*

8. See Steven Vogel, *Freer Markets, More Rules* (Ithaca: Cornell University Press, 1996).

9. Francis Fukuyama, *State-Building* (Ithaca: Cornell University Press, 2004), 6–10.

10. My definition here follows the excellent analysis in Michael E. Levine and Jennifer L. Florence, "Regulatory Capture, Public Interest, and the Public Agenda: Toward

a Synthesis," *Journal of Law, Economics and Organization*, vol. 6 (Special Issue 1990): 167–98. Following scholars as diverse as Gary Becker, Martha Derthick, Paul Quirk, and R. Douglas Arnold, I focus on policies with general or diffuse benefits, and avoid more abstract and inevitably contested discussions of the "public good" or "the general will."

11. David R. Mayhew, *Congress: The Electoral Connection* (New Haven: Yale University Press, 1974), 165–67.

12. *Ibid.*

13. Richard Posner, *Law, Pragmatism, and Democracy* (Cambridge: Harvard University Press, 2003), 202.

14. *Ibid.*

15. Consider "inefficient redistribution" in the agricultural sector. If society wishes to boost farmers' incomes, it can impose production quotas in exchange for price supports. But this indirect redistributive approach costs society much more (e.g., through higher consumer prices, restrictions on crop use, idled land, etc.) than farmers gain. Hence, it is inefficient. Leaving aside the normative issue of whether farmers today should receive public subsidies, it should be possible to boost farmers' incomes *at lower cost* (e.g., through simple lump sum transfers). In theory, at least, the incomes of farmers can be held constant while making everyone else better off. In a similar vein, lump sum grants to manufacturers are much less market-distorting than tariffs on international trade. Of course, there could be good *political* reasons (including policy-sustainability reasons) why lawmakers prefer to employ opaque methods to redistribute wealth from the public to narrow clientele groups, but that is a separate issue. On the politics of "inefficient" redistribution, see Amahi Glazer and Lawrence S. Rothenberg, *Why Government Succeeds and Why It Fails* (Cambridge: Harvard University Press, 2001).

16. For an analogous discussion of the two phases of nation-building, see Francis Fukuyama, "National Building 101" in Ted Halted, ed., *The Real State of the Union* (New York: Basic Books, 2004).

17. For an insightful analysis of shifts in pathways of influence in American national policymaking, see Paul Posner, Timothy Conlan, and David R. Beam, "The Politics that Pathways Make: A Framework for Contemporary Federal Policymaking," paper presented to the 2002 Annual Meeting of the American Political Science Association. Boston, MA, August 29–31, 2002.

18. In a hugely influential article, economist Gary Becker argues that political competition among interest groups limits the costs of rent-seeking behavior, very much as the pluralist theorists once claimed that interest groups check and balance one another to produce socially acceptable outcomes. Becker creates a stylized model in which interest groups vie for favors by supporting candidates with their votes and contributions. Each group promotes its favored candidates and tries to control free riding within its own organization. While smaller compact groups will tend to enjoy organizational advantages over larger groups, Becker argues that there is a limit to the particularistic benefits narrow groups can obtain without triggering counter-mobilizations from the majority and ultimately destroying the economic production that makes their subsidies possible. Gary S. Becker, "A Theory of Competition Among Pressure Groups for Political Influence, *The Quarterly Journal of Economics*, vol. 98, no. 3 (August 1983): 371–400. See also Gary Becker, "Comment," *Journal of Law and Economics*, 19 (August 1976): 245–48.

19. For evidence, see the essays contained in Alan S. Gerber and Eric M. Patashnik, eds., *Promoting the General Welfare: New Perspectives on Government Performance* (Washington, D.C.: The Brookings Institution), 2006.

20. Becker's model has three important empirical implications. First, it suggests that policy reforms will often be driven by exogenous economic or technological shifts that reduce the benefits to clientele groups of maintaining inefficient policies. Second, narrow groups will often be the prime movers behind general-interest reforms. Finally, the steady progression of inefficiencies creates a demand for reform, which the government quickly satisfies. The empirical basis for each of these claims is shaky. Exogenous shocks can make reform more attractive by lowering the payoffs available to powerful groups from the maintenance of inefficient policies, but there are often long lags between the onset of the shocks and the passage of reform legislation. This suggests that political considerations, not just technological or economic factors, drive the reform process. In addition, narrow clientele groups often devote considerable resources to preserving their existing privileges, even though they sometimes make last-minute strategic decisions to go on record in support of reforms when their passage becomes inevitable. Finally, inefficient policies may persist over long periods of time, in part because rent-seeking groups invest in their stock of political capital to secure additional rents in the future. (On this last point, see Clifford Winston and Vikram Mareshi, "Persistent Inefficiencies of Public Policy," Brookings Institution Working Paper, 2006).

While Becker's model is a vast improvement over simplistic bureaucratic capture models, it nonetheless fails to incorporate central features of democratic politics. Becker's model assumes that political transaction costs are zero; that the government is essentially a black box without independent influence of its own; that public spending is subject to a balanced-budget rule; that there is no slippage between the actions of interest group leaders and the preferences of group members; and that current officeholders who wish to "buy out" interest groups as part of reform packages can successfully bind their successors. *All of these assumptions are questionable.* For criticisms of Becker's model, see Sam Peltzman, Michael E. Levine, and Roger G. Noll, "The Economic Theory of Regulation After a Decade of Deregulation," *Brookings Papers on Economic Activity Microeconomics*, (1989), 1–59; and especially William C. Mitchell and Michael C. Munger. "Economic Models of Interest Groups: An Introductory Survey." *American Journal of Political Science*, 13, no. 2 (1991): 512–46. See also Paul J. Quirk, "In Defense of the Politics of Ideas," *The Journal of Politics*, vol. 50, no. 1 (February 1988): 31–41.

21. For a synthetic treatment, see Noll, "Comments on 'The Economic Theory of Regulation a Decade After Deregulation,'" 48–58. See also Levine and Forrence, "Regulatory Capture, Public Interest, and the Public Agenda: Toward a Synthesis."

22. For an excellent discussion of political entrepreneurship, see Adam D. Sheingate, "Political Entrepreneurship, Institutional Change, and American Political Development." *Studies in American Political Development*, 17 (Fall 2003): 185–203.

23. Martha Derthick and Paul Quirk, *The Politics of Deregulation* (Washington, D.C.: The Brookings Institution, 1985), 243.

24. Noll, "Comments on 'The Economic Theory of Regulation a Decade After Deregulation,'" 51–52.

25. R. Kent Weaver, "The Politics of Blame Avoidance," *Journal of Public Policy*, 6, no. 4 (1986): 371–98.

26. R. Douglas Arnold, *The Logic of Congressional Action* (New Haven: Yale University Press, 1990).

27. It is rare for compensation schemes to hold losers completely harmless. Total compensation for policy changes seems to be incompatible with the political and institutional context in which reform legislation is crafted. *Partial* compensation schemes are more common. See Dorothy Robyn, *Braking the Special Interests: Trucking Deregulation and the Politics of Policy Reform* (Chicago: University of Chicago Press, 1987).

28. For a defense of the strategic use of subsidies to build reform coalitions, see John W. Ellwood and Eric M. Patashnik, "In Praise of Pork," *The Public Interest* (Winter 1993): 19–33.

29. Anthony Downs, "Up and Down with Ecology: The Issue Attention Cycle." *The Public Interest*, 28, (1972): 38–50

30. On media attention spasms, see Frank R. Baumgartner and Bryan D. Jones, *Agendas and Instability in American Politics* (Chicago: University of Chicago Press, 1993).

31. Much literature exists on the use of restrictive procedures to promote the goals of current majorities, although scholars disagree over whether the power resides in the majority party caucus or the larger chamber. Leading participants in this debate include Sarah Binder, Eric Schickler, Gary Cox and Mathew McCubbins, and Keith Krehbiel.

32. On the positive relationship between majority size and the durability of laws, see the insightful analysis in Forrest Maltzman and Charles R. Shipan, "Continuity, Change, and the Evolution of the Law," *American Journal of Political Science*, forthcoming.

33. On the surprising advantages of comprehensive reform over incremental reform, see Arnold, *The Logic of Congressional Action*, 110. See also Jacob Hacker, "Learning from Defeat: Political Analysis and the Failure of Health Care Reform in the United States," *British Journal of Political Science*, vol. 31, no. 1 (2001): 61–94.

34. Terry M. Moe, "The Politics of Structural Choice: Toward a Theory of Public Bureaucracy," in Oliver Williamson, ed., *Organization Theory from Chester Barnard to the Present and Beyond* (New York: Oxford University Press, 1990).

35. For example, policymakers may announce a tight money policy to lower inflation expectations, only to find themselves subsequently compelled to increase the money supply when economic activity slows, resulting in larger inflation expectations than if policymakers could credibly commit themselves to honoring their promises.

36. Finn Kydland and Edward Prescott, "Rules Rather than Discretion: The Inconsistency of Optimal Plans" *Journal of Political Economy* (June 1977).

37. Compensation schemes also can send the wrong signals to interest groups, making them skeptical that the reform process will continue. Ideally, constituencies should adjust themselves to the new regime. They should shift resources away from rent-seeking and into more socially productive activities. They need to develop a new "cognitive mind set" in which group leaders believe their economic fates no longer depend upon artificial subsidies. Reforms may do little to promote this new mindset if compensation payments are not credibly tied to the reform's maintenance.

38. For a related discussion, see William N. Eskridge & John Ferejohn, *Super-Statutes*, 50 *Duke L.J.*, 1215 (2001): 1215–76.

39. Stephen Skowronek, *Building a New American State: The Expansion of National Administrative Capacities, 1877–1920* (New York: Cambridge University Press, 1982).

40. The literature on procedural or structural control is voluminous. See, for example, Mathew McCubbins, Roger Noll, and Barry Weingast, "Administrative Procedures as Instruments of Political Control," *Journal of Law, Economics, and Organization*, vol. 3, no. 2 (Fall 1987): 243–78 and Terry M. Moe "The Politics of Bureaucratic Structure," in *Can the Government Govern?* John E. Chubb and Paul E. Peterson, eds., (Washington, D.C.: Brookings Institution Press, 1990).

41. See David E. Lewis, "The Politics of Agency Termination: Confronting the Myth of Agency Immortality," *The Journal of Politics*, vol. 64, no. 1 (February 2002), 89–107.

42. See Avinash K. Dixit, *The Making of Economic Policy: A Transaction-Cost Politics Perspective* (Cambridge, MIT Press, 1996); see also David Epstein and Sharyn O'Halloran, *Delegating Powers: A Transaction Cost Politics Approach to Policy Making Under Separate Powers* (New York: Cambridge University Press, 1999).

43. Lawrence Becker, *Doing the Right Thing: Collective Action and Procedural Choice in the New Legislative Process* (Columbus, Ohio: Ohio State University Press, 2005).

44. On venue change, see Baumgartner and Jones, *Agendas and Instability in American Politics.*

45. *Ibid.*

46. Glazer and Rothenberg, *Why Government Succeeds and Why It Fails.*

47. Michael Bailey, Judith Goldstein, and Barry R. Weingast. "The Institutional Roots of American Trade Policy: Politics, Coalitions, and International Trade," *World Politics*, 49, no. 3 (1997): 309–38.

48. See Paul Pierson, *Politics in Time* (Princeton: Princeton University Press, 2004), 103–32.

49. Eric Schickler, *Disjointed Pluralism* (Princeton: Princeton University Press, 2001).

50. Joseph A. Schumpeter, *The Theory of Economic Development: An Inquiry into Profits, Capital, Credit, Interest, and the Business Cycle* (Oxford: Oxford University, 1969).

51. Marc K. Landy and Martin A. Levin, "Creating Competitive Markets: The Politics of Market Design," in Marc K. Landy, Martin A. Levin, and Martin Shapiro, eds., *Creating Competitive Markets* (Washington, D.C.: Brookings Institution Press, 2007), 17.

52. Sheingate, "Political Entrepreneurship, Institutional Change, and American Political Development."

53. Schickler, *Disjointed Pluralism.*

54. By markets, I mean the social process of voluntary, self-regarding exchange. It is important to distinguish the market process from both the actors who participate in markets (e.g., firms, workers, etc.) and from the political-institutional foundations and auxiliaries (e.g., property rights, courts) that lower transaction costs and enable markets to function. See Eric M. Patashnik, "The Day After Market Oriented Reform, or What Happens When Economists' Ideas Meet Politics," in Landy, Levin, and Shapiro, eds., *Creating Competitive Markets*, 267–89.

55. Mayhew stresses that members of Congress have an incentive to win victories only on legislation dealing with particularized benefits. On other laws, the electoral credit comes from being on the right side, not the winning one. Mayhew, *Congress: The Electoral Connection*, 114 and *passim.*

56. The literature is voluminous. For an early summary statement, see Theda Skocpol. "The Origins of Social Policy in the United States," in *The Dynamics of American Politics*, Lawrence C. Dodd and Calvin Jillson, eds., (Boulder, Colorado: Westview Press, 1994), 182–206. For an excellent literature review, see Suzanne Mettler and Joe Soss, "The Consequences of Public Policy for Democratic Citizenship: Bridging Policy Studies and Mass Politics," *Perspectives on Politics*, vol. 2, no. 1 (March 2004): 55–73; see also Joe Soss, Jacob S. Hacker, and Suzanne Mettler, editors, *Remaking America: Democracy and Public Policy in an Age of Inequality* (New York: Russell Sage Foundation, 2007).,

57. E. E. Schattschneider, *Politics, Pressure, and the Tariff* (New York: Prentice-Hall, 1935), 288.

58. Theodore Lowi, "American Business, Public Policy, Case-Studies, and Political Theory." *World Politics*, 16 (1964): 677–715; James Q. Wilson, *Political Organizations* (New York: Basic Books: 1973).

59. Examples of key works include Theda Skocpol, *Protecting Soldiers and Mothers: The Political Origins of Social Policy in the United States* (Cambridge: Harvard University Press, 1992); Paul Pierson "When Effect Becomes Cause: Policy Feedback and Political Change," *World Politics*, vol. 45, no. 4 (July 1993): 595–628; Andrea Louise Campbell, *How Policies Make Citizens: Senior Political Activism and the American Welfare State* (Princeton: Princeton University Press, 2003); Suzanne B. Mettler, "Bringing the State Back in to Civic Engagement: Policy Feedback Effects of the G.I. Bill for World War II Veterans," *American Political Science Review*, vol. 96, no. 2 (June 2002): 351–65; Joe Soss and Sanford F. Schram, "A Public Transformed? Welfare Reform as Policy Feedback," *American Political Science Review*, vol. 101, no. 1 (February 2007): 111–27; and Paul Pierson and Theda Skocpol, eds., *The Transformation of American Politics: Activist Government and the Rise of Conservatism* (Princeton: Princeton University Press, 2007).

60. Not all social programs generate positive feedback on mass political behavior, however. The former AFDC program, for example, had a negative impact on recipients' sense of external political efficacy and reduced their voter turnout. Joe Soss, "Lessons of Welfare: Policy Design, Political Learning, and Political Action," *American Political Science Review*, vol. 93, no. 2 (1999): 363–80.

61. Campbell, *How Policies Make Citizens*.

62. Mettler, "Brining the State Back in to Civic Engagement."

63. Hacker, *The Divided Welfare State*.

64. For an excellent analysis of the conditions under which policies should be expected to generate feedback in the mass public, see Soss and Schram, "A Public Transformed? Welfare Reform as Policy Feedback."

65. Interestingly, the original focus of the feedback literature was on the mindsets of officeholders and the goals of organized interests. In her 1992 book *Protecting Soldiers and Mothers*, for example, Skocpol showed that party-based corruption associated with Civil War pensions created a negative precedent against the subsequent enactment of old-age pensions in the United States. Skocpol, *Protecting Soldiers and Mothers*.

66. On interest-group "spoils," see Pierson, *Dismantling the Welfare State*, 40.

67. Clifford Winston stimulated me to think about this point.

68. A related issue is whether the cognitive mindsets of officeholders themselves change after reform.

69. It is especially challenging to alter cognitive mindsets when the government retains a residual role in a reformed sector.

70. On the social construction of clientele groups, see Anne Schneider and Helen Ingram. "Social Construction of Target Populations: Implications for Politics and Policy," *American Political Science Review*, vol. 87, no. 2 (June 1993): 334–48.

71. Baumgartner and Jones, *Agendas and Instability in American Politics*.

72. For other efforts to think systemically about the conditions under which positive and negative feedback can be expected to arise, see Hacker, "Privatizing Risk Without Privatizing the Welfare State: The Hidden Politics of Welfare State Retrenchment in the United States; and Soss and Schram, "A Public Transformed? Welfare Reform as Policy Feedback."

73. Skocpol, "The Origins of Social Policy in the United States."

74. See Hugh Heclo, "Issue Networks and the Executive Establishment," in Anthony King, ed., *The New American Political System* (Washington, D.C.: American Enterprise Institute, 1978), 87–125.

75. John P. Heinz, Edward O. Laumann, Robert L. Nelson, and Robert H. Salisbury, *The Hollow Core* (Cambridge: Harvard University Press, 1993).

76. Pierson, *Politics in Time*.

77. Kathleen Thelen, "Historical Institutionalism in Comparative Politics." *American Review of Political Science*, 2 (1999): 369–404.

78. I owe this phrase to an anonymous referee.

79. This is a dynamic akin to what other scholars have termed "layering." See, for example, Hacker, "Privatizing Risk Without Privatizing the Welfare State: The Hidden Politics of Welfare State Retrenchment in the United States;" Orren and Skowronek, *The Search for American Political Development*; and Schickler, *Disjointed Pluralism*.

80. An example from the education reform arena would be the durable implementation of a new K–12 standardized testing regime that shifts teachers' course preparations and lesson plans, but does not otherwise alter the power or political behavior of parents, administrators, or teachers' unions. In contrast, school choice programs, if sustained, would be an example of reconfiguration.

CHAPTER 3
EXPERT IDEAS MEET POLITICS: REFORMING THE TAX CODE

1. Alan Greenspan, quoted in Jeffrey H. Birnbaum and Alan S. Murray, *Showdown at Gucci Gulch* (New York: Vintage Books, 1988).

2. Michael J. Graetz, "Tax Reform Unraveling," *Journal of Economic Perspectives*, vol. 21, no.1 (Winter 1997): 72.

3. Christopher Howard, *The Hidden Welfare State: Tax Expenditures and Social Policy in the United States* (Princeton: Princeton University Press, 1997).

4. This paragraph draws on W. Elliott Brownlee, *Federal Taxation in America: A Short History, 2nd Edition* (New York: Cambridge University Press, 2004), 130.

5. Paul R. McDaniel and Stanley S. Surrey, *Tax Expenditures* (Cambridge: Harvard University Press, 1985).

6. John F. Witte, *The Politics and Development of the Federal Income Tax* (Madison: University of Wisconsin Press, 1985), 364.

7. Sheldon D. Pollack, *The Failure of U.S. Tax Policy* (University Park, Pennsylvania: Penn State Press, 1996), 74.

8. The Tax Reform Act of 1969 is an important exception. See Julian E. Zelizer, *Taxing America* (New York: Cambridge University Press, 1998).

9. Birnbaum and Murray, *Showdown at Gucci Gulch* (New York: Vintage Books, 1988), 14.

10. Witte, *The Politics and Development of the Federal Income Tax*, 292.

11. Ibid., 242–43; and Zelizer, *Taxing America*, 308–11.

12. C. Eugene Steuerle, *The Tax Decade* (Washington, D.C.: The Urban Institute, 1992), 33.

13. Pollack, *The Failure of Tax Policy*, 82.

14. Witte, *The Politics and Development of the Federal Income Tax*, 349.

15. As John F. Witte argued—quite correctly—in 1985, there was "nothing, absolutely nothing in the history or politics of the income tax that indicates that any of these [fundamental tax reform] schemes has the slightest hope of being enacted in the forms proposed. *Ibid.*, 380.

16. Eileen Shanahan, "House Overwhelmingly OKs Tax Overhaul Bill," *Congressional Quarterly Weekly Report*, " September 27, 1986, 2255; Eileen Shanahan, "Senate Clears Massive Tax Overhaul Measure, Technical Corrections Pose Minor Hang-up," *Congressional Quarterly Weekly Report*, October 4, 1986, 2344.

17. Timothy J. Conlan, David R. Beam, Margaret Wrightson, "Policy Models and Political Change: Insights from the Passage of Tax Reform," Marc K. Landy and Martin A. Levin, eds., *The New Politics of Public Policy* (Baltimore: Johns Hopkins University Press, 1995), 135. See also Pollack, *The Failure of U.S. Tax Policy*, 126.

18. *Ibid.*, 168–72.

19. John H. Makin and Norman J. Ornstein, *Debt and Taxes* (New York: Times Books, 1994), 194.

20. Birnbaum and Murray, *Showdown at Gucci Gulch*, 23–31.

21. Timothy J. Conlan, David Beam, and Margaret Wrightson, "Policy Models and Political Change," 315, n. 46.

22. Ronald Reagan, address before a Joint Session of the Congress on the State of the Union, January 25, 1984, in Public Papers of the Presidents: Ronald Reagan, 1994 (Washington, D.C. Government Printing Office, 1986), 87.

23. U.S. Department of the Treasury, *Tax Reform for Fairness, Simplicity, and Economic Growth*, Washington, D.C., November 1984. The tax reform issue was politically sensitive enough with the public, and with Republican constituencies, that Reagan insisted that the proposal not be released until after the 1984 election.

24. Joseph White and Aaron Wildavsky, *The Deficit and the Public Interest* (Berkeley: University of California Press, 1989), 476.

25. On the bill's legislative odyssey, see Birnbaum and Murray, *Showdown at Gucci Gulch*; and David E. Rosenbaum, "The Tax Reform Act of 1986: How the Measure Came Together; A Tax Bill for the Textbooks," *The New York Times*, October 23, 1986, D16.

26. R. Douglas Arnold, *The Logic of Congressional Action* (New Haven: Yale University Press, 1990), 213.

27. *Ibid.*, 218.

28. The 15 percent rate was phased out for taxpayers with relatively high incomes

and eliminated completely for those with the highest incomes. A 5 percent surtax on income was imposed on taxpayers subject to the phase-out. Taxpayers in this phase-out range were thus subject to a top marginal tax rate of 33 percent.

29. For a summary of the reform's major provisions, see "Major Provisions of the Tax Reform Act," *Congressional Quarterly Weekly Report*, (October 4, 1986), 2350.

30. Gary Klott, "Rostenkowski Opposes Big '87 Tax Changes," *The New York Times*, October 22, 1986, D2.

31. Steuerle, *Contemporary U.S. Tax Policy*, 175.

32. Graetz, "Tax Reform Unraveling," 70.

33. Barbara Bradley, "Tax Pruning Due Creates Opportunity," *Christian Science Monitor*, March 20, 1987, B6. In fiscal 1986, the federal deficit stood at 5 percent of GDP and the out years looked even bleaker.

34. Joseph White and Aaron Wildavsky describe the improbable triumph of tax reform as a "counterpoint" to the deficit wars of the 1980s and early 1990s. See White and Wildavsky, *The Deficit and the Public Interest*, chapter 21.

35. Randall Weiss, "The Tax Reform Act of 1986: Did Congress Love it or Leave It?" *National Tax Journal*, vol. 49, no. 3 (September 1996): 455.

36. On the 1990 Act, see White and Wildavsky, *The Deficit and the Public Interest*, 577–89; and Pollack, *The Failure of U.S. Tax Policy*, 117–20.

37. On the 1993 Act, see Paul Pierson, "The Deficit and the Politics of Domestic Reform," in Margaret Weir, editor, *The Social Divide* (Washington, D.C.: The Brookings Institution, 1998), 126–80.

38. Alan Auerbach, "The U.S. Tax Reform Experience," comments prepared for presentation at the Workshop on Tax Reform in Japan, Economic and Social Research Institute, September 12, 2002, 7.

39. Steven Greenhouse, "Squaring off on Taxes; Clinton Proposals Are Drawing Fire from Supporters of the 1986 Reform law," *The New York Times*, May 6, 1993, D1.

40. President's Advisory Panel on Federal Tax Reform, *Simple, Fair, and Pro-Growth: Proposals to Fix America's Tax System*, chapter 2, 15.

41. Alison E. Post and Paul Pierson, "How a Law Stays a Law: The Durability of U.S. Tax Breaks, 1967–2003," prepared for presentation at the annual meeting of the American Political Science Association, September 1–4, 2005. Washington, D.C.

42. Quoted in Zelizer, *Taxing America*, 309.

43. Michael J. Graetz, *The Decline (and Fall?) of the Income Tax* (New York: Norton, 1997), 142.

44. "America's Tax Laws, Vastly Simplified Three Years Ago, Are Slipping Back into Their Bad Old Ways," *The Economist*, October 7, 1989, 16.

45. David S. Cloud, "Clinton Strategy Renews Debate over Investment Tax Credit," *Congressional Quarterly Weekly Report*, November 14, 1992, 3637. Most mainstream economists scoffed at this prediction of future job growth, and the investment credit was not enacted. See David E. Rosenbaum, "Rejection Is Seen for a Tax Credit Aimed at Business," *The New York Times*, April 10, 1993, A1.

46. Greenhouse, "Squaring off on Taxes; Clinton Proposals Are Drawing Fire from Supporters of the 1986 Reform law," D1.

47. Leslie B. Samuels, "Clinton Won't Undo 1986 Tax Reforms, Treasury Nominee Tells Finance Panel," *The Bond Buyer*, April 27, 1993, 1.

48. Anne Swardson, "Lawmakers Clamor Anew for Tax Breaks," *The Washington Post*, April 17, 1988, H1.

49. Howard Gleckman, "Tinkering with Tax Reform: A Bad Idea that Will just Get Worse," *BusinessWeek*, November 6, 1989, 104.

50. *Ibid.*

51. Allen Schick, *The Federal Budget—Revised Edition* (Washington, D.C.: The Brookings Institution, 2000), 151.

52. The President's Advisory Panel on Tax Reform, *Simple, Fair, and Pro-Growth: Proposals to Fix America's Tax System*, chapter 2, ("How We Got Here"), 16.

53. U.S. General Accountability Office, *Government Performance and Accountability: Tax Expenditures Represent a Substantial Federal Commitment and Need to Be Reexamined* GAO05-690, September 2005, 22.

54. See Jill Barshay, "Corporate Tax Bills, Stuffed, Scorned—and Supported," *Congressional Quarterly Weekly Report*, June 26, 2004, 1540; Jonathan Weisman, "President Signs Corporate Tax Legislation," *The Washington Post*, October 23, 2004, A10.

55. The TRA did not target any of the major existing social tax expenditures (e.g., the home mortgage interest deduction) for outright repeal; the provisions were considered too politically sensitive.

56. Eric Lukus, "Education Tax Package Offers Middle-Class Families a Break; But Experts Worry Tuition Inflation Could Wipe Out Any Gains." *The Baltimore Sun*, April 5, 1A.

57. Since the late 1980s, the public has consistently ranked the federal income tax as the first or second worst major tax (the local property tax has edged out the income tax for bottom billing in some recent surveys—unsurprising given the rapid increase in property values). For survey data, see John Kincaid and Richard L. Cole, "Changing Public Attitudes on Power and Taxation in the American Federal Tax System," *Publius*, vol. 31, no. 3 (Summer 2001): 205–14.

58. Poll data cited in W. Lance Bennett and Erik Asard, "The Marketplace of Ideas: The Rhetoric and Politics of Tax Reform in Sweden and the United States," *Polity*, vol. 28, no. 1 (Fall 1988), fn 55, 14.

59. *Ibid.*

60. David E. Rosenbaum, "Tax Simplification Proves Elusive," *The New York Times*, March 4, 1990, Section 3, 13.

61. Graetz, *The Decline (and Fall?) of the Income Tax*, 139.

62. Members of the House Ways and Means and Senate Finance Committee received two times as much money from political action committees in 1985 ($6.7 million) as they did in 1983 ($2.7 million), according to a Common Cause study. See Anne Swardson, "Tax Writers Reportedly in the Money," *The Washington Post*, February 11, 1986, A13.

63. Poll data cited in Kevin Phillips, *The Politics of Rich and Poor* (New York: Random House, 1990), 247.

64. Alan J. Auerbach and Joel Slemrod, "The Economic Effects of the Tax Reform Act of 1986," *Journal of Economic Literature*, (June 1997): 589–632.

65. Graetz, *The Decline (and Fall?) of the Income Tax*, 136.

66. Auerbach and Slemord, "The Economic Effects of the Tax Reform Act of 1986," 626–27.

67. Tax reform and realizations of capital gains in 1986. Leonard E. Burman, Kim-

berly A. Clausing, and John F. O'Hare. *National Tax Journal*, vol. 47, no. 1 (March 1994): 1–18.

68. *Ibid.*; see also Eric M. Engen and William G. Gale, "Tax Preferred Assets and Debt and the Tax Reform Act of 1986: Some Implications for Fundamental Tax Reform," *National Tax Journal*, vol. 49, no. 3 (September 1996): 331–39.

69. *Ibid.*

70. www.hrblock.com/presscenter/about/fastFacts.jsp

71. For a prescient and skeptical assessment of the likelihood that TRA was a true policy watershed signaling a long-term change in legislative incentives and institutions, see John F. Witte, "The Tax Reform Act of 1986: A New Era in Tax Politics?" *American Political Quarterly*, vol. 19, no 4 (October 1991): 438–57.

72. For the Treasury Department's view on the TRA's impact, see www.ustreas .gov/education/fact-sheets/taxes/ustax.html.

73. Carol Matlack, "Coming Unglued," *National Journal*, November 4, 1989, 2692.

74. On the high value of seats on the tax writing panels, see Tim Groseclose; Charles Stewart III, "The Value of Committee Seats in the House, 1947–1991," *American Journal of Political Science*, vol. 42, no. 2 (April 1998), 453–74; and Keith M. Edwards and Charles Stewart III, "The Value of Committee Assignments in Congress Since 1994," prepared for the 2006 Annual Meetings of the Southern Political Science Avocation, Atlanta, Georgia, January 5–7, 2006. These studies show the tax-writing panels consistently at or near the top in terms of members' own rankings. Of course, other items within the tax panels' jurisdiction—such as entitlement spending—have also grown in importance over time.

75. Jeffrey Milyo, "Electoral and Financial Effects of Changes in Committee Power: The Gramm-Rudman-Hollings Budget Reform, The Tax Reform Act of 1986, and The Money Committees in the House," *Journal of Law and Economics*, vol. 40, no. 1 (April 1997): 105.

76. Graetz, *The Decline (and Fall?) of the Income Tax*, 289.

77. Unlike farm subsidies provided in response to declining prices, tax expenditures could not be framed as "emergency spending" exempt from budget enforcement rules.

78. See Eric M. Patashnik, "Budgets and Fiscal Policy," in Paul J. Quirk and Sarah A. Binder, eds., *The Legislative Branch* (New York: Oxford University Press), 382–406.

79. Graetz, "The Unraveling of Tax Reform," 82. George K. Yin has produced hard data on the decline. Between 1981 and 1986, net losses reported by limited partnerships (a vehicle for many tax sheltering activities) increased by 123 percent, while net income reported by limited partnerships increased by 115 percent over that period. In contrast, from 1986 to 1996, net income from limited partnerships and LLCs increased over 600 percent, but net losses reported were essentially constant. See George K. Yin, "Getting Serious About Corporate Tax Shelters: Taking a Lesson from History," 54 *SMU L. Rev.* (2001): 209–38.

80. Joseph Bankman, "The New Market in Corporate Tax Shelters," Tax Notes, June 21, 1999, 1776.

81. Graetz, "The Unraveling of Tax Reform," 82.

82. Remarks of Treasury Secretary Lawrence H. Summers, "Tracking the Growth of Corporate Tax Shelters," Federal Bar Association, Washington, D.C., February 28, 2000, www.ustreas.gov/press/releases/ls421.htm.

83. Bankman, "The New Market in Corporate Tax Shelters," 1784.

84. Proceedings of "The 1986 Tax Reform Act—What Are the Lessons for Today?" A Tax Analysts Conference Series, Washington, D.C., April 1, 2005, 1.

85. Karen Orren and Stephen Skowronek, *The Search for American Political Development* (New York: Cambridge University Press, 2004), 129.

86. Jonathan Chait, "Bush's Fake Tax Reform. Bait And. . .." *The New Republic*, January 17, 2005, 17.

87. Robert Hall and Alvin Rabushka, *The Flat Tax* (Palo Alto: The Hoover Institution Press, 1995).

88. See William G. Gale and Peter R. Orszag, "Bush Administration Tax Policy: Down Payment on Tax Reform?" *Tax Notes*, November 8, 2004, 879–84.

89. See Michael J. Graetz, "A Fair and Balanced Tax Code for the 21st Century," paper delivered at American Enterprise Institute Tax Policy Conference, February 11, 2005.

90. See William G. Gale and Peter R. Orszag, "Bush Administration Tax Policy: Down Payment on Tax Reform?" *Tax Notes*, November 8, 2004, 879–84.

91. The President's Advisory Panel on Tax Reform, *Simple, Fair, and Pro-Growth: Proposals to Fix America's Tax System* (Washington, D.C.: Government Printing Office, November 2005, chapter 2, ("How We Got Here"), 14.

92. Jeffrey H. Birnbaum, "Commission Proposes Changes in Tax System," *The Washington Post*, November 2, 2005, A01.

93. Sandra Fleischman, "Deduction Eruption," *The Washington Post*, November 12, 2005, F01.

94. Edmund L. Andrews, "Bush Expected to Postpone Tax Overhaul Until 2007," *The New York Times*, December 6, 2005, 3; and Joseph J. Schatz, "The Power of the Status Quo on Taxes," *Congressional Quarterly Weekly Report*, February 6, 2006, 322.

95. "A Tax Law to Hail. Yes, a Tax Law," *The New York Times*, October 22, 1986, A30.

96. Peter Passell, "Back Door Attack on 'Tax Reform,'" *The New York Times*, September 28, 1988, D2.

97. On this institutional reform idea, see Alan S. Blinder, "Is Government too Political?" *Foreign Affairs*, (November/December 1997): 115–20. See also John F. Witte, *The Politics and Development of the Federal Income Tax*, 379–85. Constitutional issues might also be raised by any effort to delegate control over tax policy.

98. Quoted in Fred S. McChesney, *Money for Nothing: Politicians, Rent Extraction, and Political Extortion* (1997), 94.

Chapter 4
Freedom to Farm? The Mixed Case of Agricultural Reform

1. David Sanger, "Reversing Course, Bush Signs Bill Raising Farm Subsidies," *The New York Times*, May 14, 2002, 16; Mike Allen, "Bush Signs Bill Providing Big Farm Subsidy Increases," *The Washington Post*, May 14, 2002, A1.

2. David Hosansky, "Farm Subsidies," *CQ Researcher*, May 17, 2002, 435.

3. "Cringe for Mr. Bush," *The Washington Post*, May 31, 2002, A20.

4. David Orden, "U.S. Agricultural Policy: The 2002 Farm Bill and WTO DOHA Round Proposal," International Food Policy Research Institute Discussion Paper No. 109, February 2003, 2.

5. My discussion of the political development of U.S. farm policy draws heavily on the following excellent studies: David Orden, Robert Paarlberg, and Terry Roe, *Policy Reform in American Agriculture* (Chicago: University of Chicago Press, 1999); Adam D. Sheingate, *The Rise of the Agricultural Welfare State* (Princeton, New Jersey: Princeton University Press, 2001); Graham K. Wilson, *Special Interests and Policymaking* (London: John Wiley & Sons, 1977); and Bruce L. Gardner, *American Agriculture in the Twentieth Century* (Cambridge, Massachusetts: Harvard University Press, 2002).

6. The CCC loans in effect gave farmers a free "put" option, enabling them to sell their crops at a prespecified price.

7. Gardner, *American Agriculture*, 218.

8. Orden, Paarlberg, and Roe, *Policy Reform in American Agriculture*, 22.

9. Graham Wilson, "To Market, To Market. . . .and Back Again: Change and Fluctuation in Agricultural Policy and Politics in the United States," paper prepared for the Conference on the Politics and Economics of the Market, Brandeis University, February 4–5, 2005, 4.

10. Sheingate, *The Rise of the Agricultural Welfare State*, 193.

11. John Mark Hansen, *Gaining Access: Congress and the Farm Lobby, 1919–1981* (Chicago: University of Chicago Press, 1991).

12. Orden, Paarlberg, and Roe, *Policy Reform in American Agriculture*, 70–71; see also Sheingate, *The Rise of the Agriculture Welfare State*, 142.

13. Orden, Paarlberg, and Roe, *Policy Reform in American Agriculture*, 68–69, 232.

14. *Ibid.*, 72–82.

15. The CRP program was the result of an emerging logrolling relationship between environmental groups and farm interests. This program is not analyzed in this study, but suffice it to say that its net social benefits are a matter of controversy among policy analysts.

16. Gardner, *American Agriculture*, 216–17.

17. U.S. Department of Agriculture, *Agriculture Statistics*, various years.

18. Suzanne Steel, "Farm to Market," *Columbus Dispatch*, February 26, 1995, 3H.

19. See James Bovard, *The Farm Fiasco* (San Francisco: Institute for Contemporary Studies, 1989). According to another study, 73 percent of the $15.2 billion in farm payments in 1999 went to 263,537 farm households with farm crop and livestock sales over $100,000. These households comprised less than 15 percent of all farm households and only 0.2 percent of the nation's population. Payments averaged $42,020 on these farms. Luther Tweeten, "Farm Commodity Programs: Essential Safety Net or Corporate Welfare," in Luther Tweeten and Stanley R. Thompson, eds., *Agriculture Policy in the 21st Century* (Ames: Iowa State Press, 2002), 1–34.

20. Lee S. Friedman, "Wither, or Whither, Agricultural Crop Subsidies," keynote luncheon address, American Agricultural Economics Association, Montreal, Canada, July 2, 2003, 10.

21. *Ibid.* These risk-hedging mechanisms would allow farmers to sell their crops at a preset future price. Futures contracts are typically standardized and traded in an exchange. Forward contracts are privately negotiated.

22. Orden, Paarlberg, and Roe, *Policy Reform in American Agriculture*, 82.

23. Luther Tweeten, Testimony on "Farm Programs: Are Americans Getting What They Pay For?" Senate Committee on Agriculture, Nutrition, and Forestry, Washing-

ton, D.C., March 9, 1995. See also Thomas A. Fogarty, "Freedom to Farm? Not Likely," *USA Today*, January 3, 2002, 2B.

24. James Bovard, "The 1995 Farm Follies," *Regulation*, www.cato.org/pubs/regulation/regv18n3/reg18n3-bovard.html.

25. Quoted in *Congressional Almanac* (1996), 3–15.

26. The vote was bipartisan in the House (R 211-17; D 106-72), but not in the Senate (R 52-1; D 22-25).

27. Associated Press, "Clinton Signs Farm Bill Ending Subsidies," *The New York Times*, April 5, 1996, A22.

28. For excellent analyses of Freedom to Farm's passage, see Orden, Paarlberg, and Roe, *Policy Reform in American Agriculture*;125–95; and Sheingate, *The Rise of the Agriculture Welfare State*, 201–7.

29. David Hosansky, "Clinton and Congress Divided Over Farmers' Safety Net," *Congressional Quarterly Weekly Report*, December 9, 1995, 3730.

30. David Hosansky, "Panel Rejects Farm Overhaul in a Rebuke to Leadership," *Congressional Quarterly Weekly Report*, September 23, 1995, 2875.

31. Guy Gugilotta, "Democratic Tactics Prove Useful to GOP Leaders," *The Washington Post*, October 8, 1995, A04.

32. Sheingate, *The Rise of the Agricultural Welfare State*, 203.

33. *Ibid.*, 208–9.

34. Quoted in Jonathan Rauch "Cash Crops," *The National Journal*, May 4, 1996, 978.

35. Orden, Paarlberg, and Roe, *Policy Reform in American Agriculture*, 147–50.

36. Bruce Gardner, Personal Communication, December 15, 2003.

37. *Congressional Record*, March 28, 1996, 3151.

38. Guy Gugilotta, "Spending Limits May Nibble at Hill Effort to Aid Farmers," *The Washington Post*, March 7, 1999, A4.

39. Sue Kirchhoff and Alan Greenblatt," Economic Surplus Leavers Farmers Disgruntled with Congress, '96 Farm Law," *Congressional Quarterly Weekly Report*, May 30, 1998, 1461.

40. By treating these new farm payments as "emergency spending," Congress was able to circumvent tough budget enforcement rules.

41. Quoted in Charles Pope, "When Markets Fail the Farm," *Congressional Quarterly Weekly Report*, March 4, 2000, 452–54.

42. Rauch, "Cash Crops," 978.

43. David Orden, "Reform's Stunted Crop," *Regulation*, Spring 2002, 26–32,

44. "'02 Farm Bill Revised Subsidies," *2002 Congressional Quarterly Almanac* (Washington, DC: CQ Press, 2003), 4:3–4:6.

45. The Administration evidently felt sheepish enough about the bill to hold the signing ceremony away from the White House and at the ungodly hour of 7:45 a.m. Presidential adviser Karl Rove insisted on a low profile ceremony to avoid drawing media attention in Washington, joking at one point that the president might sign the bill by candlelight. A more positive reason for the early morning signing ceremony was to ensure the news would be picked up in early crop broadcasts in farm states. Mike Allen, "Bush Signs Bill Providing Big Farm Subsidy Increases," *The Washington Post*, May 14, 2002, A1.

46. Lawrence Lindsay, "A Farm Bill Worth Signing," *The Wall Street Journal*, May 14, 2002, A18.

47. Quoted in Charles Johnson, "House Passes $170 Billion Farm Bill, Backs Target Prices," *Western Farm Press*, October 20, 2001, 20.

48. Quoted in Gebe Martinez, "Free-Spending Farm Bill: A Triumph of Politics," *Congressional Quarterly Weekly Report*, May 4, 2002, 1148.

49. Bruce L. Gardner, "Economists and the 2002 Farm Bill: What Is the Value-Added of Policy Analysis," *Agricultural and Resource Economics Review*, vol. 31, no. 2 (October 2002): 139–46.

50. Eric Pianin and Juliet Eilperin, "Congress Approves Farm Aid Package," *The Washington Post*, May 26, 2000, A1. On the politics of "bidding up," see John B. Gilmour, "The Bidding-Up Phenomenon: Bargaining Between Congress and the President." Presented at the 1990 Annual Meeting of the American Political Science Association, San Francisco.

51. John E. Frydenlund, "The Erosion of Freedom to Farm," *The Heritage Foundation Backgrounder 1523*, May 8, 2002.

52. David Orden, "U.S. Agricultural Policy: The 2002 Farm Bill and WTO DOHA Round Proposal," in Diaz-Bonilla, Eugenio, Soren E. Frandsen, and Sherman Robinson eds., *WTO Negotiations and Agricultural Trade Liberalization: The Effect of Developed Countries' Policies on Developing Economies* (Cambridge, MA: CABI, 2006), 80–102.

53. On committee property rights, see David C. King, *Turf Wars* (Chicago: University of Chicago Press, 1997).

54. David Hosansky, "Farm Policy on the Brink of a New Direction," *Congressional Quarterly Weekly Report*, March 23, 1996, 786.

55. Bruce L. Gardner, "Agricultural Policy: Pre- and Post-Fair Act Comparison," paper prepared for Luther Tweeten Symposium, Ohio State University, September 10, 2000.

56. Dan Morgan, "Farm Revolution Stops at Subsidies," *The Washington Post*, October 3, 2004, A3.

57. Stephen Blakely, "Seeds of Change for Farmers: The New Law Phasing Out Various Federal Subsidies Is Altering the Landscape for Agriculture," *Nation's Business*, December 1996, vol. 84, no. 12, 43–45.

58. Statement of Dusty Tallman, National Association of Wheat Growers, "Formulation of the 2002 Farm Bill," House of Representatives, Committee on Agriculture, Washington, D.C., July 17, 2001, at http://commdocs.house.gov/committees/ag/hag107G.000/hag107G_0f.htm. Retrieved November 11, 2002.

59. "Directions for Farm Policy: The Role of Government in Support of Production Agriculture," Commission on 21st Century Production Agriculture, Washington, D.C., Government Printing Office, January 2001, 18.

60. Mary Clare Jalonick, *Congressional Quarterly Weekly Report*, February 14, 2004, 354.

61. Sara Schaefer Munoz, "Bush Agriculture Plan Divides Farm Lobby," The Wall Street Journal, March 7, 2005, A4.

62. Dan Morgan, "Farm Subsidies May Not Face Limits," *The Washington Post*, April 15, 2005, A23.

63. For a hopeful assessment of the prospects for farm reform by a realist, see

Jonathan Rauch, "The Farm Bill Is a Bad Joke with a Good Punch Line," *National Journal*, May 18, 2002.

CHAPTER 5
REFORMING THE AMERICAN WELFARE STATE: ERISA AND THE MEDICARE
CATASTROPHIC COVERAGE ACT

1. The literature on the American welfare state is voluminous. Two of the best works are Jacob S. Hacker, *The Divided Welfare State: The Battle over Public and Private Social Benefits in the United States* (New York: Cambridge University Press, 2002); and Christopher Howard, *The Welfare State Nobody Knows* (Princeton: Princeton University Press, 2007).

2. "Pension Security," *The New York Times*, March 6, 1974, 36.

3. Craig Copeland, "Employment-Based Retirement Plan Participation: Geographic Differences and Trends, 2005," *Employee Benefit Research Institute Issue Brief*, (November 2006), 7.

4. Marilyn Moon, *Medicare: A Policy Primer* (Washington, D.C.: The Urban Institute Press, 79).

5. James A. Wooten, *The Employee Retirement Income Security Act of 1974: A Political History* (Berkeley: University of California Press, 2004), 3.

6. Steven A. Sass, *The Promise of Private Pensions* (Cambridge: Harvard University Press, 1997), 221.

7. This and the following paragraph are based on Sylvester J. Scheiber, "The Evolution and Implications of Federal Pension Regulation," in *The Evolving Pension System*, William G. Gale, John B. Shoven, and Mark J. Warshawsky, eds., (Washington, D.C.: Brookings Institution Press, 2005), 11–49.

8. Sass, *The Promise of Private Pensions*, 179.

9. Scheiber, "The Evolution and Implications of Federal Pension Regulation," 16.

10. Wooten, *The Employee Retirement Income Security Act of 1974*, 76–77.

11. "The widest possible scope should be given to private decision-making in the design of private pension plans, consistent with the public interest in preventing abuses," Ford stated. Quoted in Sass, *The Promise of Private Pensions*, at 200.

12. Wooten, *The Employment Retirement Income Security Act of 1974*, 80–115.

13. On the development of the proposal, see Edwin. Dale, Jr., "Government Study Proposed Reforms for Pension Plans," *The New York Times*, May 12, 1967, 67.

14. See John W. Finney, "Bill Would Widen Private Pensions," *The New York Times*, May 3, 1968, 35.

15. Wooten, *The Employment Retirement Income Security Act of 1974*, 7–8.

16. James Atwood of Equitable Life, quoted in *Ibid.*, 150.

17. Hacker, *The Divided Welfare State*, 150.

18. *Ibid.*, 149.

19. This paragraph draws on Howard, *The Welfare State Nobody Knows*, 77–80.

20. Quoted in Wooten, *The Employee Retirement Income Security Act of 1974*, 181.

21. Howard, *The Welfare State Nobody Knows*, 80.

22. Sass, *The Promise of Private Pensions*, 219.

23. Javits would later recall that his office received 20,000 letters of support for his reform efforts during one two-week period. Howard, *The Welfare State Nobody Knows*, 79.

24. Wooten, *The Employee Retirement Act of 1974*, 13.

25. "Congress Clears Bill to Regulate Pensions," *1974 CQ Almanac* (Washington, D.C.: CQ Press, 1975), 244–53.

26. Richard D. Lyons, "Pension Reform Bill Signed by President on 'Historic Day,'" *The New York Times*, September 3, 1974, 73.

27. See "Congress Clears Bill to Regulate Pensions," *1974 CQ Almanac*, 244–53.

28. Paul J. Graney, "Pension Benefit Guaranty Corporation: A Fact Sheet," *CRS Report for Congress*, 95-118 EPW, updated January 5, 2005.

29. In a defined benefit plan, benefits are calculated according to a formula or rule, usually based on years of service and a percentage of pay. In a defined contribution plan, contributions are allocated according to a predetermined formula. Individual benefits are equal to account contributions (minus withdrawals). See Employee Benefit Research Institute, *Facts from EBRI*, April 2005.

30. Hacker, *The Divided Welfare State*, 157.

31. Wooten, *The Employee Retirement Income Security Act of 1974*, 281.

32. Daniel I. Halperin and Alicia H. Munnell, "Ensuring Retirement Income for all Workers," in *The Evolving Pension System* (Washington, D.C.: Brookings Institution Press, 2005), 155–89, at 161. See also Hacker, *The Divided Welfare State*, 153–57.

33. For a quantitative study of ERISA's impact, see Johannes Ledoleter and Mark L. Power, "A Study of ERISA's Impact on Private Retirement Plan Growth," *The Journal of Risk and Insurance*, vol. 51, no. 2 (June 1984): 225–43.

34. Dennis E. Logue, *Legislative Influence on Corporate Pension Plans* (Washington: American Enterprise Institute, 1979), 67.

35. *Ibid.*

36. Other policy reforms, including affirmative action laws and occupational safety regulations, were also responsible for these changes in corporate governance during this time period. See Frank Dobbin and Frank R. Sutton, "The Strength of the Weak State: The Rights Revolution and the Rise of Human Resources Management Divisions," *The American Journal of Sociology*, vol. 104, no. 2 (September 1998), 441–47.

37. *Ibid.*

38. *Ibid.*, 449.

39. *Ibid.*

40. *Ibid.*, 454.

41. Howard, *The Hidden Welfare State*, 132.

42. *Ibid.*, 135; and Wooten, *The Employment Retirement Act of 1974*, 275.

43. See Richard A. Ippolito, "How to Reduce the Cost of Federal Pension Insurance," *Policy Analysis*, no. 523, Cato Institute, August 24, 2004.

44. "Pension Benefit Guaranty Corporation, *Structural Problems Limit Agency's Ability to Protect Itself from Risk*. Testimony of David M. Walker, Comptroller General of the United States, before the Subcommittee on Government Management, Finance, and Accountability, Committee on Government Reform, House of Representatives, March 2, 2005. This figure is for single-employer plans only. The PBGC runs another program for "multiemployer" plans, which cover employees of different companies in the same industry.

45. The PBGC's financial woes also reflect unanticipated shifts in the economy. When Congress passed ERISA, it was focused on the bankruptcy of isolated firms. It did not envision that entire industries like steel or the airlines would face bankruptcy and be unable to deliver on pension promises. See "Pension Crisis," *CQ Researcher*, February 17, 2006, 148.

46. Ariel Battelheim, "Moving to Close the Pension Gap," *Congressional Quarterly Weekly Report*, October 3, 2005, 2624.

47. David Wessel, "The Big Pension Bill: Is that All There Is?" *The Wall Street Journal*, August 3, 2006, A2.

48. Hacker, *The Divided Welfare State*, 157. The ERISA Industry Committee, a lobby group representing the interests of large employers, has advocated a higher interest rate to calculate the present value of future pension obligations to make liabilities appear smaller. "Discount Them at Your Peril," *The Economist*, February 15, 2003.

49. Richard A. Ippolito, "How to Reduce the Cost of Federal Pension Insurance," Cato Institute: *Policy Analysis*, no. 523, August 24, 2004.

50. There is no *legal* requirement for a taxpayer bailout of the PBGC, but experts consider it very likely.

51. Indeed, Wooten argues, "If PBGC cannot meet its obligations, taxpayers will end up bearing the burden. And to the extent that taxpayers bear the liability, the PBGC's premium payers will be off the hook. In sum, healthy employers in the single-employer insurance program may be better off if PBGC fails than if it survives." Labor unions also don't have a large stake in a well-funded PBGC. The most direct way to stabilize the PBGC's funding would be to rein in the growth of its liabilities. Yet, as Wooten notes, "liabilities that are costs for the PBGC are benefits for union members." It should be noted that while labor does not have a stake in a stabilized PBGC, it certainly does have a stake in termination insurance. See James A. Wooten, "A Historical Perspective on the 'Crisis' of Private Pensions," Twenty-Second Annual Carl A. Warns, Jr. Labor and Employment Law Institute Lecture, June 16, 2005.

52. On political battles over PBGC funding, see Drew Douglas, "The Pension System: Can Its Promises Be Kept?" *Congressional Quarterly Weekly Report*, April 11, 1987, 647. Janet Hook, "Retirement Income at Stake," *Congressional Quarterly Weekly Report*, March 10, 1984, 559.

53. Peter Baker, "Bush Signs Sweeping Revision of Pension Law," *The Washington Post*, August 18, 2006, D01; Sue Kirchhoff, "Pension Act: Does It Add to Instability?" *USA Today*, August 7, 2006, 4B.

54. The legislation also included provisions to allow companies to automatically enroll employees in 401(k) plans.

55. Michael R. Crittenden, "Pension Rewrite Clears After a Long Battle," *Congressional Quarterly Weekly Report*, August 7, 2006, 21.

56. Daniel I. Halperin and Alicia H. Munnell, "Ensuring Retirement Income for All," 155.

57. For an analysis, see EBRI, "An Evolving Pension System: Trends in Defined Benefit and Defined Contribution Plans, *EBRI Issue Brief* 249, September 2002.

58. Edward A. Zelinsky, "The Defined Contribution Paradigm," *Yale Law Review*, vol. 114, no. 3 (2004): 451–534.

59. William G. Gale, Leslie E. Papke, and Jack VanDerhei, "The Shifting Structure of Private Pensions," in William G. Gale, John B. Shoven, and Mark J. Warshawsky,

eds., *The Evolving Pensions System* (Washington, D.C.: The Brookings Institution, 2005), 63.

60. Jacob Hacker, *The Great Risk Shift* (New York: Oxford University Press, 2006), 54. While IRAs were originally available only to workers without private pension coverage, eligibility rules were broadened under Ronald Reagan in 1981. Just five years later, the Tax Reform Act of 1986 tightened eligibility rules and reduced the IRA deductions that taxpayers could claim. However, participation rules were liberalized and the permissible uses of accounts were broadened to include housing and education in the 1997 tax legislation. See also Hacker, *The Divided Welfare State*, 163–73.

61. Zelinsky, "The Defined Contribution Paradigm," 482.

62. James A. Wooten, "A Legislative and Political History of ERISA Preemption, Part 1," *Journal of Pension Benefits* (Autumn 2007): 31–35, at 31.

63. Michael S. Gordon, "The History of ERISA's Preemption Provision and Its Bearing on the Current Debate over Health Care Reform," *EBRI Issue Brief*, March 1993, 29.

64. Hacker, *The Divided Welfare State*, 257.

65. Daniel M. Fox and Daniel C. Shaffer, "Semi Preemption in ERISA: Legislative Process and Health Policy," *American Journal of Tax Policy* (Spring 1988), 52. The authors argue that health insurance lobbyists and members of Congress with health expertise, were not involved in the final deliberations and therefore did not grasp the stakes. Wooten disputes this finding. See Wotten, *The Employee Retirement Income Security Act of 1974*, 281.

66. Elizabeth A. Palmer, "How ERISA Backfired," *Congressional Quarterly Weekly Report*, June 13, 1992, 1707.

67. Hacker, *The Divided Welfare State*, 257.

68. Mary Ann Chirba-Martin and Troyen A. Brennan, "The Critical Role of ERISA in State Health Reform," *Health Affairs* (Spring 1994): 142–56, at 146.

69. *Ibid.*

70. Hacker, *The Divided Welfare State*, 61.

71. See Testimony of Rand E. Rosenblatt, "ERISA: A Quarter Century of Providing Workers Health Insurance," hearing before the Subcommittee on Employer-Employee Relations of the Committee on Education and the Workforce, U.S. House of Representatives, February 24, 1999.

72. Chirba-Martin and Brennan, "The Critical Role of ERISA in State Health Reform." See also, Kate Schuler, "High Court Rules Against State Efforts to Broaden Patients' Legal Rights," *Congressional Quarterly Weekly Report*, June 26, 2004, 1558.

73. This capacious understanding of the preemption clause is discussed in Edward A. Zelinsky, Travelers, Reasoned Textualism, and the New Jurisprudence of ERISA Preemption, 21 *Cardozo L. Rev.* 807 (1999): 815–27.

74. Spencer Rich, "State Health Reform Hits ERISA Law," *The Washington Post*, December 1, 1994, A10.

75. Matthew Mosk and Ylan Q. Mui, "Judge Invalidates Md. 'Wal-Mart Law,'" The Washington Post, July 20, 2006, B01.

76. If they do not want to administer the programs themselves, employers could set up "Section 125" accounts to permit workers to purchase coverage directly through a state "connector."

77. Alan Greenblatt, "Gimme Coverage," *Governing Magazine*, June 2007, 40.

78. Howard, *The Hidden Welfare State*, 133.

79. The ERISA Industry Committee grew out of the Washington Pension Report Group. See Wotten, *The Employee Retirement Income Security Act*, 119.

80. See Robert Pear, "States Seek a Voice in Company Health Plans," *The New York Times*, December 1, 1994, A28.

81. Address by Kevin Flatly, in *ERISA: 20 Years later—A Look Back, A look Ahead*, December 6, 1994, Hyatt Regency on Capitol Hill, 13.

82. Marie Gottschalk, *The Shadow Welfare State* (Ithaca Cornell University Press, 2000) 54.

83. Hacker, *The Divided Welfare State*, 296.

84. The term ERISA litigation generates more than 1.5 million hits on Google.

85. Rovner, "Congress's 'Catastrophic' Attempt to Fix Medicare," 150.

86. In 1981, the Reagan Administration tentatively proposed cuts in early Social Security benefits. The Senate repudiated the Administration by a vote of 96-0. See David Stockman, *The Triumph of Politics* (New York: Harper & Row), 192.

87. U.S. Department of Health and Human Services, Catastrophic Illness Expenses. Report to the President (Washington, D.C.: Government Printing Office, 1986).

88. Jonathan Oberlander, *The Political Life of Medicare* (Chicago: University of Chicago Press, 2003), 55.

89. Himelfarb, *Catastrophic Politics*, 24.

90. By the time Congress had finished its work, the five-year price tag of the measure had climbed from $13 to $30 billion. *Ibid.*, 31.

91. Oberlander, *The Political Life of Medicare*, 61.

92. Quoted in Paul Blustein, "'Catastrophic' Measure to Raise Taxes for Elderly," *The Washington Post*, July 1, 1988, G1.

93. Julie Rovner, "Conference Nearing a Conclusion: Dispute over Drug Benefit Slows Catastrophic Costs Bill," *Congressional Quarterly Weekly Report*, May 14, 1988, 1290.

94. Julie Rovner, "Conference Nearing a Conclusion: Dispute over Drug Benefit Slows Catastrophic Costs Bill," *Congressional Quarterly Weekly Report*, May 14, 1988, 1290.

95. Himelfarb, *Catastrophic Politics*, 62.

96. Allegations were made that the Pharmaceutical Manufacturers Avocation spent tens of millions of dollars to defeat the legislation. Rovner, "Congress's 'Catastrophic Attempt,'" 167; Moon, *Medicare: A Policy Primer*, 85.

97. See "Catastrophic Health Insurance Bill Enacted," *1988 Congressional Quarterly Almanac*, 281–92. Three of the ten Republican conferees—Senator Robert Dole (KS) and Reps. Norman F. Lent (NY) and John J. Duncan (TN) refused to sign the conference report. But House Minority Leader Robert H. Michel (R-IL), who had led opposition to the original House-passed version, urged adoption of the measure.

98. Spencer Rich, "President Reagan Signs Historic 'Catastrophic' Illness Bill, *The Washington Post*, July 1, 1988, July 2, 1988, A4.

99. Himelfarb, *Catastrophic Politics*, 73.

100. Oberlander, *The Political Life of Medicare*, 69.

101. Susan Dentzer, "A Health Care Debacle," *U.S. News & World Report*, October 9, 1989, 16. The Department of Health and Human Services did send out several mail-

ings but this campaign was evidently too limited to reach many seniors. A 1989 survey of beneficiaries found that while most respondents were quite familiar with the main Medicare program, only 36 percent were aware of the new prescription drug benefit. Ironically, less than half of the respondents (47 percent) knew about the surtax. See Spencer Rich, "Catastrophic-Health Law Unfamiliar to Elderly," *The Washington Post*, October 17, 1989, A25.

102. "Catastrophic-Coverage Law Is Repealed," *1989 CQ Almanac*, 150.

103. *Ibid.*

104. Robin Toner, "Back at Grass Roots, Congressman Is All Ears," *The New York Times*, August 18, 1989, A1.

105. AP, "House Panel Leader Jeered by Elderly in Chicago," *The New York Times*, August 19, 1989, A8.

106. David Dahh, "Catastrophic Coverage: Lawmaking Gone Awry," *St. Petersburg Times*, December 17, 1989, 1D.

107. Rovner, "How Congress," 165–66.

108. "Catastrophic Coverage Act Is Repealed," *1989 Congressional Quarterly Almanac*, 149–56.

109. Supporters lost much of their will to defend the package after the Congressional Budget Office released updated projections showing that the cost of the MCAA would be much higher than anticipated. See Moon, *Medicare: A Policy Primer*, 86; and Himelfarb, *Catastrophic Politics*, 89.

110. The final measure left intact a few Medicaid expansions that had been included in the original Act, including protections against spousal impoverishment.

111. Brian J. Donnelly (D-MA) quoted in Martin Tolchin, "Congress Rescinds Long-Term Care Before Adjourning," *The New York Times*, November 22, 1989, A1.

112. On policy learning in health policy, see Mark A. Peterson, "The Limits of Social Learning: Translating Analysis into Action," *Journal of Health Politics, Policy, & Law* (August 1997): 107–14. See also the excellent discussion in Thomas R. Oliver, Philip R. Lee, and Helene L. Lipton, "A Political History of Medicare and Prescription Drug Coverage," *The Milbank Quarterly*, vol. 82, no. 2 (2004): 335–41.

113. See "Analysis: Comparison of New Medicare Bill to One in 1988," December 8, 2003, *NPR Morning Edition*, at www.house.gov/schakowsky/Article_12_08_03 _Medicare_Bill_in_1988.html.

114. The new prescription drug benefit (Medicare Part D) will be financed by approximately 25 percent from beneficiary premiums and the remaining 75 percent from general revenues. The program will also be financed in part by state subsidies for low-income beneficiaries.

115. Oliver, Lee, and Lipton, "A Political History of Medicare and Prescription Drug Coverage," 338.

116. Nancy Weaver, "Caught in Drug Plan's Hole," *Sacramento Bee*, August 24, 2006, B1.

117. Moon, *Medicare: A Policy Primer*, 105.

118. See, for example, "Drug Plan for Seniors Risks Replay of 'Catastrophic' Past," *USA Today*, July 28, 2003, 12A; Deirdre Shesgreen, "Drug Plan for Elderly Could Help or Backfire on GOP," *St. Louis Post-Dispatch*, November 23, 2003, B1.

119. These costs will only increase if Congress closes the unpopular doughnut hole.

CHAPTER 6
UNCLE SAM GOES SHOPPING: REINVENTING GOVERNMENT PROCUREMENT

1. Federal Procurement Data Center, *Federal Procurement Report* (U.S. Government Services Administration, 2005).

2. Scott Lilly, A *Return to Competitive Contracting: Congress Needs to Clean Up the Procurement Mess*, Center for American Progress, May 2007, 3.

3. James Q. Wilson and John J. DiIulio, Jr., *American Government*, 9th *Edition* (New York: Houghton Mifflin Company, 2004), 398.

4. Martha Angle, "CQ Roundtable: Fewer Rules May Curb Procurement Abuses," *Congressional Quarterly Weekly Report*, March 12, 1994, 638.

5. In 1998, the Brookings Institution issued a five-year report card on the reinventing government initiative. While the report found that many reform objectives had not been achieved, it awarded the only full "A" to procurement reform, concluding that the system was now far more efficient than it used to be. Donald F. Kettl, *Reinventing Government: A Fifth-Year Report Card* (Washington, D.C.: The Brookings Institution, September 1998).

6. See the detailed analyses in Steven Kelman, *Unleashing Change: A Study of Organizational Renewal in Government* (Washington, D.C.: The Brookings Institution, 2005).

7. For a similar discussion of the threat of the political environment to the maintenance of flexible regulatory enforcement, see Eugene Bardach and Robert A. Kagan, *Going by the Book: The Problem of Regulatory Unreasonableness* (Philadelphia, PA: Temple University Press, 1982), especially chapter 7.

8. James W. Fesler and Donald F. Kettl, *The Politics of the Administrative Process*, 2nd *Edition* (Chatham, New Jersey: Chatham House), 302.

9. Donald F. Kettl, *Sharing Power: Public Governance and Private Markets* (Washington, D.C.: Brookings Institution Press, 1993).

10. Christopher Foreman, "Reinventing Politics? The NPR Meets Congress" in Donald F. Kettl and John J. DiIulio, Jr., *Inside the Reinvention Machine* (Washington, D.C.: The Brookings Institution, 1995), 162.

11. *Ibid.*, 4.

12. Steven Kelman, *Procurement and Public Management: The Fear of Discretion and the Quality of Government Performance* (Washington, D.C.: American Enterprise Press, 1990).

13. See Pat Towell, "Hill Weighs Bills to Avert Procurement Abuses," *Congressional Quarterly Weekly Report*, July 16, 1988, 1975.

14. On the myth of the $435 hammer, see James Q. Wilson, *Bureaucracy: What Government Agencies Do and Why They Do It* (New York: Basic Books, 1989), 319.

15. William B. Scott, "Defense Acquisition Policies Hinder Contractors' Ability to Innovate," *Aviation Week & Space Technology*, March 14, 1988, 68.

16. As one reviewer points out, there is a touch of irony in an 1800-page report about making government simpler and more efficient!

17. Department of Defense Acquisition Law Advisory Panel ["Section 800 Panel"]. "Streamlining Defense Acquisition Laws," January 1993.

18. Fred Kaplan, "Cheney Unveils Reforms, but $39b Trim Is Doubted," *The Boston Globe*, January 12, 1990, 4.

19. On the role of "reinventing government" in Clinton's governing agenda, see the perceptive essay, Margaret Weir, "Political Parties and Social Policymaking," in Margaret Weir, ed., *The Social Divide* (Washington, D.C.: The Brookings Institution, 1998), 1–48.

20. The literature on reinventing government is vast. See, for example, National Performance Review, *From Red Tape to Results: Creating a Government that Works Better and Costs Less* (Government Printing Office, 1993); Donald F. Kettl, *Reinventing Government: A Fifth Year Report Card*, CPM 98-1 (Brookings Center for Public Management, 1998); James Q. Wilson, "Reinventing Public Administration," *P.S.: Political Science & Politics*, 27, no. 4 (December 1994); and Ronald C. Moe, "The Reinventing Government Exercise: Misinterpreting the Problem, Misjudging the Consequences," *Public Administration Review*, 54, no. 2 (May/June 1994).

21. Inspiration for the Administration's reform thrust came from David Osborne and Ted Gaebler, *Reinventing Government* (New York: Addison Wesley, 1992).

22. Office of the Vice President, *From Red Tape to Results: Creating a Government that Works Better and Costs Less. Report of the National Performance Review.* (Washington, D.C.: Government Printing Office, 1993).

23. Gwen Ifill, "Gore Jumps into the Job of Cutting U.S. Waste," *The New York Times*, August 20, 1993, A20.

24. Gary Fields, "Gore a Smash Hit on Letterman," *USA Today*, September 9, 1993, 1A.

25. Kelman, *Procurement and Public Management.*

26. Anthony Flint, "Kennedy School Teacher Gets a Key Budget Post," *Boston Globe*, July 30, 1993, 7.

27. *Ibid.*, 18.

28. While corruption must be aggressively punished, it is impossible to eliminate every abuse in the vast federal contracting system. Too many dollars are at stake, and there will always be a few bad apples who will seek to exploit the rules. Just as the socially efficient level of pollution is not zero (which would require the government to shut down every factory in the nation), the bitter truth is that some level of waste is unavoidable.

29. For a critique of the 1990s procurement reforms from an orthodox perspective, see Steven L. Schooner, "Fear of Oversight: The Fundamental Failure of Businesslike Government," *American University Law Review*, 50, (2001): 627–723.

30. The distinguished bureaucracy scholar James Q. Wilson had also written about the urgent need to selectively "deregulate government" as a way to improve service delivery. See James Q. Wilson, *Bureaucracy*; see also Mark Moore, *Creating Public Value: Strategic Management in Government* (Cambridge: Harvard University Press, 1995).

31. Like President Clinton's larger "reinventing government" agenda, Kelman's criticisms of antibureaucratic controls was a "third way" approach that cut across traditional left-right ideological divisions. It was probably helpful to his nomination, however, that his book was published by the American Enterprise Institute, a center-right think tank with ties to business organizations. This probably made it harder for conservative Republicans to dismiss procurement reform as a state-building scheme of an activist-leaning Administration. Kelman's nomination was approved by the Senate Government Affairs Committee by voice vote. Al Kamen, "White House Faces a Painful Extraction," *The Washington Post*, November 19, 1993, A27.

32. See Stephanie Smith, "Civilian Procurement Efforts," CRS Report for Congress, 96-598 GOV, July 3, 1996; and "Procurement Bill Simplifies Buying," *1994 CQ Almanac* (Washington, D.C.: CQ Press, 1995), 144–47.

33. Mark Lewyn, "Washington Bogs Down in Booting Up," *Business Week*, June 6, 1994, 116.

34. Christopher J. Dorobek, "Is It Curtains at Last for the Brooks Act," *Government Computer News*, December 11, 1995, vol. 14, no. 26, 6; Christopher J. Dorobek, "Congress Passes IT Overhaul," *Government Computer News*, February 5, 1996, vol. 15, no. 3, 1; Kevin Power, "In Wake of Cohen Bill, One Thing Is for Sure: Uncertainty," *Government Computer News*, June 24, 1996, vol. 15, no. 4, 12.

35. Robert A. Kagan, *Adversarial Legalism* (Cambridge: Harvard University Press, 2001).

36. Amy Borrus, "To Overhaul Pentagon Purchasing, Bill Perry Will Have to Go to War," *BusinessWeek*, September 6, 2003, 60; GoExec.com, "Details of the New Procurement Law," www.govexec.com/archdoc/prs95/0195prs2.htm.

37. On these strategies, see R. Douglas Arnold, The Logic of Congressional Action (New Haven: Yale University Press, 1990); see also my discussion in chapter 2.

38. Stephen Barr, "Fast Track to Streamlined Procurement?" *The Washington Post*, October 25, 1993, A17.

39. Pat Towell, "Bill to Simplify Purchasing Wins Senate Approval," *Congressional Quarterly Weekly Report*, August 27, 1994.

40. Under existing law, contacts under $25,000 were normally reserved for small businesses. The House proposed eliminating the small business preference altogether, but the U.S. Chamber of Commerce pushed to retain a set-aside. Ultimately, the reform reserved most contracts between $2,500 and $10,000 for small businesses. The $2,500 threshold was intended to permit government to make small purchases from local chain stores. See Laura Livan, "Federal Procurement Reform Moves Closer to Enactment," *Nation's Business*, August 1994, 8.

41. Tom Icniowski, "Driven to Reform," Engineering News-Record, September 5, 1994, 82.

42. "The Federal Acquisition Streamlining Act of 1994," Congressional Record, vol. 140, June 8, 1994, S6565–99.

43. See Statement of Robert P. Murphy, "Procurement Reform: H.R. 1670, Federal Acquisition Reform Act of 1995," testimony before the Committee on Government Reform and Oversight and the Committee on National Security, U.S. House of Representatives, May 25, 1995.

44. For evidence of the DoD's pleasure at the ending of the GSA's authority over IT procurements, see "FY96 Defense Authorization Bill Hailed as Victory for Acquisition Reform," at www.defenselink.mil/releases/1996/b021396_bt0201ac.html.

45. Kathleen Day, "Uncle Sam's Buying Power: Effort to Change Spending Rules Spurs Debate About Competition," *The Washington Post*, November 17, 1995, D1.

46. See U.S. Congress, Committee on Government Reform and Oversight. Federal Acquisition Reform Act of 1995. House Report 104-222, Part 1, August 1, 1995, Washington, D.C.: U.S. Government Printing Office, 1995.

47. Pat Towell, "Defense Authorization: GOP Takes Another Swing at Procurement Overhaul," October 7, 1995.

48. "House Passes Bill to Revise Government Purchasing," *Congressional Quarterly Weekly Report*, September 16, 2005, 2803.

49. The text of Clinton's veto message is reprinted in *Congressional Quarterly*, January 6, 1996, 68.

50. Pat Towell, "Senate Clears Compromise Bill, Clinton Expected to Sign," *Congressional Quarterly Weekly Report*, January 27, 1996, 225.

51. Kathleen Day, "Streamlining Procurement Begins Phase 2: Behind-the Scenes Wrangling Centers on Shaping of Rules," *The Washington Post*, February 9, 1996, A19.

52. Vago Muradian, "New Rules Would Fundamentally Change Acquisition Process," *Defense Daily*, August 8, 1996.

53. Vago Muradian, "ABA, Chamber of Commerce Oppose Acquisition Changes," *Defense Daily*, October 10, 1996.

54. Vago Muradian, "Government Releases New Acquisition Rules, Seeks Comment," *Defense Daily*, September 13, 1996.

55. Quoted in Vago Muradian, "Opposition Turns to Support for New Acquisition Reform Rules," *Defense Daily*, January 3, 1997.

56. General Accounting Office, Federal Procurement: Spending and Workforce Trends: Report to the Committee on Government Reform, House of Representatives, and the Committee on Governmental Affrays, U.S. Senate, April 2003 GAO-03-443.

57. General Accountability Office, *Federal Procurement: Spending and Workforce Trends*, Report to the Committee on Government Reform, House of Representatives and the Committee on Governmental Affairs, U.S. Senate, April 2003, GAO-03-443, 13.

58. *Ibid.*, 18.

59. Schooner, "Fear of Oversight," 645.

60. *Ibid.*, 646.

61. In 1994, twenty-five civilian agencies, the military services, and the Defense Logistics Agency conducted pilot tests of the idea of using past performance data. A study by the Office of Management and Budget showed that on thirty contracts re-competed using past performance information, the average customer satisfaction level increased 21 percent over the previous contract. Anne Laurent, "All Eyes on Acquisition Reform," GovExec.com, August 30, 1999, http://govexec.com/procure/articles/97top/97topacq.htm. Some experts I interviewed, however, question the impact of past performance data on government decision-making, arguing that evaluations have been subject to "grade creep" (i.e., contract officers are reluctant to award low marks).

62. General Accounting Office, *Federal Procurement: Spending and Workforce Trends*, Report to the Committee on Government Reform, House of Representatives, and the Committee on Governmental Affairs, U.S. Senate, April 2003 GAO-03-443, 19–20.

63. Bethany Stott and Oliver Zlomislic, "Single Bid Awards Under the GSA Service Schedule," report to the U.S. General Services Administration, John F. Kennedy School of Government, Harvard University.

64. The government also committed more than $20 billion to New York city for rebuilding efforts. See U.S General Accountability Office, "U.S. General Accounting Office, September 11: Overview of Federal Disaster Assistance to the New York City Area," GAO Rep. No. GAO-04-72 (October 2003).

65. Interview with a Republican committee staff member, October 18, 2005.

66. Kelman, *Unleashing Change*, 213.

67. Shane Harris, "Federal Acquisition Workforce Ill-equipped for Procurement Reforms," GovExec.com, May 23, 2001.

68. Stephen Losey, "Problems with Interagency Contracting," February 28, 2005, www.fedearltimes.com/index2.php?s=68595.

69. United States General Accounting Office, "Acquisition Workforce: Status of Agency Efforts to Address Future Needs," Report to the Senate Committee on Government Affairs, (December 2002), GAO 03-55.

70. Professional Services Council, *2002 PSC Procurement Policy Survey* (Washington, D.C., 2002), 6.

71. Confidential interview with senior Democratic Senate staff member, October 18, 2005.

72. See Daniel P. Carpenter, *The Forging of Bureaucratic Autonomy* (Princeton, New Jersey: Princeton University Press, 2001).

73. While government waste and abuse obviously exists, the mainstream media's coverage of the topic is generally very superficial. For a scholarly study, see Fred Thompson and W. T. Stanbury, "The Political Economy of Government Waste," *Public Administration Review*, 55/5 (September/October 1995) 418–27.

74. See, for example, James F. Nagle, A History of Government Contracting (Washington, D.C.: George Washington University, 1992).

75. Ironically, some critics of the 1990s reform have questioned whether this cycle would repeat itself, suggesting that perhaps oversight mechanisms had been so degraded that the buying system would become virtually scandal-proof. This seems unlikely, given the media's insatiable appetite for stories about government waste, fraud, and abuse, and the reality that the prodigious sums spent on federal contracts really does lead some actors to play fast and loose with the rules. See Schooner, "Fear of Oversight," 712.

76. Griff Witte and Renae Merle, "Contactors Face More Scrutiny, Pinched Purses," *The Washington Post*, November 28, 2006, D1.

77. Phone interview with Congressman Tom Davis, June 22, 2007.

78. Stephen Barr, "Bush Initiative Has Employees Feeling Exposed at Interior," *The Washington Post*, November 28, 2001, B02.

79. Edward Walsh, "OMB Details 'Outsourcing' Revision," *The Washington Post*, May 30, 2003, A21.

80. Angela Styles, Nominee for Administrator, Testimony, Senate Government Affairs Committee, November 17, 2001.

81. Shane Harris, "The Procurement Reform Pendulum," Government Executive, November 15, 2002, at www.govexec.com/story_page.cfm?articleid=24292&printer-friendlyVers=1&.

82. "An Assessment of Today's Procurement System," remarks of Stephen Daniels, chairman, General Services Board of Contract Appeals, Office of Federal Procurement Policy Lecture Series, August 15, 2002; http://www.pogo.org/m/cp/cp-daniels2002.pdf.

83. Anita Reddy, "Law Aims to Change Acquisitions," *The Washington Post*, November 24, 2003, E07.

84. Jason Peckenpaugh, "Where might David Safavian Lead White House Procurement Policy?" GovExec.com, June 15, 2004, www.govexec.com/story_page.cfm?articleid=28805.

85. Safavian was alleged to have improperly used his influence at GSA in 2002 to

help Republican lobbyist Jack Abramoff obtain two federal properties. R. Jeffrey Smith and Susan Schmidt, "Bush Official Arrested in Corruption Probe," *The Washington Post*, September 20, 2005, A1.

86. Michael Hardy, "Procurement Chief's Arrest Leaves Leadership Void," *Federal Computer Week*, September 25, 2005, www.fcw.com/article90908-09-26-05-Print.

87. However, another reason for the controversy is that contract officers sometimes tried to use commercial contracting vehicles for large military purchases, such as the acquisition of a C130 cargo plane. This drew a harsh reaction from Senator John McCain in 2005. See Amy Klamper, "Air Force Tells Senator It Will Alter C130J Contract," *Congress Daily*, April 14, 2005.

88. I thank Donald F. Kettl for clarifying this important point in a personal communication.

89. Erik Eckholm, "Democrats Step Up Criticism of Halliburton Billing in Iraq," *The New York Times*, June 28, 2005, 12.

90. Erik Eckholm, "Army Contract Official Critical of Halliburton Pact Is Demoted," *The New York Times*, August 29, 2005, 9.

91. David Brooks, "Cynics Without a Cause," *The New York Times*, November 11, 2003, 21; David Ivanovich, "Halliburton Awarded Iraq Firefighting Contract," *The Houston Chronicle*, March 23, 2005, 1.

92. See Opening Statement of Chairman Tom Davis, Committee on Government Reform, "Contracting and the Rebuilding of Iraq: Part IV," July 22, 2004; Testimony of Dr. Steven Kelman, before the House Committee on Government Reform, July 21, 2004; and Steven Kelman, "No Cronyism in Iraq," *The Washington Post*, November 6, 2003, A33.

93. Jeff Gerth and Don Van Natta, Jr., "The Struggle for Iraq; Postwar Rebuilding," *The New York Times*, December 29, 2003, 1.

94. David M. Walker, Contract Management: Contracting for Iraqi Reconstruction and for Global Logistics Support, testimony before the Committee on Government Reform, House of Representatives, June 15, 2004.

95. Erik Eckholm, "Ex-Halliburton Man Charged with Defrauding U.S. of $3.5 Million," *The New York Times*, March 18, 2005, 10.

96. Opening Statement of Chairman Tom Davis, Committee on Government Reform, "Contracting and the Rebuilding of Iraq: Part IV," July 22, 2004.

97. Griff Witte, "Army to End Expansive, Exclusive Halliburton Deal," *The Washington Post*, July 12, 2006, A1.

98. See "Executive Summary: An Investigation of the Abu Ghraib Detention Facility and the 205th Military Brigade," MG George R. Fay, available at www.findlaw.com; see also Shane Harris, "From Contract to Oversight," the Army mismanaged interrogators at Abu Ghraib, Govexec.com, September 15, 2004.

99. General Accountability Office, Interagency Contracting: Problems with DoD's and Interior's Orders to Support Military Operations, April 2005, GAO 05-201.

100. Chris Storm, "Officials Fear Contracting Abuses in Wake of Hurricane Katrina," GovExec.com, September 27, 2005, www.govexec.com/dailyfed/0905/092705c1.htm.

101. Eric Lipton and Ron Nixon, "Many Contracts for Storm Work Raise Questions," *The New York Times*, September 26, 2005, 1.

102. "House Democrats Introduce Bill Establishing Ant-Fraud Commission," *Capitol Hill Press Release*, September 20, 2005.

103. U.S. Department of Justice Fact Sheet: Hurricane Katrina Fraud Task Force, October 20, 2005; http://releases.usnewswire.com/GetRelease.asp?id=55339.

104. Robert Hernandez and Eric Lipton, "In Shift, FEMA Will Seek Bids for Gulf Work," *The New York Times*, October 7, 2005, 1.

105. Amelia Gruber, "White House Returns Purchase Card to Pre-Katrina Levels," October 3, 2005, GovExec.com, www.govexec.com/dailyfed/1005/100305a2.htm.

106. Kelman reports he received the following e-mail from a contract officer: "Those of us involved in [Hurricane Katrina relief contracting] have been talking among ourselves that contracting officers are criticized if they award things quickly for wasting money—fleecing America. And if they try to step back and take a day or two to complete something, they are inflexible bureaucrats who aren't getting help to the public. Who would want to work in that environment?" Steve Kelman, "An Open Letter to 1102s," *Federal Computer Week*, October 31, 2005, www.fcw.com/article91249-10-31-05-Print.

107. Testimony of Stan Soloway, President, Professional Services Council, before the Committee on Government Reform, June 21, 2005, http://72.14.207.104/search?q=cache:kxL-ha4ruGMJ:reform.house.gov/UploadedFiles/Soloway%2520Testimony.pdf+stan+soloway+professional+services&hl=en.

108. The Democratic attacks predated their takeover of Congress. See John Berlau, "Democrat Attacks on Contractors," *Insight on the News*, March 1, 2004, 18.

109. Quoted in Scott Shane and Ron Nixon, "In Washington, Contacting Take on Biggest Role Ever," *The New York Times*, February 4, 2007, 24.

110. Amy Doolittle, "House Targets Contractor Abuses," *Federal Times*, May 21, 2007.

111. Alice Lipowicz, "Waxman Bill Sparks Industry Fears," *Washington Technology*, March 9, 2007.

112. Jason Miller, "Has Contracting Gotten Out of Hand?" *Washington Technology*, May 15, 2007. See also Lilly, *A Return to Competitive Contracting*.

113. Kim Hart and Renae Merle, "As Military Contracts Grow, so Do Protests," *The Washington Post*, February 27, 2007, D1.

114. Kelman, *Unleashing Change*, 212.

115. Confidential interview with a Republican congressional staff member, October 18, 2005.

CHAPTER 7
UNSHACKLING AN UNSTABLE INDUSTRY: AIRLINE DEREGULATION

1. Michael E. Levine and Jennifer L. Forrence, "Regulatory Capture, Public Interest, and the Public Agenda: Toward a Synthesis," *The Journal of Law, Economics, and Organization*, 6, (Special Issue 1990), 174, 176ff.

2. Alfred E. Kahn, "Surprises of Airline Deregulation," *The American Economic Review*, 78, no. 2 (May 1988): 316.

3. See, for example, Adam Bryant, "Why Flying Is Hell," *Newsweek*, April 23, 2001, 34–37.

4. Michael E. Levine, personal communication, April 1, 2005. This chapter was

drafted prior to my correspondence with Levine, but the final version has benefited enormously from his comments and from reading his own writings on the topic.

5. Regulation of airline safety and the operation of the air traffic control system were a responsibility of another agency.

6. Civil Aeronautics Act of 1938, 52 Stat. 973.

7. Richard H. K. Vietor, "Contrived Competition: Airline Regulation and Deregulation, 1925–1988," *Business History Review*, 64, no. 1 (Spring 1990): 61–108, at 67.

8. *Ibid*.

9. W. Kip Viscusi, John M. Vernon, and Joseph E. Harrington, Jr., *Economics of Regulation and Antitrust, 3rd Edition* (Cambridge: MIT Press, 2000), 554–55.

10. *Ibid*.

11. Early on, the CAB tried on several occasions to actually hold tariff hearings, but since carrier costs differed, the industry environment changed rapidly, and the costing issues were very complex, it abandoned the practice. At one time, it took up establishing a fare formula, but abandoned that effort as well. In the early 1970s the tariff coordination system was declared illegal (*Moss v. CAB*) and the Board was forced to embark on another general hearing. The result (*Domestic Passenger Fare Investigation*) was so rigid and labyrinthine that it contributed to the environment that created airline deregulation. Michael Levine, personal communication, February 17, 2007.

12. Elizabeth E. Bailey, David R. Graham, and Daniel P. Kaplan, *Deregulating the Airlines* (Cambridge, MA: The MIT Press, 1985), 16–17.

13. Vietor, "Contrived Competition," 78-79.

14. Paul L. Joskow and Roger G. Noll, "Economic Regulation" in Martin Feldstein, ed., *American Economic Policy in the 1980s* (Chicago: University of Chicago Press, 1994), 393.

15. Bailey, Graham, and Kaplan, Deregulating the Airlines, 27–28.

16. Michael E. Levine, "Is Regulation Necessary? California Air Transportation and National regulatory Policy," *Yale Law Journal*, 74 (July 1965): 1416–47.

17. Martha Derthick and Paul J. Quirk, *The Politics of Deregulation* (Washington, D.C.: The Brookings Institution, 1985), 36.

18. Vietor, "Contrived Competition," 81.

19. Derthick and Quirk, *The Politics of Deregulation*, 47.

20. Vietor, "Contrived Competition," 83.

21. *Ibid*., 82.

22. Bailey, Graham, and Kaplan, *Deregulating the Airlines*, 32.

23. See Derthick and Quirk, *The Politics of Deregulation*.

24. Vietor, "Contrived Competition," 82.

25. In fact, the CAB removed by policy statement and regulations virtually all entry restrictions within a few months of enactment.

26. Michael E. Levine, "The Economic Theory of Regulation After a Decade of Deregulation: Comments and Discussion," *Brookings Papers on Economic Activity—Microeconomics*, (1989): 47; Derthick and Quirk, *The Politics of Deregulation*, 163; Vietor, "Contrived Competition," 83

27. In the event, the compensation provisions were never funded because it was impossible for the government to separate out the impact of deregulation from other economic factors affecting the industry.

28. Senators from rural states voted for airline deregulation by a margin of 2-1; those from urban and moderately urban states voted for it by a margin of 4-1. Derthick and Quirk, *Politics of Deregulation*, 137.

29. Bailey, Graham, and Kaplan, *Deregulating the Airlines*, 34.

30. Again, the CAB acted by policy and regulation to make fare freedom virtually unlimited by 1980.

31. For a critique of such functionalist arguments, see Paul Pierson, *Politics in Time* (Princeton, New Jersey: Princeton University Press, 2005).

32. Melvin A. Brenner, James O. Leet, Elihu Schott, *Airline Deregulation* (Westport, CT: ENO Foundation for Transportation, Inc., 1985), 20.

33. Janet L. Fix, "Airline Deregulation Wasn't Supposed to Turn Out this Way," *Detroit Free Press*, March 22, 2001,1A.

34. Brenner, Leet, and Schott, *Airline Deregulation*, 20

35. John E. Robson, "Airline Deregulation: Twenty Years of Success and Counting," *Regulation*, 21, no. 2 (1998): 20.

36. Steven A. Morrison and Clifford Winston, "The Remaining Role for Government Policy in the Deregulated Airline Industry," in Sam Peltzman and Clifford Winston, *Deregulation of Network Industries: What's Next?* (Washington: The Brookings Institution, 2000), 9.

37. Brenner, Leet, and Schott, *Airline Deregulation*, 66.

38. Robson, "Airline Deregulation: Twenty Years of Success and Counting," 19. Even that percentage overstates the degree of capacity utilization, since under regulation most aircraft had many fewer seats installed than they could accommodate.

39. Steven Morrison and Clifford Winston, *The Economic Effects of Airline Deregulation* (Washington: The Brookings Institution, 1986), 5–10.

40. Vietor, "Contrived Competition," 86.

41. Brenner, Leet, and Schott, *Airline Deregulation*, 95.

42. Stacey Kole and Kenneth Lehn, "Deregulation, the Evolution of Corporate Governance Structure, and Survival," *The American Economics Review*, 87, no. 2 (May 1997): 422.

43. *Ibid.*

44. Brenner, Leet, and Schott, *Airline Deregulation*, 61–62.

45. Elizabeth E. Bailey, "Airline Deregulation: Confronting the Paradoxes," *Regulation*, 15, no. 3 (Summer 1992), www.cato.org/pubs/regulation/regv15n3/reg15n3-bailey.html.

46. *Ibid.*

47. Vietor, "Contrived Competition," 101.

48. Kahn, "Surprises from Deregulation," 319.

49. Steven Morrison and Clifford Winston, *The Evolution of the Airline Industry* (Washington: The Brookings Institution Press, 1995).

50. Air Transport Association, www.airlines.org/econ/d.aspx?nid=6207. Retrieved April 5, 2005.

51. Michael E. Levine, "No Clear Way Forward for Airlines," *The New York Times*, December 6, 2002, 35.

52. A number of legacy carriers have resorted to Chapter 11 to modify their labor contracts and to ease their pension liabilities. United and US Airways used bankruptcy to turn over their defined-benefit plans to the Pension Guaranty Insurance Corporation, and Delta and Northwest in 2006 successfully lobbied for permission to amortize

their pension deficits over a longer period of time. (Delta subsequently terminated its plan.) See "Pension Reform Still Requires Equal Treatment, "Aviation Week and Space Technology," August 14, 2006, 58.

53. See Alexandra Marks, "Critics of Airline Mergers Launch Countermoves," *The Christian Science Monitor*, March 29, 2001, 2.

54. Another air carrier known as Frontier Airlines was in existence between 1950 and 1986. The Frontier Airlines of the 1990s was founded by previous executives of this firm.

55. Dan Reed, "Low-Fare Carriers Service Bests Big Rivals," *USA Today*, April 5, 2004, 2B.

56. As Alfred Kahn points out, "The essential of the case for competition is the impossibility of predicting most of its consequences. The superiority of the competitive market is the positive stimuli it provides for constantly improving efficiency, innovating, and offering consumers diversity of choices." See Alfred E. Kahn, "Deregulation and Vested Interests: The Case of Airlines," in Roger G. Noll and Bruce M. Owen, eds., *The Political Economy of Deregulation* (Washington, D.C.: American Enterprise Institute, 1993, 140).

57. See Steven Morrison and Clifford Winston, "The Remaining Role of Government Policy in the Airline Industry."

58. Air Transport Association, www.airlines.org/econ/d.aspx?nid=1032. Retrieved April 7, 2005.

59. Alfred E. Kahn, "Airline Deregulation," *The Concise Encyclopedia of Economics*. retrieved at www.econlib.org/library/Enc/AirlineDeregulation.html, March 28, 2005.

60. See *CQ Researcher*, "Airline Industry Problems," September 24, 1999, vol. 9, no. 36, 825–48.

61. See *Consumer Reports*, "Deregulation: Dethroning the Customer," Consumer Reports, July 2002, 30–35.

62. For criticism of these interventions, see the editorial, "Halt Government's Creep Back into the Airlines," *USA Today*, April 30, 2004, 20A.

63. Michael E. Levine, "Why Weren't the Airlines Reregulated," *Yale Journal on Regulation*, vol. 23, 2 (2006), 286–87.

64. Matsushita Elec. Indus. Co. v. Zenith Radio Corp., 475 U.S. 574, 588–90 (1986).

65. Michael E. Levine, "Regulation, the Market, and Interest Group Cohesion: Why Airlines Were Not Reregulated," in Marc K. Landy, Marin A. Levin, and Martin Shapiro, eds., *Creating Competitive Markets: The Politics of Regulatory Reform* (Washington, D.C.: Brookings Institution Press, 2007), 215–46, at 225–26.

66. *Ibid*.

67. *Ibid*., 227.

68. Michael Levine, personal communication, April 5, 2005. See also *supra* n. 61, 286.

69. Paul Starobin, "Deregulation: New Doubts, Damage Control," *Congressional Quarterly Weekly Report*," July 11, 1987, 1489.

70. Carolyn Lochhead, "Fears of Monopolies in the Sky," *The San Francisco Chronicle*, May 6, 1998, A1.

71. Mark. S. Kahn, statement before the U.S. Senate Committee on Commerce, Science, and Transportation, Subcommittee on Aviation, April 23, 1998, 2.

72. Frank Swoboda, "Airline Rules Put on Shelf," *The Washington Post*, June 25, 1998, C05.

73. Greg Gordon, "Airline Panel Doesn't Clear Air," *Minneapolis Star Tribune*, July 31, 1999, 1D.

74. Frank Swoboda, "American's Tactics Against Discounters Legal, Judge Says," *The Washington Post*, April 28, 2001, E1.

75. Statement of Carol B. Hallett, President, Air Transport Association, ATA Press Release, April 30, 1999.

76. David Armstrong, "Travelers Say Airline Reforms Are Way Behind Schedule," *The San Francisco Chronicle*, March 30, 2001, B1.

77. "Air Travelers Say Major Airlines Are Earning Their Wings," The Gallup Poll, August 9, 2005. http://poll.gallup.com/content/default.aspx?ci=17740.

78. CQ Researcher, *Airline Industry Problems*, September 21, 1999, 827.

79. Cited in Congers Daily / A.M., "Reid Introduces Bill to Improve Airline Travel for Passengers," January 30, 2001.

80. Community Regional Airline News, ""GAO Report Questions Value of EAS Program," March 31, 2003, vol. 21, no. 13, 1.

81. Lochhead, "Fears of Monopolies in the Sky."

82. Testimony of John V. Coleman, House Committee on Transportation and Infrastructure, Subcommittee on Aviation, May 25, 2000.

83. In 2003, the federal government gave the airlines another $3.8 billion in assistance, $2.3 billion of which was partial reimbursement for security-related taxes and costs incurred by the industry after the September 11 attacks.

84. Leslie Wayne and Michael Moss, "Bailout for Airlines Showed the Weight of a Mighty Lobby," *The New York Times*, October 10, 2001, A1.

85. See General Accounting Office, "Commercial Aviation," Testimony of Jay Etta Z. Hecker, Director, Physical Infrastructure, before the Subcommittee on Aviation, Committee on Transportation and Infrastructure, House of Representatives, GAO-04-837T, June 3, 2004.

86. James C. Benton and Peter Cohn, "Hill Clears Aid for Airlines," *Congressional Quarterly Weekly Report*, September 221, 2001, 2206.

87. See, for example, the lead editorial in *USA Today*, June 9, 2004, 10A.

88. Stephen Labaton, "Trying to Hand Out Life Jackets Over, Under, and Around Politics," *The New York Times*, June 29, 2004, C1.

89. The business loan problem is one of the main dilemmas of policy implementation described in Jeffrey Pressman and Aaron Wildavsky, *Implementation* (Berkeley: University of California Press, 1973).

90. Quoted in Labaton, "Trying to Hand Out Life Jackets Over, Under, and Around Politics," *The New York Times*, June 29, 2004, C1.

91. "Micheline Maynard, "Federal Help for United Appears to Be Less Likely," *The New York Times*, June 22, 2004, C1.

92. Air Transportation Stabilization Board Decision P0-3670, December 4, 2002.

93. Air Transportation Stabilization Board Decision JS-1733, June 17, 2004.

94. Micheline Maynard, "United Again Denied U.S. Aid to Emerge from Chapter 11," *The New York Times*, June 29, 2004, C1.

95. Micheline Maynard, "New Scrutiny for Airline Bailout Plan Three Years After Sept. 11," *The New York Times*, September 15, 2004, C1.

96. Kathryn A. Wolfe, "Senior Lawmaker Says Airlines Will Get No More Federal Aid," *Congressional Quarterly Weekly Report*, June 5, 2004, 1355.

97. Scott McCartney, "Airline Loan-Guarantee Deal Ends with a Profit," *The Wall Street Journal*, May 30, 2006, D4.

98. As Vietor writes, "Competition scarcely appears more 'perfect' in the airline industry than regulation; the problems are just different." Vietor, "Contrived Competition," 108.

CHAPTER 8
MAKING POLLUTION CONTROL PAY: EMISSIONS TRADING FOR ACID RAIN

1. For early statements of the virtues of market-based environmental policies, see J. D. Dales, *Pollution, Property, and Prices* (Toronto: University of Toronto Press, 1968); and David W. Montgomery, "Markets in Licenses and Efficient Pollution Control Programs," *Journal of Economic Theory*, 5, no. 3 (1972): 395–418. Another market-based approach is to impose a tax on emissions. While cap-and-trade programs establish a fixed limit on total emissions and allow the market price of permits to fluctuate, taxes impose a constant price on emissions and allow the total level of emissions to rise or fall. In theory, the two approaches can produce identical results. However, the two methods may have different real-world effects for both the actual level of emissions and the overall economist costs of pollution reductions if there is uncertainty over the shape of firms' marginal cost curves. Many economists (including some who support the acid rain program) believe that taxes are a superior approach to curbing greenhouse gases. The two approaches may also have different implications for political sustainability. See my discussion of this point in chapter 9.

2. See Charles L. Schultze, *The Public Use of Private Interest* (Washington, D.C. The Brookings Institution, 1977). Schultze in his discussion of pollution control emphasizes the possible use of effluent taxes.

3. They did not fail entirely, however. As noted in the following, there were some important, albeit modest, experiments with market approaches within the overall command-and-control framework.

4. See Peter Passell, "Economic Watch; Sale of Air Pollution Permits Is Part of Bush Acid-Rain Plan," *The New York Times*, May 17, 1989, A1.

5. This chapter focuses on the emissions trading market for sulfur dioxide, the main precursor to acid rain. The Clean Air Act of 1990 also sought to curb nitrogen oxide emissions—a secondary contributor to acid precipitation—through standard command-and-control regulations. However, the innovative cap-and-trade concept was subsequently extended to nitrogen oxide emissions at the local level, as noted in the following.

6. U.S. Environmental Protection Agency, *EPA Acid Rain Program: 2002 Progress Report* (EPA 430-R-03-011), November 2003. The acid rain program stopped the pollution of lakes and streams in the Northeast from getting worse and created the potential for a sustained recovery under the CAIR program (discussed in the following).

7. For a thoughtful discussion of the tension between public support for environmental policy and opposition to its implementation, see R. Shep Melnick, "Risky Businesses: Government and the Environment After Earth Day," in Morton Keller and R. Shep Melnick, eds., *Taking Stock: American Government in the Twentieth Century* (New York: Woodrow Wilson Center and Cambridge University Press, 1999), 157–86.

8. In a 2003 Pew survey, 86 percent of respondents agreed that "there needs to be stricter laws and regulations to protect the environment," but 57 percent agreed that "continuing environmental improvements should be made regardless of cost. www .publicagenda.org/issues/major_proposals_detail.cfm?issue_type=environment&list=1.

9. For a detailed history of the political jockeying leading to the passage of the 1990 Clean Air Act Amendments, see Richard E. Cohen, *Washington at Work: Back Rooms and Clean Air*, 2nd Edition, (Boston: Allyn and Bacon, 1995).

10. "Western Coal Darkens Ohio's Mining Future," *BusinessWeek*, May 2, 1977, 28.

11. Bruce A. Ackerman and William T. Hassler, *Clean Coal / Dirty Air* (New Haven: Yale University Pres, 1981).

12. "Cleaning Up the Big Dirties: The Problem of Acid Rain," Kennedy School of Government Case Program, C15-99.1514.0, 5.

13. Dallas Burtraw and Karen Palmer, "The Paparazzi Take a Look at a Living Legend: The SO_2 Cap-and-Trade Program for Power Plants in the United States," Resources of the Future Discussion Paper 03-15, April 2003, Washington D.C., 4.

14. Dingell, who represented an auto industry district, blocked Waxman's acid rain measures in part to preserve his bargaining leverage in a future rewrite of the Clean Air Act. See Cohen, *Washington at Work*, 37.

15. *Ibid.*, 38–49; see also "Cleaning Up the Big Dirties: The Problem of Acid Rain, 6–8.

16. Michael Weisskopf, "Acid Rain Legislation Dies After Compromise Effort Fails; 'Rigid and Unyielding' Environmentalists Blamed," *The Washington Post*, October 5, 1988 A2; Rochelle L. Stainfield, "For Acid Rain, 'Wait Till Next Year,'" *National Journal*, October 15, 1988, 2606.

17. Peter Hoffmann, "Senator Mitchell Throws in Towel on Clean Air Bill," *Engineering News-Record*, October 13, 1988, 7.

18. "Acid Rain Controls Examined," *The New York Times*, June 21, 1984, A18.

19. For an excellent discussion of the adoption of emissions trading, see Kevin M. Sterling, *The Political Economy of Expertise* (Ann Arbor: University of Michigan Press, 2004), chapter 6.

20. "The Greening of George Bush," *The Economist*, June 17, 1989, 29.

21. Michael Weisskopf, "Bush's EPA Choice Declares 'New Era,'" *The Washington Post*, February 1, 1989, A7.

22. See Text of President Bush's Speech to Congress, February 10, 1989, *The Washington Post*, A20. Bob Hepburn, "Bush Pledges Action over Acid Rain," *The Toronto Star*, February 10, 1989, A1.

23. Michael Weisskopf, "A Changed Equation on Pollution," *The Washington Post*, June 7, 1989, A1.

24. Richard W. Stevenson "Concern over Bush Clean Air Plan," *The New York Times*, June 14, 1989, D1.

25. Cohen, *Washington at Work*, 64.

26. Esterling, *The Political Economy of Expertise*, 130–34; See also Robert Hahn, "Economic Prescriptions for Environmental Problems: How the Patient Followed the Doctor's Orders," *Journal of Economic Perspectives*, vol. 3, no. 2 (1989), 95–114; and Blas Pérez-Henríquez, "Creating a Market in Sulfur Emission Allowances," in *Creating Competitive Markets*, Marc Landy, Martin A. Levin, and Martin Shapiro, eds., (Washington: Brookings Institution Press, 2006).

27. *Ibid.*

28. R. Shep Melnick, *Regulation and the Courts: The Case of the Clean Air Act* (Washington, D.C.: The Brookings Institution, 1983).

29. Cohen, *Washington at Work*, 64.

30. Michael Weisskopf and Ann Devroy, "Bush Sets Clean Air Strategy," *The Washington Post*, June 13, 1989, A1; Phillip Shabcoff, "President Urges Steps to Tighten Law on Clean Air,' *The New York Times*, June 13, 1989, A1.

31. Quoted in Marshall Yates, "Congress Approves Historic Clean Air Legislation," *Public Utilities Fortnightly*, December 6, 1990, 53.

32. Richard W. Stevenson, "Concern Over Bush Clean Air Plan," *The New York Times*, June 14, 1989, D1.

33. For early mixed reactions to Bush's trial balloon, see Marie Coco, "Pollution Bill May Let Dirty Plants Benefit from Clean Ones," *The St. Louis Post Dispatch*, March 14, 1989, B1.

34. *Ibid.*

35. "Clean Air Act Rewritten, Tightened," *1990 Congressional Quarterly Almanac*, (Washington, D.C.: Congressional Quarterly, 1990), 229–79. Michael Weisskopf, "Bush Signs Sweeping Air Pollution Controls into Law," *The Washington Post*, November 16, 1990, A6.

36. Esterling, *The Political Economy of Expertise*, 158 and *passim*.

37. A. Denny Ellerman, Paul L. Joskow, Richard Schmalensee, Juan-Pablo Montero, and Elizabeth M. Bailey, *Markets for Clean Air: The U.S. Acid Rain Program* (New York: Cambridge University Press, 2000), 24.

38. Larry Tye, "Bush, Pledging to Clean Air, Presents Tough Antipollution Plan," *The Boston Globe*, June 13, 1989, 1.

39. *1990 CQ Almanac*, "Clean Air Act Rewritten, Tightened," 236–38. Some conservative lawmakers voted for the Byrd Amendment in hopes it would pass and cause Bush to carry out his treat to veto the measure. See Ellerman *et al.*, *Markets for Clean Air*, 29, fn. 35.

40. The bill authorized $250 million over five years, but the money was made available to workers in all industries who were unemployed, not just miners. In addition, the funds were classified as discretionary spending, rather than as mandatory entitlements. See Cohen, *Washington at Work*, 186–87; and Michael Mills, "Aiding Displaced Workers," *Congressional Quarterly Weekly Report*, October 27, 1990, 3589.

41. Plants that use scrubbers to meet their Phase I reduction requirements were permitted either to postpone compliance until 1997 or receive an early-reduction bonuses allowance for reductions achieved between 1995 and 1997. See Marshall Yates, "Congress Approves Historic Clean Air Legislation," Public Utilities Fortnightly, December 6, 1990, 53.

42. Esterling, *The Political Economy of Expertise*, 157-158.

43. Margaret E. Kriz, "Dunning the Midwest," *National Journal*, April 14, 1990: 893–97. It should be noted that the free allocation of allowances took place in the context of the regulated cost of service rules. The market was not yet competitive. Today, this type of free giveaway of allowances would be much more controversial and would have efficiency consequences. I thank Dallas Salisbury for this insight.

44. "Independent Generators Seeking Assurance on Access to Allowances," Independent Power Report, March 9, 1990, 10; "House Panel Clean Air Bill Likely Set for

Early May Floor Date," *Electric Utility Weekly*, April 16, 1990, 11. For a detailed analysis of the key program design issue, see Karl Hausker, "Coping with a Cap: How Auctions Can Help the Allowance Market Work," *Public Utilities Fortnightly*, May 24, 1990, 28.

45. "Senate Passes Clean Air Bill that Permits Growth for Independents," *Independent Power Report*, April 6, 1990, 1; Marshall Yates, "Congress Approves Historic Clean Air Measure," *Public Utilities Fortnightly*, December 6, 1990, 53. The final bill also included a Direct Sales Reserve that required the offered allowances at a fixed price of $1,500 (adjusted for inflation). While any unit could buy allowances in the direct sale, independent power producers had first priority. The EPA shut down the direct sale in 1997 because it proved unnecessary. See www.epa.gov/airmarkets/arp/overview.html.

46. See www.epa.gov/airmarkets/auctions/factsheet.html.

47. Cohen, *Washington at Work*, 146–49.

48. On Reilly's displeasure, see *Ibid.*, 186; and Michael Weisskopf, "With Pen, Bush to Seal Administration Split on Clean Air Act," *The Washington Post*, November 15, 1990, A23.

49. *1990 CQ Almanac*, 278.

50. Ellerman *et al.*, *Markets for Clean Air*, chapter 3, offers a superb analysis of the political economy of allowance allocations.

51. *Ibid.*, 75.

52. Lauraine G. Chesnut and David M. Mills, "A Fresh Look at the Benefits and Costs of the U.S. Acid Rain Program," *Journal of Environmental Management*, vol. 77, no. 3 (November 2005): 252–66. These social benefits arise from the emissions of acid rain and nitrogen oxides, as well as from reduced mercury emissions as power plants switched to low-sulfur coal and/or installed scrubbers.

53. See U.S. General Accounting Office, *Acid Rain: Emissions Trends and Effects in the Eastern United States* GAO/ RCED—00-47, March 2000. See also U.S. Environmental Protection Agency, *Acid Rain Program: 2004 Progress Report*. Government Printing Office, 2005, 3.

54. A. Danny Ellerman, Paul L. Joskow, and David Harrison, Jr. "Emission Trading in the U.S," prepared for the Pew Center on Global Climate Change, May 2003, 14.

55. Indeed, some environmentalists were open to emission trading, but were so fearful of hotspots that they proposed multiple trading regions to ensure reductions in environmentally sensitive areas in the East Coast.

56. Burtraw and Palmer, "The Paparazzi Take a Look at a Living Legend," 10.

57. Testimony of Michael O. Leavitt, Administrator, EPA, hearing on implementation of air quality standards, Senate Environment and Public Works Committee, April 1, 2004.

58. Matthew L. Wald, "Utility Is Selling Right to Pollute," *The New York Times*, May 12, 1992, A1.

59. Matthew L. Wald, "Acid-Rain Pollution Credits Are Not Enticing Utilities," *The New York Times*, July 5, 1995, A11.

60. One environmentalist quipped to a reporter, "What's next? The L.A. Police Department trying to buy civil rights credits from Wisconsin?" See "Power Plant Emissions," *Public Utilities Fortnightly*, August 1997, 30.

61. *Ibid.*

62. *Acid Rain Program: 2004 Progress Report*, 7.

63. *Ibid.*

64. Testimony of Peter F. Guerrero, Director, Environmental Protection Issues, U.S. General Accounting Office. *Air Pollution: Overview and Issues on Emissions Allowance Trading Programs.* GAO/T-RCED-97-183, July 9, 1997, 3.

65. *Public Utilities Fortnightly,* June 15, 2003, 36. This figure includes NO_X emission allowances.

66. Dallas A. Burtraw, David A. Evans, Alan Krupnick, Karen Palmer, and Russell Toth, *Economics of Pollution Trading for SO_2 and NO_X,* Resources for the Future Discussion Paper, Washington, D.C. 2005, 18.

67. *Ibid.*

68. "Exchange Gets OK for SO_2 Futures Treating," *Megawatt Daily,* November 11, 2004, 1.

69. The organizations are Clean Air Conservancy Trust, Acid Rain Retirement Fund, Adirondack Council, and the Environmental Resources Trust. See www.epa .gov/airmarket/trading/buying.html.

70. Barnaby J. Feder, "Sold: The Rights to Air Pollution," *The New York Times,* March 30, 1993, D1.

71. Laurie Morse, "Pollution Rights Go to Auction," *The Financial Times,* March 29, 1993, 4.

72. In 2006, the Chicago Board of Trade notified the EPA that it no longer wished to host the auction going forward. The EPA managed the auction itself in 2006. "Chicago Board of Trade to Stop Hosting EPA's Yearly Sulfur Dioxide Emission Rights Auctions," *Foster Electric Report,* May 11, 2005, 16.

73. Section 403(f) of the 1990 Clean Air Act.

74. Jim Johnston, "We Told You So," *Regulation,* no. 3, 1995.

75. Markus W. Gehring and Charlotte Streck, "Emissions Trading: Lessons from SO_X and NO_X Emissions Allowance and Credit Systems Legal Nature, Title, Transfer, and Taxation of Emission Allowance and Credits," *Environmental Law Reporter,* 35 (2005): 10200–10234.

76. Ellerman *et. al,* *Markets for Clean Air,* 32, fn. 2.

77. Daniel H. Cole, "Clearing the Air: Four Propositions About Property Rights and Environmental Protection," *Duke Environmental Law and Policy Forum,* 10, (1999): 103–30.

78. Burtraw *et al.,* "Economics of Pollution Trading for SO_2 and NO_X," 14.

79. Ellerman *et al.,* *Markets for Clean Air,* 104.

80. Tom Fowler, "Rising Price of Pollution," *The Houston Chronicle,* March 29, 2005, B1.

81. Gregory Zuckerman, "High-Sulfur Coal Comes Back in Favor," *The Wall Street Journal,* April 24, 2006, C1.

82. "Lawsuits and Lack of Tracking System Add to Allowance Market University," *Utility Environmental Report,* July 9, 1993, 1.

83. *Acid Rain: 2004 Progress Report,* 12.

84. Testimony of Peter F. Guerrero, Director, Environmental Protection Issues, U.S. General Accounting Office. *Air Pollution: Overview and Issues on Emissions Allowance Trading Programs.* GAO/T-RCED-97-183, July 9, 1997, 12.

85. *2004 Acid Rain Report,* 8.

86. Ellerman *et al.,* Markets for Clean Air, 318.

87. See R. Shep Melnick, *Regulation and the Courts* (Washington, D.C: The Brookings Institution, 1983).

88. Christine Todd Whitman, EPA Administrator, Testimony on Clear Skies Act, Senate Environment and Public Works Committee, April 8, 2003.

89. Testimony of Peter F. Guerrero, Director, Environmental Protection Issues, U.S. General Accounting Office. *Air Pollution: Overview and Issues on Emissions Allowance Trading Programs*. GAO/T-RCED-97-183, July 9, 1997, 3.

90. This paragraph is based on Environmental Defense Fund, *From Obstacle to Opportunity: How Acid Rain Emissions Trading Is Delivering Cleaner Air*, Washington, D.C., September 2000, 19.

91. Vikas Bajaj, "Are Storm Clouds Massing? These Traders Need to Know," *The New York Times*, May 17, 2006, G2.

92. "Allowance Market Players Create Group to Promote Emissions Trading Programs," *Utility Environment Report*, January 17, 1997, 9. The group later changes its name to Environmental Markets Association.

93. Erik Haites, "Banking on Reductions," *Environmental Finance*, February 2005, 28.

94. Burtraw and Palmer, "The Paparazzi Take a Look at a Living Legend," 8.

95. Christine Todd Whitman, EPA Administrator, Testimony on Clear Skies Act, Senate Environment and Public Works Committee, April 8, 2003.

96. EPA, *Clearing the Air: The Facts About Capping and Trading Emissions*, Washington, Government Printing Office, 2002, 9.

97. See www.aqmd.gov/reclaim/reclaim.html.

98. See "EPA Reports Success with NO_X Cap, Trading Program," *Environmental Laboratory Washington Report*, September 23, 2004, 1.

99. Vikas Bajaj, "Are Storm Clouds Massing? These Traders Need to Know," 2.

100. For a summary, see James E. McCarthy, *Clean Air Act Issues in the 109th Congress*, *CRS Issue Brief for Congress*, IB10137. Updated May 3, 2006.

101. For support of Clear Skies, see "A. Denny Ellerman and Paul L. Joskow, "Bush Has a Good Plan for Cleaner Air," *San Diego Union-Tribune*, May 2, 2002, B15

102. Shankar Vedantam, "Senate Impasse Stops Clear Skies Measure," *The Washington Post*, March 10, 2005, A04.

103. Rick Weiss, "EPA Enacts Long-Awaited Rule to Improve Air Quality, Health," *The Washington Post*, March 11, 2005, A1.

104. *Acid Rain: 2004 Progress Report*, 23.

105. *Federal Register*, vol. 69, no. 20, January 20, 2004, 4630.

106. *Ibid*.

107. Allowances of all vintages retain their full value for emissions in states not covered by CAIR. Trading between facilities covered by CAIR and noncovered facilities is permitted.

108. See "EPA's CAIR Emissions Rules Face Court Challenges," *Foster Electric Report*, July 20, 2005, 15.

109. *Federal Register*, April 26, 2006, 25308.

110. Even during the program's early years, when trading volume was low, there has never been any serious discussion of scrapping the program.

111. Necessary conditions include accurate emissions monitoring, strict enforcement, clearly defined allowances, and the ability to trade without time-consuming preapproval of trades by regulators. See Denny Ellerman, Paul L. Joskow, and David

Harrison, *Emissions Trading in the U.S*, Prepared for the Pew Center on Global Climate Change, May 2003.

CHAPTER 9
CONCLUSIONS: THE PATTERNS AND PARADOXES OF POLICY REFORM

1. Sarah A. Binder, "Can Congress Serve the General Welfare?" in Alan S. Gerber and Eric M. Patashnik, eds., *Promoting the General Welfare: New Perspectives on Government Performance* (Washington, D.C.: Brookings Institution Press, 2006), 199–219.

2. R. Douglas Arnold, *The Logic of Congressional Action* (New Haven: Yale University Press, 1990).

3. On the weak incentives to do this kind of work, see Eugene Bardach's discussion of "fixers" in *The Implementation Game* (Cambridge, MA: The MIT Press, 1977).

4. See David Lewis, *Politicizing Administration* (Princeton: Princeton University Press, 2008).

5. Terry M. Moe, "The Politics of Bureaucratic Structure," in John E. Chubb and Paul E. Peterson, eds., *Can the Government Govern?* (Washington, D.C.: The Brookings Institution, 1989), 267–329. For a critique from a slightly different angle, see Daniel P. Carpenter, *The Forging of Bureaucratic Autonomy* (Princeton: Princeton University Press, 2001), 357–59.

6. On this point, see Paul Pierson, *Politics in Time: History, Institutions, and Social Analysis* (Princeton: Princeton University Press, 2004).

7. Kathleen Thelen, *How Institutions Evolve: The Political Economy of Skills in Germany, Great Britain, the United States, and Japan* (New York: Cambridge University Press, 2004).

8. *Ibid.*, 293.

9. The strongest versions of the theory in political science can be found in Stephen Krasner, "Sovereignty: An Institutional Perspective," *Comparative Political Studies*, 21 (1988): 66–94. A far more nuanced version is offered in Frank Baumgartner and Bryan D. Jones, *Agendas and Instability in American Politics* (Chicago: University of Chicago Press, 1993). Although my analysis departs from Baumgartner and Jones's 1993 model in key respects, it is heavily indebted to it in many ways; further, as I note later, Baumgartner and Jones's more recent work addresses a number of the issues I raise.

10. See the insightful analysis in Patrick McGuinn, "Swing Issues and Policy Regimes: Federal Education Policy and the Politics of Policy Change," *Journal of Policy History*, vol. 18, no. 2 (2006): 205–40.

11. Jacob S. Hacker, *The Divided Welfare State: The Battle Over Public and Private Social Benefits in the United States* (New York: Cambridge University Press, 2002).

12. McGuinn, "Swing Issues and Policy Regimes," 211. In more recent work, Baumgartner and Jones have considerably broadened their discussion of positive and negative types of feedback to include greater attention to longer-run processes of policy development. See, for example, Frank R. Baumgartner and Bryan D. Jones, eds., *Policy Dynamics* (Chicago: University of Chicago Press, 2002).

13. *Ibid.*

14. On congressional reform, see, for example, Eric Schickler, *Disjoined Pluralism* (Princeton: Princeton University Press, 2001) and Julian E. Zelizer, *On Capitol Hill*

(New York: Cambridge University Press, 2006); on the expansion of administrative capacities, see Steven Skowronek, *Building a New American State* (New York: Cambridge University Press, 1982); on policy feedback in welfare state policy, see, for example, Andrea Louise Campbell, *How Policies Make Citizens: Senior Political Activism and the American Welfare State* (Princeton: Princeton University Press, 2003).

15. For a start to this integration, see the essays contained in Marc K. Landy, Marin A. Levin, and Martin Shapiro, eds., *Creating Competitive Markets* (Washington, D.C.: Brookings Institution Press, 2007).

16. Paul Pierson, "The Study of Policy Development," *Journal of Policy History*, vol. 17, no. 1 (2005): 35.

17. Paul Pierson, "Ahead of Its Time: On Martha Derthick's Policymaking for Social Security," *P.S.*, July 2004, 441.

18. Martha Derthick, *Policymaking for Social Security* (Washington, D.C.: Brookings Institution, 1979), 9.

19. On this crucial point, see Pierson, *Politics in Time*, 165–66; *and* also the excellent analysis in Jacob S. Hacker, "Privatizing Risk Without Privatizing the Welfare State: The Hidden Politics of Social Policy Retrenchment in the United States," *American Political Science Review*, 98, 2 (May 2004): 243–60.

20. See the empirical analyses contained in: David E. Lewis, *Presidents and the Politics of Agency* Design (Palo Alto: Stanford University Press, 2003); Forrest Maltzman and Charles R. Shipan, "Continuity, Change, and the Evolution of the Law," *American Journal of Political Science*, forthcoming; and Christopher R. Berry, Barry C. Burden, and William G. Howell, "Matters of Life and Death: The Durability of Discretionary Programs, 1970–2004," presented at the 2006 Meeting of the Midwest Political Science Association, Chicago, Illinois. I caution that these are a family of arguments, and different studies stress different explanatory variables.

21. Reviewing the factors associated with the durability of major laws, Mayhew suggests that "there is *some* value to the idea of extended party control" but that "it is a mistake to claim too much." See David R. Mayhew, *Electoral Realignments* (New Haven: Yale University Press, 2002), 121.

22. For example, the election of Bill Clinton in 1992 briefly restored unified Democratic control; the same partisan conditions that existed when airline deregulation was enacted under President Carter. The Clinton Administration did little to disturb the reform, but not because the issue climates during the two eras of unified Democratic control were the same. On the contrary, the public concerns that originally prompted airline deregulation's adoption (e.g., high inflation) in 1978 were no longer salient in 1993, and some Clinton Administration officials might well have preferred the government to play a more interventionist role. By the early 1990s, however, airline deregulation had been in place for more than a decade, and the economic organization of the airline industry had been thoroughly reconfigured.

23. See Paul Pierson, "The Study of Policy Development," *Journal of Policy History*, vol. 17, no. 1 (2005): 34–50.

24. See, for example, the excellent Maltzman and Shipan study, "Continuity, Change, and the Evolution of the Law." This study systematically examines why some major federal laws last in their original unamended form longer than others. It persuasively demonstrates that the partisan configurations of enacting coalitions affect the probability of subsequent amendments. The limitation of the study for an understand-

ing of the dynamics of *policy sustainability* is that it focuses on the existence of *legal change* rather than the *direction of policy evolution*. Policies may be highly sustainable even when their underlying authorizing legislation is frequently amended. Social Security is a leading example. The original 1935 Act has been modified many times over the past seven decades, but the basic program has been highly durable. In contrast, policies can be eroded even without formal repeal. The Tax Reform Act of 1986 is a prime example. Despite these significant differences, the Malzman–Shipan paper and related literature offer many valuable insights and intriguing hypotheses.

25. It is reasonable to presume that reforms enacted by large coalitions will be more sustainable than reforms passed by slim majorities, all things being equal. Yet all of the reforms examined in this book passed by large bipartisan majorities in both chambers (Table 9-1). It is of course possible that this reflects idiosyncrasies of my sample. The reforms were not selected to ensure variance based upon the size of enacting coalitions. It seems more likely, however, that the high level of political support these laws enjoyed at the outset reflects core features of U.S. policymaking, including the tendency for Washington policymakers periodically to work themselves up into a frenzy over the need to "solve" a certain problem. On this point, see David R. Mayhew, *Divided We Govern: Party Control, Lawmaking, and Investigation, 1946–1990* (New Haven: Yale University Press, 1991), 119–35. A second reason why broad majorities are commonplace is that coalition leaders have strong incentives to make deals and compromise on principles to neutralize a bill's opposition. Indeed, opposition to general-interest reforms tends to be most intense during the early stages of the legislative process, before side payments and concessions have been made. Once general-interest reforms reach chamber floors, most legislators will be reluctant to go on record against the bill's diffuse benefits.

26. On the importance of relative timing, see Paul Pierson, "Not Just What, but When: Timing and Sequence in Political Processes," *Studies in American Political Development*, (2000): 72–92.

27. While welfare reform has endured, it has not produced some of the political feedback some of its advocates hoped, such as stimulating greater public support for dramatically increased investments targeted at the "deserving poor." See the insightful analysis of Joe Soss and Sanford F. Schram, "A Public Transformed? Welfare Reform as Policy Feedback," *American Political Science Review*, 101, 1, (2007): 111–27.

28. See Karen Orren and Stephen Skowronek, *The Search for American Political Development* (New York: Cambridge University Press, 2004), 127–28.

29. A mixed case is the Pension Benefit Guaranty Corporation. On the one hand, the PBGC has increased the chances that a vested worker will receive defined pension benefits. On the other hand, the financial risks of pension plan failures have largely been shifted to general taxpayers because the PBGC lacks the authority to impose market-based insurance premiums.

30. Similarly, while preventing members of Congress from engaging in irresponsible blame-casting and micromanagement was an implicit goal of procurement reform, reform advocates were understandably reluctant to directly attack the authority or motivations of powerful committee chairs. Instead, they focused on the benefits of better "customer service."

31. On the importance of investments, see Pierson, *Politics in Time*, 148.

32. See Hacker, *The Divided Welfare State*.

33. David Truman, *The Governmental Process* (New York: Knopf, 1951).

34. Samuel P. Huntington, *American Politics: The Promise of Disharmony* (Cambridge: Harvard University Press, 1981).

35. Andrew S. McFarland, "Interest Groups and Political Time: Cycles in America," *British Journal of Political Science*, 21 (1991): 257–84.

36. Richard Rose, "Models of Change," in *The Dynamics of Public Policy: A Comparative Analysis*, Richard Rose, ed., (London: Sage Publications, 1976), 16–18.

37. See also the critical discussion of cycle theory in Baumgartner and Jones, *Agendas and Instability in American Politics*, 243–46.

38. On the sources of resilience over time, see Pierson, *Politics in Time*, 150–53.

39. Baumgartner and Jones, *Agendas and Instability in American Politics*, 243–46.

40. *Ibid.*, 161–64.

41. McFarland, "Interest Groups and Political Time," 264.

42. Eugene S. Bardach, "Policy Dynamics," in Michael Moran, Martin Rein, and Robert E. Goodin, eds., *The Oxford Handbook of Public Policy* (New York: Oxford University Press, 2006), 346–47.

43. For a defense of these tactics in building support for general-interest reforms, see John W. Ellwood and Eric M. Patashnik, "In Praise of Pork," *The Public Interest* (Winter, 1993), 19–33; and see the excellent empirical analysis, Diana Evans, *Greasing the Wheels: Using Pork Barrel Projects to Build Majority Coalitions in Congress* (Cambridge University Press, 2004).

44. I thank Steve Teles for this point.

45. See Daniel Shaviro, *When Rules Change* (Chicago: University of Chicago Press, 2000).

46. For a summary of these changes, see Marc K. Landy and Martin A. Levin, eds., *The New Politics of Public Policy* (Baltimore: Johns Hopkins University Press, 1995).

47. Martha Derthick and Paul J. Quirk, *The Politics of Deregulation* (Washington, D.C.: Brookings Institution Press, 1985), 246.

48. Bruce Gardner, personal communication, December 15, 2003.

49. Epstein and O'Halloran report that the Tax Reform Act of 1986 has one of the lowest delegation ratios (provisions with executive delegation divided by total provisions) of any major law in their sample. Many other tax laws also feature low delegation ratios. See David Epstein and Sharyn O'Halloran, *Delegating Powers* (New York: Cambridge University Press, 1999), Table 5-3, 96.

50. To be sure, Congress sometimes chooses to delegate control over distributive policy areas, but generally only when doing so serves political goals, such as party-building. Barry R. Weingast, Judith Goldstein, and Michael A. Bailey, "The Institutional Roots of American Trade Policy: Politics, Coalitions, and International Trade," *World Politics*, vol. 49, no. 3 (April 1997), 309–38.

51. Jacob S. Hacker, "The Politics of Risk Privatization in U.S. Social Policy," in Landy, Levin, and Shapiro, eds., *Creating Competitive Markets*, 83–109.

52. Eugene Bardach, "Why Deregulation Succeeds or Fails," in *Ibid.*, 337.

53. Michael E. Levin, "Regulation, the Market, and Interest Group Cohesion: Why Airlines Were Not Reregulated," in *Ibid.*, 235–37.

54. Eric M. Patashnik, "The Day After Market-Oriented Reform; Or, What Happens When Economists' Reform Ideas Meet Politics," in *Ibid.*, 286.

55. Aaron Wildavsky, *Speaking Truth to Power: The Art and Craft of Policy Analysis* (New Brunswick, N.J: Transaction Press, 1979).

56. For very useful insights on these issues, see Bardach, "Why Deregulation Succeeds or Fails"; Dani Rodrik, "Understanding Economic Policy Reform," *Journal of Economic Literature* (March 1996): 9–41; and Jennifer H. Hochschild, "You Win Some, You Lose Some: Explaining the Pattern of Success and Failure in the Second Reconstruction," in Morton Keller and R. Shep Melnick, eds., *Taking Stock: American Government in the Twentieth Century* (Washington, D.C: Woodrow Wilson Center Press, 1999), 219–48.

57. For additional practical suggestions, see Bardach, "Why Deregulation Succeeds or Fails."

58. See Joel S. Hellman, "Winners Take All: The Politics of Partial Reform in Postcommunist Transitions," *World Politics*, vol. 50, no. 2 (1998): 203–34.

59. Levine, "Regulation, the Market, and Interest Group Cohesion," 226.

60. Patricio Navia and Andres Velasco, "The Politics of Second-Generation Reforms," in Pedro-Pablo Kuczynski and John Williamson, eds., *After the Washington Consensus: Restarting Growth and Reform in Latin America* (Washington, D.C.: Institute for International Economics, 2003), 301.

61. The electricity restructuring in California attempted to redistribute income to consumers in ways that hindered the market's efficient operation. Utilities were prevented from using forward contracts to lock in supplies at fixed prices and from passing on higher electricity costs to customers. See statement of Paul N. Joskow before the Committee on Government Affairs, United States Senate, November 12, 2002, http://web.mit.edu/ceepr/www/2002-010.pdf.

62. Hugh Heclo, "A Political Science Perspective on Social Security Reform," in *Framing the Social Security Debate*, R. Douglas Arnold, Michael J. Graetz, and Alicia H. Munnell, eds., (Washington, D.C.: National Academy of Social Insurance, 1998), 84.

63. Ibid., 86.

64. On relational contracting, see Oliver E. Williamson, *The Economic Institutions of Capitalism* (New York: Free Press, 1985).

65. For an excellent analysis of game playing in the implementation process, see Bardach, *The Implementation Game*.

66. Marc K. Landy and Marin A. Levin, "Creating Competitive Markets: The Politics of Market Design," in Landy, Levin, and Shapiro, *Creating Competitive Markets*, 20–21.

67. Steve M. Teles, "Paradoxes of Welfare-State Conservatism," *The Public Interest*, Fall 2000, 17–40.

68. Ibid.

69. As Dani Rodrik points out, reformers sometimes give too much attention to eliminating distortions that "simply affect static resource allocation" and do not pay enough attention to "stimulating the dynamic forces" that lie behind economic growth. See his essay, "Goodbye Washington Consensus, Hello Washington Confusion?" *Journal of Economic Literature*, December 2006, 976.

70. While the cap-and-trade market for sulfur dioxide emissions only had to govern a single sector (just 445 coal-fired power plants), a comprehensive emissions trading for greenhouse gases would have to apply to a wide range of sectors across the economy. If

the marginal costs and benefits of carbon reductions were known with certainty, policymakers could use either carbon taxes or cap-and-trade to achieve the same result. But since these benefits and costs are unknown, there is concern about making a mistake. Many economists argue that the costs of a mistake would be higher under cap-and-trade, because if policymakers set the tax rate too low, they could (in theory) raise it quickly, without doing much harm to the environment (a temporary excess in emissions makes little difference to the overall path of global warming). But if policymakers err by creating the wrong number of permits, the prices of carbon emissions could skyrocket, imposing great harm to the economy. See "Tradable Emissions Permits Are a Popular, but Inferior, Way to Tackle Global Warming," *The Economist*, June 16, 2007, 86; and William Pizer, "Choosing Price or Quantity Controls for Greenhouse Gases," *Climate Issues Brief*, no. 17, Resources for the Future, July 1999; and Kenneth P. Green, Steven F. Hayward, and Kevin A. Hassett, "Climate Change: Caps vs. Taxes," *Environmental Policy Outlook*, no. 2, American Enterprise Institute for Public Policy Research, June 2007.

71. Robert Lempert, "Creating Constituencies for Long-Term Radical Change," John Brademas Center for Congress, *Research Brief*, no. 2, March 2007, 9.

72. *Ibid.*

73. C. Eugene Steurele, *The Tax Decade* (Washington, D.C.: The Urban Institute Press, 1992), 190–91.

Index

AARP, 86, 87

Abu Ghraib incident, 102, 105

Accountability in Contracting Act (2007), 107

acid rain (acid deposition), 17, 136, 137; acid rain proposals of George H. W. Bush, 140–44; market-based approach to the problem of, 141–42; and organized labor, 137–38. *See also* emissions trading (acid rain program)

"adversarial legalism," 97

AFL-CIO, 77, 82

Agendas and Instability in American Politics (Baumgartner and Jones), 223n9

Agricultural Adjustment Act (AAA [1933]), 56

Agricultural Adjustment Act (AAA [1949]), 56

agricultural deregulation, effect of on private-sector investment, 68–69

agricultural reform, 13, 158, 169, 170, 175, 178; and farm subsidies, 59, 70–71, 197n19; and "inefficient redistribution," 186n15; timing of, 163. *See also* farm bill (2002); Freedom to Farm Act (1996)

Agricultural Welfare State, The (Sheingate), 9

Aid to Families with Dependent Children (AFDC) program, 190n60

Air Transportation Association (ATA), 126, 127

Air Transportation Stabilization Board, 130–33; critics of, 132; loan guarantees provided by, 132

airline deregulation, 21, 30, 110–11, 133–35, 157, 159, 162, 167, 168, 169, 170, 172, 213n27; 214n28; 224n22; benefits of for consumers, 122–23; effect of on travel agents, 117–18; failure of "competitive guidelines," 127–28; and frequent flyer programs, 118; and hub-and-spoke networks, 116–17, 126, 169; and legacy carriers' resorting to Chapter 11, 214–15n52; and low-cost carriers, 115–16, 120–22, 176; and market forces, 28; and mergers and bankruptcies, 118–20; and the phasing out of the Civil Aeronautics Board, 124–25; and policymaking, 125–26; politics of, 112–14; the pre-reform situation, 111–14, 128; and reservation systems, 117–18; sustainability of, 111; and yield management systems, 118. *See also* airline reregulation

Airline Deregulation Act (1978), 110, 114

airline reregulation, 123–26, 213n5, 214n38; in the aftermath of 9/11, 124, 128–29, 130, 216n83 (*see also* Air Transportation Stabilization Board); inhibition of by the deregulated market, 133–35; and the passenger bill of rights, 128; and passenger service, 128–29; and predatory pricing, 126–28; and small-community service subsidies (the Essential Air Service [EAS] program), 129–30

American Enterprise Institute, 12, 207n31

American Jobs Creation Act (2004), 44

American Political Development (APD): implications for the study of, 159–61; literature of, 159

American Society of Travel Agents, 128

antitrust policy, 119

Arnold, R. Douglas, 8–9, 21, 39, 156, 179

Auerbach, Alan J., 50

Barbour, Haley, 131

Bardach, Eugene, 171, 175

Baumgartner, Frank, 4, 27, 170, 182n14, 223n9, 223n12

Beam, David R., 38

Becker, Gary, 186n18, 187n20

Berry, Christopher, 4

Biden, Joseph, 142

Binder, Sarah, 188n31

Bowen, Otis R., 85–86

Bradley, Bill, 38, 44, 156, 157

Brady, Henry, 13

Brandt, Roden, 127

Breyer, Stephen, 113

Brian, Danielle, 107

Brookings Institution, 12, 36, 53, 206n5

Brooks Act (1965), 96–97

Brown, Lawrence D., 185n4

Budget Enforcement Act (1990), 52

PRINCETON STUDIES IN AMERICAN POLITICS:

HISTORICAL, INTERNATIONAL, AND
COMPARATIVE PERSPECTIVES

Series Editors

Ira Katznelson, Martin Shefter, and Theda Skocpol, eds.